THE PERILS OF EMPIRE

THE PERILS OF EMPIRE

AMERICA AND ITS IMPERIAL PREDECESSORS

JAMES LAXER

VIKING
CANADA

VIKING CANADA

Published by the Penguin Group

Penguin Group (Canada), 90 Eglinton Avenue East, Suite 700, Toronto, Ontario,
   Canada M4P 2Y3 (a division of Pearson Canada Inc.)

Penguin Group (USA) Inc., 375 Hudson Street, New York, New York 10014, U.S.A.
Penguin Books Ltd, 80 Strand, London WC2R ORL, England
Penguin Ireland, 25 St Stephen's Green, Dublin 2, Ireland
   (a division of Penguin Books Ltd)
Penguin Group (Australia), 250 Camberwell Road, Camberwell, Victoria 3124,
   Australia (a division of Pearson Australia Group Pty Ltd)
Penguin Books India Pvt Ltd, 11 Community Centre, Panchsheel Park,
   New Delhi – 110 017, India
Penguin Group (NZ), 67 Apollo Drive, Rosedale, North Shore 0745, Auckland,
   New Zealand (a division of Pearson New Zealand Ltd)
Penguin Books (South Africa) (Pty) Ltd, 24 Sturdee Avenue, Rosebank, Johannesburg
   2196, South Africa

Penguin Books Ltd, Registered Offices: 80 Strand, London WC2R ORL, England

First published 2008

1 2 3 4 5 6 7 8 9 10 (RRD)

Manufactured in the U.S.A.

ISBN-13: 978-0-670-06361-1
ISBN-10: 0-670-06361-4

Library and Archives Canada Cataloguing in Publication data available upon request.

Visit the Penguin Group (Canada) website at **www.penguin.ca**

Special and corporate bulk purchase rates available; please see
www.penguin.ca/corporatesales or call 1-800-810-3104, ext. 477 or 474

To Sandy

CONTENTS

INTRODUCTION The American Empire in a Perilous Time 1

PART 1: THE EMPIRE DEBATE 9
ONE Facing Up to Empire 11

PART 2: HOW EMPIRES RISE AND FALL 35
TWO The Empire in History 37
THREE Egypt: The Secret of Longevity 45
FOUR The Athenian Empire: Reducing Allies
to Subjects 59
FIVE China: An Affair of State 71
SIX Rome: Military Supremacy 81
SEVEN Spain: The First World Empire 93
EIGHT The British Empire: Cultural Superiority 115

PART 3: THE CRISIS OF THE AMERICAN EMPIRE 135
NINE Imperial Overstretch 137
TEN Islam and Oil 153
ELEVEN Latin America: Taken for Granted 169
TWELVE The Coming Sino-American Collision 177
THIRTEEN Resisting Empire 189
FOURTEEN The Legitimacy of Empire in the Twenty-First
Century 207

Acknowledgments 233
Notes 235

The American Empire in a Perilous Time

America, in this young century, proclaims
liberty throughout all the world and to all the
inhabitants thereof.
— PRESIDENT GEORGE W. BUSH,
SECOND INAUGURAL ADDRESS,
JANUARY 20, 2005

On May 2, 2003, only six weeks after the American military assault on Iraq, President George W. Bush landed in a warplane on the deck of the USS *Abraham Lincoln*. After the tail hook landing, the president climbed out of the plane and was greeted by a huge banner that read "mission accomplished." Dressed in the fatigues of a Navy fighter pilot, Bush swaggered across the deck. The president, who had avoided combat in Vietnam as a member of the Texas Air National Guard, was presiding over a quickly won military triumph.

Four years later, however, Iraq was sinking into civil war. Four million Iraqis had fled their homes to refugee camps in Syria and Jordan and to less warlike regions of their own country. The American occupiers had been reduced almost to the level of spectators as sectarian violence drove Iraq toward balkanization. In December 2006, political elders Republican James Baker and Democrat Lee Hamilton issued the report of their Iraq Study Group, which had been established to seek a graceful way out of Iraq for the Bush administration. The report parted company with the Bush administration's view that the Iraq War should be fought to victory, calling instead for a negotiated peace to include Iran and Syria and for the withdrawal of U.S. troops beginning in 2008. Disillusioned with the war and the broader vision of the administration, American voters punished the Republicans when they handed control of both houses of Congress to the Democrats in the elections of November 2006.

Facing a military quagmire in Iraq and rising political discontent at home, Bush made his next move. In an address to the American people on January 10, 2007, he announced that the United States would send an additional 21,500 troops to Iraq, a surge whose purpose was to halt the country's descent into chaos, particularly in Baghdad. The mission of the troops was to go into Baghdad's toughest neighborhoods. Holding out hope that increased force could do the job, Bush said that in the past "there were too many restrictions on the troops we did have" and that this time "we will have the force levels we need to hold the areas that have been cleared."

Bush's decision to send more troops to Iraq should not be interpreted as determination on the part of Washington to fight through to final victory. Indeed, Bush hinted at that in his speech when he said that "victory will not look like the ones our fathers and grandfathers achieved. There will be no surrender ceremony on the deck of a battleship." Talk of "mission accomplished" was no longer a part of the chastened U.S. administration's vocabulary.

PRESIDENT GEORGE W. BUSH presides over the most powerful enterprise in the history of humanity, the American Empire. Its military, economic, technological, and cultural prowess is without parallel. Empires have risen and fallen over the millennia. Empires are gargantuan enterprises, behemoths. To those who live in the dominant center of an empire and to those who are ruled by one and live in its periphery, it is difficult to imagine that such a mighty entity can ever stumble and fall. But like all human creations, empires are transitory. In the end, they do stumble and fall.

Some empires endure for thousands of years, while others flash and fail quickly. The proto-empire of Adolf Hitler rose and crashed into oblivion in a mere twelve years. Because it happened less than twenty years ago and can be remembered by many of us, the collapse of the Soviet Empire provides even more stunning evidence that empires fall. While the Nazi Empire was conquered by a more powerful coalition of states, the Soviet Empire, although challenged from without, crumbled from within.

Because the essence of empire is the rule of one people over others, empires are prone to crisis. The lives of empires are punctuated by collisions—collisions successfully negotiated that lead on to greater things, and collisions that weaken or even terminate an empire.

Today the American Empire is in crisis, the consequence of military, economic, and political collisions that point toward an uncertain future. While collisions with external forces play a major role in the crisis of the American Empire, its essence is the disagreement among Americans and their elites about the role of the United States in the world. The American Empire is experiencing a crisis of legitimacy. From the crisis it confronts in the dog days of the administration of George W. Bush, the empire can be re-floated under more astute management, or it can founder, perhaps convincing Americans that the career of their country as an imperial power has been more trouble than it was worth.

In the halcyon days of the 1990s, the sorry state to which America has sunk in the world would have seemed unimaginable. The invasion of Iraq in 2003 was a matter of choice rather than necessity. George W. Bush and his top advisers believed that the United States would emerge stronger from the conflict, not only in the Middle East but in the world. The invasion of Afghanistan in the weeks following the terror attacks of September 11, 2001, was less optional, not because it was strategically necessary or has turned out well for the United States—it has not—but because it would have been difficult for any American president to have refrained from unleashing maximum force against the regime that harbored Al Qaeda and Osama bin Laden in a time of such understandable American popular fury.

George W. Bush was not just any American president. Whatever his personal strengths and weaknesses, he headed up the most determinedly right-wing regime in American history. It is not that his Republican predecessors, Ronald Reagan and George Bush, the elder, did not command right-wing regimes. It is that George W. Bush's regime has been more unilateralist in its outlook, believing more fervently than its forerunners in the salutary benefits of the use of force. "Give war a chance" could not unfairly be deemed to have been the watchword of Vice-President Dick Cheney, Secretary of Defense Donald Rumsfeld, and Deputy Secretary of Defense Paul Wolfowitz, in addition to the influential members of the neo-conservative intellectual chorus, William Kristol, Richard Perle, Robert Kagan, David Frum, and other armchair warriors.

The Bush team despised Europe, fervently believing that the Western alliance was more a hindrance than a benefit to America. The trouble with the Europeans, in their eyes, was that they had lost the martial virtues of their ancestors. With the exception of the Brits, who produced Margaret Thatcher, the "iron lady," they had become weak-willed compromisers, too inclined to see the other fellow's point of view. Moreover, they had fallen so far behind the United States in military capability that they were no longer much use on a battlefield. Mostly, they were only worth inviting to a war after it had been won and someone was needed to help clean up. The tone was captured in January 2003, when Donald Rumsfeld airily dismissed Western European opposition to the impending invasion: "You look at vast numbers of other countries in Europe, they're not with France and Germany ... they're with the U.S. You're thinking of Europe as Germany and France. I don't. I think that's old Europe."

The members of the Bush administration were, more than anything else, committed to the American imperial project in a more visionary, far-sighted, and ruthless way than their predecessors had been. That is what makes the disastrous record of the members of this administration so important, not just as an American political saga, but as a test of their approach to managing an empire.

More than the Bush administration was in crisis. The global position of the United States has been threatened. The U.S. military is over-stretched. Iran appears to be the major winner as a consequence of the Iraq debacle, more likely than ever to become a more powerful regional player. North Korea defied the will of the international system with its nuclear test in the autumn of 2006. Washington had to rely on China, its ultimate global rival, to rein in Pyongyang. In February 2007, at six-party talks in Beijing, China brokered a deal with the regime of Kim Jong-Il under which North Korea agreed to disable nuclear facilities in return for energy aid.

The financial position of the United States in the global system grows ever more imperiled, in need of a major correction. Americans owe over $2 trillion more to foreigners than is owed by foreigners to them. More than a trillion dollars in U.S. securities are held by the Chinese and the Japanese. The position of the dollar as the world's reserve currency is in doubt.

When we pull back from the details, what snaps into focus is the fact that the American Empire is in crisis. The United States faces problems remarkably similar to those experienced by previous empires. Empires are prone to overstretch, which sometimes leads to collapse and sometimes to successful reorganization.

ONE OF THE GREATEST CHALLENGES for people in any epoch is to imagine vast changes to the political and societal order in which they live. Ask the expert or the layperson whether a great empire will crumble or falter, or whether it could be overtaken by the rise of another empire and a new constellation of power relationships in the world, and they will almost always forecast only minor changes, alternatives within the existing order of things. If we stand back to observe the course of history, however, even if only over a relatively short period such as the last fifty to one hundred years, it is evident that vast transformations in the relations of the powers occur frequently. While it is exceedingly difficult to forecast the extent and even the direction of changes, there is no doubt that great changes will occur.

A major benefit, therefore, of studying the present dominant empire, that of the United States, in relation to the empires that came before—the purpose of this book—is that it helps to expose the basic factors that cause empires to rise and fall, that make it possible for them to endure or push them toward swift decline. Among those factors, of course, are material realities, the size of a state's economic output and its technical sophistication, the relative strength of its armed forces in relation to those of its rivals, the advantages and disadvantages of its geographical position. In addition to these factors are the ideas on which an empire is established, the ways its leaders seek to legitimate their rule over other peoples.

I have been using the term "American Empire" as though it is self-evident that the United States does preside over an empire. Although an increasing number of scholars—those who look with favor on the role the United States plays in the world as well as those who criticize it—acknowledge the existence of an American Empire, Americans rarely employ the term in their political discourse. In my view, for them to understand the global predicament they face, Americans would be much better off if they dispensed with the fiction that there is no American Empire.

This book probes the strengths and weaknesses of the American Empire as it navigates the turbulent seas of the twenty-first century.

SINCE THE DAWN OF RECORDED HISTORY, before the rise of the American Empire, there were three types of empires—slave/peasant empires (Egypt, Athens, Rome, Han-Chinese); mercantile empires (Spanish, early French and British); and capitalist empires (British, French, German, and Japanese).

While Egypt, Athens, Rome, and the Han-Chinese empires shared broad similarities, their cultures and circumstances made each of them unique. With the pyramids they built to house their dead rulers, the Egyptians achieved solidity and unparalleled imperial longevity, protected from frequent collisions with other powers by their geographic remoteness. The Athenians, at the height of their brilliant civilization, created a short-lived empire in which they converted allies into subjects. Their rise and the problems they encountered bring to mind the dilemmas of imperial America. The ancient empire most often compared to America's was Rome, whose dominion over the whole of the Mediterranean world was built on the strength of its military superiority. The Han-Chinese Empire began the construction of the Chinese state, whose enduring influence was indispensable to the creation of the world's most populous nation.

The great example of the mercantile empires was that of Spain, whose imperium was the first to span the globe, an empire that relied on slavery, the lust for profit in early capitalist Europe, and military supremacy financed by the gold and silver plundered from the peoples of the New World.

The capitalist empires of the late nineteenth century collided with each other in what is often regarded as the classic age of imperialism. The British Empire, which prided itself on its supposed cultural superiority over those it ruled, served as the role model for the empires of France, Germany, Japan, and other lesser powers.

The American Empire, which came to fruition in the postwar decades, and particularly following the collapse of the Soviet Union, is a fourth type of imperial venture. This is an empire over which the Stars and Stripes does not fly but throughout which the United States succeeds to a greater or lesser extent in achieving the long-term outcomes it seeks in economic, political, military, and cultural realms. Part One of the book introduces the debate that swirls around the American Empire today.

Part Two explores the empires that preceded that of America. Part Three analyzes the perils that face the American Empire in the twenty-first century. The book concludes with an assessment of whether the United States, with its democratic heritage, is suited to sustaining an empire.

More than any other kind of ruling arrangement, an empire makes claims to power, and to longevity, if not to eternity. Both the rulers and the ruled in an empire glory in, or resign themselves to, these certainties, depending on their circumstances. If all empires make these assertions, throughout history empires have faced a range of challenges that greatly affect their capacity for survival.

In the West, our image of an empire that made credible claims to longevity is Rome. Roma Aeterna. Eternal Rome: this seems not too great a boast. That is why the sight of imperial ruins in Rome itself or elsewhere around the Mediterranean is so unsettling. A crumbling triumphal arch, erected to commemorate a battle won and to warn that future foes will face the same fate, proclaims hubris and the tragedy of the human condition. Nothing lasts forever.

But some empires endure for much longer than others. Consider this. If the Roman Empire, from the time of the creation of the original city-state—long before Rome acquired an empire—had lasted as long as the Egyptian Empire, it would still exist today. One reason the Egyptian Empire survived—despite great upheavals and reorganizations—was because during the three-thousand-year span of its empire, Egypt was comparatively isolated from external foes. By the time Rome established itself, the geopolitical world of the Mediterranean was much more crowded than it had been in Egypt's heyday. Indeed, it was the rise of Rome that finally finished Egypt off as an imperial power in the time of Cleopatra.

The British Empire did not endure nearly as long as Rome or Egypt. The empire on which the "sun never set" lasted a little longer than three and a half centuries. Britannia can make a claim to having ruled the waves from the defeat of the Spanish Armada in 1588 until the early part of the Second World War. The golden age of Royal Navy dominance lasted, with interruptions, only from the Battle of Trafalgar in 1805 to the end of the First World War.

In addition to permanence, empires pride themselves on the superior attributes—cultural, racial, or technological—that make them fit to dominate others. A proud claim of Americans is that the United States is a democracy, which makes their influence over others a veritable preparatory school for democracy. The Americans are not the first to make this claim. Several centuries before the birth of Christ, the Athenians mounted a short-lived empire that included the odd practice of imposing democratic constitutions on the city-states they conquered.

This is not a "how to" book that advises Americans to make use of the lessons of the past to manage their own empire. Comparisons among empires shed light on the nature of states and governing arrangements. But the beauty and the horror of history are that its passages are always unique, never repeated.

PART 1
THE
EMPIRE
DEBATE

Facing Up to Empire

"The Americans have had an empire since Teddy Roosevelt, yet persist in believing they do not."[1]

"The former American Secretary of State Dean Acheson famously said that Britain had lost an empire but failed to find a role. Perhaps the reality is that the Americans have taken our old role without yet facing the fact that an empire comes with it."[2]

The seminal geopolitical issue of our time is the debate about the American Empire. What does it mean for the world in the twenty-first century that one state dominates the globe as never before? Is the American Empire a necessary guarantor of democracy and free markets? Or should the quest to impose American values on humanity awaken us to the danger that the pursuit of a universal order is the road to tyranny? A major blind spot of American political leaders, in striking contrast to political thinkers, is their almost universal denial that an American Empire actually exists. In truth, the American Empire is much more similar to the empires that have preceded it over the past six thousand years than Americans think. And although the technology available to the Americans far surpasses that at the disposal of their imperial forebears, the goals of empire and the consequences are not so different.

Broadly speaking, an empire exists when one people or state conquers, subjugates, or dominates another people for an extended period of time. Military conquest is a common feature of imperial expansion, whether we are talking about ancient empires such as China and Rome or modern empires such as Britain and America. But conquest is not essential to empire. Peoples and states can fall under the sway of an empire without a shot being fired, without a single imperial soldier entering their territory. Furthermore, it is not necessary for the flag of the imperial power to be raised over a country for it to fall under the sway of the empire. Rome allowed various local governing arrangements to continue in some of the territories within its empire. Much of the British Empire comprised countries, such as Egypt and even Argentina, over which the Union Jack did not fly. Today, the American Empire is made up almost entirely of countries that are not currently occupied by U.S. troops and over which the Stars and Stripes does not fly.

An empire is first, last, and always an affair of blood. However its existence is justified to its core population and to those who come under its heel, an empire rests on the shedding of blood or the threat to shed blood. Empires have existed for thousands of years and in almost all regions of the world. Empires rose and fell long before nations, in the modern sense of the term, appeared on the historical stage. For almost as long as there have been tribes, there have been empires. In their earliest form, empires came into being when one tribe conquered a neighboring tribe and held sway over the conquered people for a lengthy period. In this way, proto-empires undoubtedly existed that have left no pictographic, hieroglyphic, or written records and no archaeological remnants that can be clearly deciphered. Sumer, Assyria, the Indus States, the States of the Yellow River, the Maya, the Aztecs, and the Incas came and went as imperial powers.

From the dawn of civilization until the end of the Cold War, the world has witnessed three kinds of empires, slave/peasant empires, mercantile empires, and capitalist empires. In the early years of the twenty-first century, we are face to face with a fourth type of empire: the American Empire. While the American Empire is novel in the extent of its global sway, it embodies a form of rule of one people over many others that is as old as recorded history.

In the mid-twentieth century, historians and social scientists were drawing the not unreasonable conclusion that empires were quickly becoming a thing of the past. The British Empire, which had ruled one-quarter of humanity at the beginning of the twentieth century, was losing its imperial holdings in rapid succession. And the French and Dutch empires, despite vicious wars to prevent their dissolution, were also disintegrating. With the three largest European imperial systems fast going to their extinction it is no wonder that analysts concluded that they were witnessing the end of empire. Mid-century speculation about the demise of empires was powerfully reinforced several decades later. In a remarkable process, between 1989 and 1991, the Soviet Empire, successor to the Empire of the Czars and the ruler of an Eastern European realm conquered by Soviet armies in the Second World War, crumbled, to be replaced by a host of successor states. It seemed that the twentieth century had been the great age of imperial dissolution.

New ideas do not emerge in a historical or societal vacuum. For more than four decades, from the mid-1940s to 1991, the case for the projection of American power in the world rested on the struggle against Communism and the Soviet Empire. The struggle was portrayed in terms of stark polarities: freedom versus totalitarianism; capitalism versus Communism; human rights versus human bondage; West versus East. This was a twilight struggle that would go on until one side vanquished the other. In a bipolar world conceived by pro-American ideologists in these terms, the arguments that could be made on behalf of American intervention on a global scale were ready to hand. America was the most powerful member of the worldwide alliance of free nations. It was *primus inter pares*, first among equals. The history of America had made it the very shrine of liberty, and its power was being used to promote freedom everywhere. American power, understood this way, did not threaten the liberty of others; it was the guarantor of that liberty. The issue, therefore, was not American domination, but rather the prospects for advancing the cause of freedom against tyranny.

While the rationale for a muscular U.S. role in the world was much harder to make at some times than at others, notably during the Vietnam War, it was a case that stood up well enough throughout the Cold War. There was no need for America's defenders to conceive of the United States as an empire and to make the case that an empire could be benign. The traditional and attractive American portrayal of the United States as the home of modern history's first anti-imperial revolution sufficed as long as an alternative world system posed a real danger.

The sudden and largely unanticipated collapse of the Soviet Union and its empire changed everything. With no superpower foe remaining as a challenger, what was the rationale for the United States continuing to exercise military and political as well as economic power around the world? In the first flush of post–Cold War euphoria, the twin ideas of the end of history and the borderless world made their appearance. This was a moment for utopian thinking. All great ideologies conceive of the world in terms of a struggle to the death against the "other," the ideological opponent that threatens to negate all that is good. Marxists talk of the withering away of the state that will follow the demise of capitalism. That is their version of the end of history and the borderless world.

Before the end of the Cold War, only those on the political left who were critics of the role the United States played in the world claimed that there was an American Empire. While it remains unthinkable for American politicians to acknowledge that the United States possesses an empire, it has become ever more common for thinkers on the political center or right to grant that an American Empire exists and to insist that it plays a useful, indeed absolutely necessary, role in the world. As debate shifts toward a much wider acceptance of the existence of an American Empire, two other debates have opened up. The first one rages about whether the American Empire can serve the broad interests of humanity, and the second one concerns whether the American Empire is sustainable.

As is the case with all empires, those at the helm of the American Empire must constantly ask themselves the crucial question: what imperial frontiers can be sustained at a cost that is not prohibitive? The Romans decided, for instance, that most Scots and Germans were not worth the outlay in blood and treasure needed to control them. In the United States, all serious shades of political opinion are committed to the continuance of the American Empire. What divides them is strategy and tactics. The so-called multilateralists are prepared to limit the extent of the empire and understand the need to use soft as well as hard power to achieve their goals, to cajole as well as to conquer. The unilateralists—the neo-conservatives who are now in power—dare to thrust the empire into exorbitantly costly conflicts on the frontiers, believing that the stick is mightier than the carrot.

The political base of the unilateralists, the red states, is the home of American isolationism, where the belief in low taxation is second only to that in godliness. The multilateralists in the blue states, culturally less distant from the rest of the world, are prepared to tolerate somewhat higher taxes.

The unilateralists are using their power to defend and extend imperial frontiers. But as a consequence of their extravagant misrule, the empire is in serious disrepair at its very center. Foreign central bankers, led by Japan and China, have their grip on America's fiscal lifeline, holding more than $1 trillion in U.S. government securities. Foreigners hold close to $4 trillion worth of U.S. financial assets. The U.S. dollar is depreciating against other currencies and its position as the world's reserve currency is in peril. Observers recognize that the American current account and government deficits are not sustainable. Unwilling to pay for their wars and the cost of their global military establishment, the affluent and the rich in the United States are living in denial as America plunges ever further into debt. (Americans now owe foreigners $2 trillion more than foreigners owe them, and that figure increases daily.)

While the benefits of empire are many, so too are the costs. No empire can be sustained for long without a ruling class that is prepared to bear its burdens. The British upper classes were willing to pay the price in the eighteenth century during their struggle against the French Empire. They paid high taxes, won, and kept their heads. The French aristocrats refused to pay, their state collapsed, and they went to the guillotine during the French Revolution. The Roman Empire also collapsed because its upper classes turned up their noses at taxes. For the British rulers there was a happy ending after Waterloo in 1815. With their enemy vanquished, they enjoyed a century of low taxation and cheap empire. Do the American upper classes, with their pronounced taste for immediate gratification, have the stomach for the coming struggle with China?

The collapse of the Soviet Union and its Eastern European empire occurred so suddenly that the United States was left in a state of considerable embarrassment. America's global footprint, which was always much larger than that of its Soviet rival, had been justified for four decades by the doctrine that the United States was containing Communism and protecting the free world.

The Soviet implosion was succeeded by American triumphalism under the utopian banner of the "end of history." It was the capitalist equivalent of the Marxist doctrine that with Communism, the state would wither away. But even during the happy days of tech stock frenzy, Americans who were not about to shut down their military bases and call home their multinational corporations needed some new way to justify the enormous role they played everywhere. The theory that the United States was the "indispensable nation" in the global system, much touted by Secretary of State Madeleine Albright during the Clinton administration, was serviceable enough during that transitional time, the so-called era of globalization, before the new age of blood and iron that began with the terror attacks on New York City and Washington, DC, on September 11, 2001.

More robust ideas to justify American hegemony were needed for a harsher age, and they have appeared. Like an imperial starship, the Bush administration's doctrine that the United States has the right to preemptive intervention anywhere against perceived threats looms over the planet. But the starship is surrounded by a halo, the shining ephemera of a new liberal justification of American empire that plays the role in our world that Christian missionaries played in the days of the old imperialism. The missionary imperialists have performed a great service for the Bush administration, making its policies palatable to many who would not otherwise regard them as legitimate.

Well before September 11, an intellectual industry was churning out works dedicated to justifying the exercise of American power in the world. Even then, the notion of the indispensable nation was being contested by the much more muscular assertions of the Project for the New American Century, a group of neo-conservative thinkers who were defining the problem of how to sustain American global hegemony into the indefinite future.

In the moment of Western triumph, it seemed that the great questions had been answered. Some version of liberal capitalism would prevail everywhere. Even in the dark corners of the unreconstructed world, it was only a matter of time. In such an era, it appeared that markets had emerged victorious over states. Perhaps the time had arrived for the American legions to come home so that the victors could enjoy the dividends of peace.

Utopianism died quickly. Even before the Soviet Union had expired, the first Gulf War was fought in 1991. In the autumn of 1992, the Americans sent forces to Somalia in a failed attempt to bring order to that war-torn country. And in the background, and sometimes in the foreground, were the wars in the former Yugoslavia. The borderless world did not go out of fashion all at once. It lingered as a tattered companion of globalization, which was understood as moving forward inexorably, driven by communications technology, during the 1990s. For those who did not believe that globalization ensured prosperity for all, there was the rise of the anti-globalization movement, which reached its peak in a series of spectacular demonstrations against the World Trade Organization, the International Monetary Fund, and the proposed Free Trade Area of the Americas, between the autumn of 1999 and the summer of 2001.

What brought down the curtain on the idea that all the basic questions had been resolved were the terror attacks on New York City and Washington, DC, on September 11, 2001. It's not that the attacks fundamentally changed the world, as was so often claimed, but that they changed how the world was interpreted. After September 11, it became plain even to those who had been dazzled by the prospect of the perpetual domination of markets that neither the state nor borders were withering away. First to feel the change—the canary in the mineshaft— was the youthful anti-globalization movement. It was snuffed out when liberal capitalism receded before the looming presence of the surveillance state and a world of perpetual war.

American power in the world was a palpable fact, economically, technologically, militarily, and culturally. Was it an anomaly or would American global power become a permanent feature of global architecture? It was these questions that opened the door to a reconsideration of the role of empires in the world, past and present.

When geopolitical conditions are transformed, so too are the ideas that are marshaled to lend legitimacy to a new structure of power. While mainstream American political discourse refuses to acknowledge the existence of an American Empire, a group of intellectuals has stepped forward to make the case for the virtues of that empire. One prominent member of the group is British historian Niall Ferguson, who has taken to lecturing the Americans, much in the manner of the Greeks who tutored the Romans. His goal is to win America's political class around to the view that the Americans do rule an empire and that that is not a bad thing.

Ferguson argues that the British Empire, warts notwithstanding, helped civilize the world and that in the twenty-first century the Americans need to do the same. "What lessons can the United States today draw from the British experience of empire?" he asks.

The obvious one is that the most successful economy in the world—as Britain was for most of the eighteenth and nineteenth centuries—can do a very great deal to impose its preferred values on less technologically advanced societies. It is nothing short of astonishing that Great Britain was able to govern so much of the world without running up an especially large defence bill. . . . This was money well spent. No doubt it is true that, in theory, open international markets would have been preferable to imperialism; but in practice global free trade was not and is not naturally occurring. The British Empire enforced it.[3]

American polemicists, ideologues, and geostrategists are also stepping forward to make the case for the American Empire, although they are more reserved than Ferguson about the use of the word "empire." Both liberals and conservatives have been making the case for the American Empire. Because there are serious disagreements between the liberals, who are usually multilateralists, and the conservatives, who are often unilateralists, the key fact that both sides in the debate are advocating empire can easily be overlooked.

In *The Grand Chessboard*, Zbigniew Brzezinski, who served as national security adviser during the presidency of Jimmy Carter from 1977 to 1981, set out the liberal, multilateralist position. He analyzed the unique position of the United States in the contemporary system of global power, compared it to earlier empires, and made a case for how Americans should use their global position: "The exercise of American 'imperial' power," he wrote, "is derived in large measure from superior organization, from the ability to mobilize vast economic and technological resources promptly for military purposes, from the vague but significant cultural appeal of the American way of life, and from the sheer dynamism and inherent competitiveness of the American social and political elites."[4]

Brzezinski's analysis of American global power was both hard-headedly realist and sentimentally utopian. If this seems contradictory, even baffling, this juxtaposition, in fact, is a common feature of the new pro-imperial writing. In it the world is first analyzed in geopolitical terms and care is taken to show that American power rests on various pillars—economic, technological, military, and cultural. Comparisons are made that show the continuities and discontinuities between America and the empires of the past. When realism gives way to utopian hopefulness, the assertion is made that while America is indeed an empire and while empires can create benefits for subject peoples and the world as a whole, the American Empire is qualitatively different from all earlier empires. American power, if used properly, can be the handmaiden to a new world that will be better for all.

Brzezinski acknowledges that American global dominance "unavoidably evokes similarities to earlier imperial systems, the differences are more essential . . . American global power is exercised through a global system of distinctively American design that mirrors the domestic American experience. Central to that domestic experience is the pluralistic character of both the American society and its political system."

In contrast to the American polity, based on pluralism, the earlier empires were established by aristocracies and were ruled by regimes that for the most part were authoritarian. The people of these imperial states usually lacked political influence, and in more recent times they became caught up in emotional support for empire and imperial symbols, such as Britain's "white man's burden" or France's "*mission civilisatrice*."[5]

Brzezinski's portrayal of the American Empire is painted in much more attractive colors. Americans, he believes, have been much less enthusiastic about the projection of American power abroad than the people in earlier imperial powers. Following the end of the Cold War, there was little gloating in the United States about its victory over the Soviet Union.

American power, according to Brzezinski, has been massively reinforced by U.S. domination of "global communications, popular entertainment, and mass culture" and by the very real clout of "America's technological edge and global military reach."[6]

In his study of the American global system, Brzezinski focuses entirely on Eurasia, which he conceives as "the chief geopolitical prize" for America. The world's largest landmass, with a population of four billion people, and over 70 percent of global economic output, Eurasia has always been central to geopolitical analysts. Early in the twentieth century, the British geographer Harold Mackinder developed the concept of Eurasia as the pivotal area for the exercise of power globally. His famous dictum went as follows: "Who rules Eastern Europe commands the Heartland; Who rules the Heartland commands the World-Island; Who rules the World-Island commands the world."[7]

In his analysis of the Eurasian states, which Brzezinski named "geostrategic players," he concluded that over time the unique position of the United States as a non-Eurasian power, able to dominate Eurasia, and therefore, the world, was certain to decline. "Since America's unprecedented power is bound to diminish over time," he argues, "the priority must be to manage the rise of other regional powers in ways that do not threaten America's global primacy."[8]

Facing a future in which its own relative power was bound to diminish, American strategy ought to be to foster pluralism in Eurasia in the hope that as great powers emerged there, they would be "strategically compatible" with the United States. If the United States played the game shrewdly, the American Empire, Brzezinski believes, was capable of making itself the last of history's empires. Through the exercise of judgment, indeed strategic brilliance, America could oversee the emergence of a world in which its values could suffuse the world order and a number of powers could genuinely share political responsibility. In this way, America could be the empire to end all empires, much as Marx saw working-class power as the portal through which humanity could end the rule of one class over another.

Brzezinski's stratospheric overview—analogous to the strategy of a chess grand master, leading ultimately to an elegant conclusion in which America stamps its character on the world for the long term, eliminating the need for empires—was not for everyone. Parting company from him were the unilateralists, the American neo-conservative thinkers whose goal was permanent American hegemony. The idea of an American Empire, followed by a world order with a collective leadership, even if that order bore an indelibly American stamp, was too platonic a vision to appeal to neo-conservatives.

An organization that has brought together neo-conservative thinkers, top military brass, lobbyists for defense contractors, and members of Congress is the Project for the New American Century. Established in 1997, the Project included political analyst Robert Kagan, neo-conservative publisher William Kristol, and Paul Wolfowitz, later to serve as deputy secretary of defense from 2001 to 2005, who were "concerned with the decline in the strength of America's defenses, and in the problems this would create for the exercise of American leadership around the globe."[9]

Participants in the Project lobbied Washington to increase U.S. defense spending at a time when the United States was spending more on its military than the next eight powers combined. Their rationale for increased spending was that

at present the United States faces no global rival. America's grand strategy should aim to preserve and extend this advantageous position as far into the future as possible. There are, however, potentially powerful states dissatisfied with the current situation and eager to change it, if they can, in directions that endanger the relatively peaceful, prosperous and free condition the world enjoys today. Up to now, they have been deterred from doing so by the capability and global presence of American military power. But, as that power declines, relatively and absolutely, the happy conditions that follow from it will be inevitably undermined.[10]

In September 2000, the Project published a report titled *Rebuilding America's Defenses: Strategy, Forces and Resources for a New Century*. The ideological bent of the report was made plain in the acknowledgment that its approach grew out of "the defense strategy outlined by the Cheney Defense Department in the waning days of the Bush Administration. The Defense Policy Guidance (DPG) drafted in the early months of 1992 provided a blueprint for maintaining U.S. pre-eminence, precluding the rise of a great power rival, and shaping the international security order in line with American principles and interests."

Lamenting that the work of Dick Cheney's Defense Department undertaken by the administration of George Bush Sr. was buried by the Clinton administration, the report stated that "the basic tenets of the DPG, in our judgment, remain sound."[11] What made the report so important was that it was written by people very close to the first Bush administration who later came to play decisive roles in the administration of George W. Bush. The role of the Project for the New American Century was to keep the interests together that had enjoyed power under Bush the elder until the time came when an administration with a similar outlook would occupy the White House. Because the report was written while these key people were in opposition, their pronouncements were more candid than would have been the case in an official document.

"The American peace has proven itself stable and durable," the report began. "It has, over the past decade, provided the geopolitical framework for widespread economic growth and the spread of American principles of liberty and democracy. Yet no moment in international politics can be frozen in time; even a global Pax Americana will not preserve itself."[12]

To sustain the Pax Americana, the authors argued, the U.S. military needed to be rebuilt around four key missions:

- the defense of the American homeland;
- the capacity to fight, and decisively win, major theater wars simultaneously;
- the performance of "constabulary" duties that arise out of the need to shape the security environment in critical regions;
- the transformation of the U.S. armed forces to exploit what the authors call the "revolution in military affairs."

The report's unilateralism was unapologetic. On nuclear weapons, the authors excoriated the Clinton administration for its support for the Comprehensive Test Ban Treaty (CTBT), which had been ratified by 150 nations. While the Clinton administration's effort to ratify the treaty was voted down by the U.S. Senate, the Clinton White House pledged that the country would behave as though it were a party to the treaty and would not test nuclear weapons. In the long term, as far as the authors of the report were concerned, this was not a tenable strategy. "If the United States is to have a nuclear deterrent that is both effective and safe," the report reads, "it will need to test."[13]

The authors of the report envisaged a defense posture in which the U.S. military's missions would range beyond defending America to winning wars far from U.S. shores and acting as global police in unstable and strategically important parts of the world. That this was a blueprint for an empire rather than a nation-state was evident in the recommendation that a key task for the U.S. forces must be to control "the new 'international commons' of space and 'cyberspace,' and pave the way for the creation of a new military service—U.S. Space Forces—with the mission of space control."[14] This group of American thinkers sought the "weaponization of space," which has been condemned by many in the world as potentially triggering a new and dangerous arms race.

The authors of the report thought in offensive, not defensive, terms about the mission of the U.S. military. They advocated building a missile defense system for the United States. At first glance it would appear that the primary goal of missile defense would be to protect the United States against a nuclear attack by a rogue state. That, however, was not uppermost in the authors' thinking. "Without it [missile defense]," the report reasoned, "weak states operating small arsenals of crude ballistic missiles, armed with basic nuclear warheads or other weapons of mass destruction, will be in a strong position to deter the United States from using conventional force, no matter the technological or other advantages we may enjoy. Even if such enemies are merely able to threaten American allies rather than the United States homeland itself, America's ability to project power will be deeply compromised."[15]

In exceedingly frank language the authors championed missile defense as a way to prevent small countries from deterring the United States from imposing its will by launching a conventional military assault on them. Seen this way, missile defense was a tool for maintaining and extending the sway of the American Empire. Military strategists have always warned against simplistic distinctions between offensive and defensive weapons systems. Apparently a defensive weapons system, missile defense was understood by the authors of the report as key to maintaining America's offensive capability against not only small and truculent states but even a looming giant such as China.

In line with the geopolitical thinking of those who wrote it, the report, which was published before the terror attacks of September 11, 2001, recognized that the global strategic center of gravity was shifting from Europe to East Asia.[16] While many of these geostrategists would soon see the key strategic task as waging war against Islamic fundamentalism—George W. Bush's "war on terror"—at the time they wrote the report, they clearly regarded China as the next major strategic threat to America.

"Raising U.S. military strength in East Asia is the key to coping with the rise of China to great-power status," the report asserted. "By guaranteeing the security of our current allies and newly democratic nations in East Asia, the United States can help ensure that the rise of

China is a peaceful one. Indeed, in time, American and allied power in the region may provide a spur to the process of democratization inside China itself."[17]

Although recommending a shift in the regional deployment of U.S. forces, the report warned that "a requirement to station U.S. forces in northern and central Europe remains." The rationale, significantly, was not that this was crucial to European security, but that it was essential to sustaining U.S. power in Europe. "This is especially important in light of the nascent European moves toward an independent defense 'identity' and policy," the report read. "It is important that NATO not be replaced by the European Union, leaving the United States without a voice in European security affairs."[18] The authors believed that maintaining the U.S. foothold in Europe was a way to shore up American imperial interests, not European stability.

With an eye on the long-term future, the report seized on the so-called Revolution in Military Affairs (RMA) that had been made possible by technological transformation and the need for the U.S. military to take advantage of technological advances. The authors linked the creation of a U.S. global system of missile defense to the larger goal of establishing American control of space and cyberspace. The report called for the construction of a system of global missile defenses. "A network against limited strikes, capable of protecting the United States, its allies and forward-deployed forces, must be constructed," it stated. "This must be a layered system of land, sea, air and space-based components."[19]

Lamenting the unwillingness of the Clinton administration to ditch the 1972 Anti-Ballistic Missile (ABM) Treaty with the Soviet Union because it blocked the development of anti-ballistic missile defenses, the report rued the decision in 1993 to terminate the "Brilliant Pebbles" project. A feature of the Reagan administration's Star Wars program, the Brilliant Pebbles project "had matured to the point where it was becoming feasible to develop a space-based interceptor capable of destroying ballistic missiles in the early or middle portion of their flight—far preferable than attempting to hit individual warheads surrounded by clusters of decoys on their final course toward their targets. But since a space-based system would violate the ABM Treaty, the administration killed the 'Brilliant Pebbles' program, choosing instead to proceed with a ground-based interceptor and radar system—one that will be costly without being especially effective."[20]

Indeed, the weaponization of space, or the further weaponization of space as they conceived it, was a crucial notion for these planners, who saw this as essential if American global pre-eminence was to be sustained. "No system of missile defenses can be fully effective without placing sensors and weapons in space," the report stated. "Although this would appear to be creating a potential new theatre of warfare, in fact space has been militarized for the better part of four decades. Weather, communications, navigation and reconnaissance satellites are increasingly essential elements in American military power."[21]

The goal, spelled out by the authors of the report, was for the United States to exercise military control of space. This would necessitate "the application of force both in space and from space" and would include, but would not be limited to, anti-missile defenses.

Maintaining control of space would require, in the opinion of the authors, the establishment of a new American military service, to be called U.S. Space Forces. They reasoned that "it is almost certain that the conduct of warfare in outer space will differ as much from traditional air warfare as air warfare has from warfare at sea or on land; space warfare will demand new organizations, operational strategies, doctrines and training schemes. Thus, the argument to replace U.S. Space Command with U.S. Space Forces—a separate service under the Defense Department—is compelling."

The posture advocated in the report was aimed at sustaining American global pre-eminence into the indefinite future. There was no hint of any need to develop a collective leadership that included other nations or to forge an international regime to guarantee the rights of all nations. Its aim was to preserve and enhance the American Empire.

A number of those who were involved in the Project for the New American Century went on to wield power during the presidency of George W. Bush. Most notable was Paul Wolfowitz, who as undersecretary of state became a key advocate of the invasion of Iraq. After the September 11 terror attacks, these hard-liners were joined in their advocacy of the invasions of Afghanistan and Iraq by a new group of pro-imperial allies from a quite different part of the political spectrum.

This latter group was composed of liberal imperialists who envisaged imperial interventions as the only way to help build viable nations in chaotic regions of the world.

An important intellectual in this group was Michael Ignatieff, a Canadian who was Carr Professor of Human Rights Practice and director of the Carr Center for Human Rights Policy at Harvard University's John F. Kennedy School of Government. In late 2005, Ignatieff gave up this post and returned to Canada, where he won a seat in Parliament in the 2006 federal general election. Several months after the defeat of the Liberal government in that election, he launched an unsuccessful campaign to succeed Paul Martin as Liberal leader.

In his analysis of the structure of global power, Ignatieff recognized the existence of an American Empire: "It is an empire lite," he wrote, "hegemony without colonies, a global sphere of influence without the burden of direct administration and the risks of daily policing. It is an imperialism led by a people who remember that their country secured its independence by revolt against an empire, and who have often thought of their country as the friend of anti-imperial struggles everywhere. It is an empire, in other words, without consciousness of itself as such. But that does not make it any less of an empire, that is, an attempt to permanently order the world of states and markets according to its national interests."[22]

Elsewhere Ignatieff wrote: "We are no longer in the era of the United Fruit Company, when American corporations needed the Marines to secure their investments overseas. The twenty-first century imperium is a new invention in the annals of political science . . . a global hegemony whose grace notes are free markets, human rights and democracy, enforced by the most awesome military power the world has ever known."[23]

Ignatieff's thesis was that the world was beset by the problems of failed states, the wreckage of the process of decolonization of earlier empires in the 1950s and 1960s. Failed states, he argued, are preyed upon by barbarians, analogous to the barbarians who tore at the perimeters of the Roman Empire. As a consequence of modern technology, the barbarians are able to strike out at the imperial heartland as they did in the terror attacks of September 11, 2001. Faced with the barbarians, the imperial center has no choice but to hit back, using force where necessary, not only to protect itself against attacks, but also to occupy failed states so that they can be led back to health. This process he called nation-building. Thus, for Ignatieff, imperialism, for a time at least, is essential.

"Those who want America to remain a republic rather than become an empire imagine rightly," Ignatieff wrote in the months before the invasion of Iraq in 2003, "but they have not factored in what tyranny or chaos can do to vital American interests. The case for empire is that it has become, in a place like Iraq, the last hope for democracy and stability alike."[24]

Ignatieff's ideas are reminiscent of European imperialism during the belle époque. His is a "civilizing mission," and one can picture him at the Congress of Berlin in 1885, planning the division of the world with Otto von Bismarck and the other statesmen of the day. Ignatieff is very much a liberal imperialist, a believer in the idea that imperial America, for its own selfish reasons to be sure, could help lead peoples out of oppression and chaos. The addition of such thinkers to the ranks of those who supported the invasions of Afghanistan and Iraq has widened the political spectrum of those willing to lend their endorsement to the imperial wars of George W. Bush. As time passed, however, and the missions, particularly the one in Iraq, bogged down into a morass in which a sustained insurgency and growing conflict within Iraqi society made U.S. success appear highly unlikely, some staunchly conservative personalities proclaimed that they were no longer on board.

In the early months of 2006, Francis Fukuyama, author of the utopian conservative testament *The End of History and the Last Man*, published a manifesto in which he announced that he was no longer a neo-conservative. As he rehearsed in the preface of his new book, *America at the Crossroads: Democracy, Power, and the Neoconservative Legacy*, he had "long regarded" himself "as a neo-conservative," believing he shared "a common worldview with many other neo-conservatives—including friends and acquaintances who served in the administration of George W. Bush." He had worked on two occasions for Paul Wolfowitz. Earlier he had been a student of Allan Bloom, author of *The Closing of the American Mind*, himself a student of Leo Strauss, the intellectual godfather of neo-conservatism.

27

Fukuyama had also attended graduate school with William Kristol and had frequently contributed to *The National Interest* and *The Public Interest*, two periodicals founded by William's father, Irving Kristol. He had written as well for *Commentary Magazine*, the flagship neo-conservative periodical, founded by Norman Podhoretz. This list of his relationships makes it clear that Fukuyama had been a neo-conservative with a rare pedigree.[25]

In his analysis, Fukuyama eviscerated the tenets of the neo-conservative American foreign policy pursued by the administration of George W. Bush. He harshly critiqued the National Security Strategy (NSS) issued by the White House in September 2002, arguing that in making the case for pre-emptive war in the new age of terrorism and weapons of mass destruction, the administration had fatally blurred the distinction between pre-emptive war and preventive war. While he was prepared to contemplate pre-emptive war on those rare occasions when the United States was clearly threatened with an imminent attack, Fukuyama had an altogether different view of preventive wars, in which the United States invaded a country to halt its capacity to mount a threat at some point in the future.

"The problem with the NSS doctrine," according to Fukuyama, "was that in order to justify stretching the definition of preemption to include preventive war against nonimminent threats, the administration needed to be right about the dangers facing the United States. As it turned out, it overestimated the threat from Iraq specifically, and from nuclear terrorism more generally."

Fukuyama continues: "The actual experience of the Iraq war ought to demonstrate that the distinction between preemptive and preventive war remains a significant one. We have not abruptly moved into a world in which rogue states routinely pass WMD to terrorists; such a world may yet emerge, but acting as if it were here now forces us into some extremely costly choices. Even under post-September 11 conditions, preventive war remains far more difficult to justify prudentially and morally than pre-emptive war and ought properly to be used in a far more restricted number of cases."[26]

The White House endorsement of the concept of preventive war, in Fukuyama's view, struck at the heart of the integrity of state sovereignty, the system that has been in place, at least in theory, since the Peace of

Westphalia brought the Thirty Years' War to a conclusion in 1648. It was the overt challenge to the concept of state sovereignty that deeply alienated European allies, Fukuyama concluded.

From the standpoint of the Europeans and many others, the American insistence on the right to launch pre-emptive and preventive wars rested on the notion of "American exceptionalism," Fukuyama wrote. "Many countries face terrorist threats," he pointed out,

> and might be inclined to deal with them through pre-emptive intervention or the overturning of regimes deemed to harbour terrorists. Russia, China, and India all fall into this category, yet if any of them announced a general strategy of preemptive/preventive war as a means of dealing with terrorism, the United States would doubtless be the first country to object. The fact that the United States granted itself a right that it would deny other countries is based, in the NSS, on an implicit judgment that the United States is different from other countries and can be trusted to use its military power justly and wisely in ways that other powers could not.[27]

Fukuyama's break with the neo-conservatives did not mean that he had ceased to support the basic fact of the American Empire. What he was calling into question was the extreme lengths to which neo-conservatives were prepared to go to shore up the perimeters of the empire in dangerous and strategically crucial regions of the world, in particular the Middle East. Fukuyama's problem with the behavior of his erstwhile collaborators was strategic, not principled. From the standpoint of the well-being of the United States in the world, he was stating, it was highly unwise to use arguments that could only be justified on the ground that the United States was an unusually moral power, with a unique role to play in safeguarding the healthy functioning of the global system. The degree of unilateralism revealed in the NSS statement and in the Iraq War had driven too many states and their peoples into expressing hostile attitudes toward the United States. This was dangerous, in Fukuyama's view, and a strategy must be found that would safeguard American interests in the world without engendering such vast antagonism. The argument was about how to run the empire, not whether there ought to be one.

Parting company with the neo-conservative school of American foreign policy, Fukuyama declared himself a Wilsonian realist, a new school of foreign policy that he hoped would take its place alongside the other major schools, as he saw them—the Wilsonians, the liberal internationalists, the Jacksonian nationalists, and the neo-conservatives. Wilsonian realists would combine the traditional Wilsonian desire to achieve an international system based on rules and institutions, with the realist appreciation of the need for power and the use of power, including military power, and even in rare cases, pre-emptive and preventive war.

He was firm in his insistence that the United States should abandon the concept of American hegemony, however benevolent, and the idea of American exceptionalism as a basis for U.S. foreign policy. Fukuyama believed that the Bush administration's pursuit of regime change in a number of countries—for instance, the "axis of evil" states of Iraq, Iran, and North Korea—was far too disruptive and created more negative effects for the United States than it was worth. He believed that, in future, U.S. foreign policy should de-emphasize military power, in favor of "soft power," whenever possible in tandem with other democracies.

Interestingly, Fukuyama distinguished himself from the realist Henry Kissinger, who had always regarded the nineteenth-century Austrian Count Metternich as the model of a realist statesman. Instead Fukuyama suggested the model for twenty-first-century America ought to be Otto von Bismarck, the Chancellor of Germany and the founder of the Second German Reich. Having unified Germany, thereby achieving a dominant position in central Europe, following two successful wars against Austria and France, Bismarck understood "that Germany's main task would be to reassure its intimidated and resentful neighbors that Germany had become a status quo power," Fukuyama wrote.[28]

Similarly, he argued, the goal of the United States should be to limit the resentment of other powers by "deliberately seeking ways to downplay its dominance." Instead of this, the Bush administration, according to Fukuyama, provoked other powers following the September 11 terror attacks. Going beyond the intervention in Afghanistan, the administration "announced an open-ended doctrine of regime change and preventive war; it withdrew from or criticized a series of international institutions; and it implicitly asserted a principle of American exceptionalism in its self-proclaimed benevolent ordering of the world."[29]

Choosing Bismarck, the man of "blood and iron," as his example made clear the extent to which Fukuyama's Wilsonianism was to be balanced with a fierce realism. In his formulation it was not military power and global dominance that America should avoid. Rather, it was a too-ready willingness to offend others for no good purpose. America should wield real power, Fukuyama believed, without rubbing others' noses in that fact.

Fukuyama's attack on neo-conservatives was echoed by other thinkers, notably Zbigniew Brzezinski, who returned to the empire debate with a new salvo titled *The Choice: Global Domination or Global Leadership*. "The peremptory manner in which the administration decided, in mid-2002, to go to war against Iraq," he wrote, "reflected the degree to which the rise of a threat with global reach—transnational terrorism—created among American officials a disposition to make far-reaching strategic decisions in a narrow circle of insiders whose true motivations are obscure to the public."

Hailing from a different part of the ideological terrain from that inhabited by Fukuyama, Brzezinski was making a similar critique: "Personal impulses, specific group interests, and political calculations produced in stealth a sudden policy lurch with major international implications, justified publicly with very dramatic and occasionally demagogic rhetoric as well as questionable evidence. The sudden and almost simultaneous surfacing of the new strategic doctrine of pre-emptive war, reversing long-established international convention, further underscored the proposition that a beleaguered hegemony suffused with heightened domestic insecurity may not be congenial to a democratically open and deliberate formulation of foreign policy."[30]

In the summer of 2007, in an article in the *New York Times Magazine*, Michael Ignatieff joined those distancing themselves from the Bush administration's foreign policy by acknowledging that he had been wrong in expecting positive consequences to flow from an invasion of Iraq.

IN THE AFTERMATH of the Iraq debacle, a fundamental debate has erupted about how to manage the American Empire, to sustain it for the longer term. The outcome of that debate will condition the strategies of future American leaders in steering their country and the world order.

In terms of the American position in the world there are both advantages and disadvantages that come with the new frankness about the reality of an American Empire. The disadvantage, and it is a large one, has to do with perception. In an age when geostrategists are fond of talking about the importance of "soft power" in the world, especially for the United States, referring to America as an empire has definite drawbacks. If hard power involves economic and technological prowess and military capability, soft power refers to the force of ideas and culture. In short, soft power is about influence. America has been said to possess an enormous reserve of soft power in comparison with earlier empires because of the attractiveness of the American way of life, its commitment to democracy and human rights, and the global reach of its popular culture. Conceding the point that America is itself an empire can be expected to diminish its attractiveness for others, because no matter how exemplary an empire might be, at its core the idea of empire involves domination over others.

The advantages of recognizing that the world's only superpower is an empire are also considerable. First, strategic thinking based on reality and not on illusion produces effective results. If America is indeed an empire, its defenders and its strategic planners will benefit greatly from the simple act of facing up to that fact. Throughout history, from the days of the earliest empires to the twenty-first-century American behemoth, elites within empires have had to debate the central question of imperial strategy—how large can the empire grow while keeping its boundaries defensible at a cost that is not prohibitive? In the American case, thinkers can be divided into three categories: isolationists, unilateralists, and multilateralists. While isolationism is and has been a sentiment shared by a large number of Americans, it can scarcely be said to serve as the basis for important strategic thinking in our time. In practice, isolationists end up supporting unilateralists more often than they support multilateralists. In practice, then, the two major groups of thinkers can be said to be unilateralists and multilateralists. Multilateralists and unilateralists do not differ about their commitment to the American Empire and their desire to promote its long-term domination of the globe. They differ on how best to achieve this end.

Multilateralists believe that America has prospered as the leader of a coalition of nations that share similar values. They see it as America's task to bind the nations of the world within a system of rules that is largely conceived in the United States but that involves other nations as well. The Bretton Woods system, developed in 1944 to plan for the post–Second World War global economy, is an ideal example of what the multilateralists believe ought to be done. The system developed at Bretton Woods, New Hampshire, designated the U.S. dollar as the reserve currency of the global economy and created the International Monetary Fund, the World Bank, and the General Agreement on Tariffs and Trade, thereby placing the United States at the center of the global economy. At Bretton Woods, the British delegation, led by John Maynard Keynes, tried to change some of the arrangements, without success. The Americans had the power and they used it, but Bretton Woods was a multilateral arrangement, not a diktat. Through multilateral arrangements, this school of thought holds, foreigners can be made to see the need for adopting American principles and programs, without having them simply imposed.

For their part, unilateralists believe that the United States is hobbled by alliances and by the obligation to play by international rules. They like to portray America as a giant Gulliver tied down by a legion of Lilliputians. Unilateralists are particularly antagonistic to America's European allies, whom they portray as fearful welfare-state countries that are unwilling to use force when necessary to defend the interests of the West. Playing the game of these alliances—especially with the involvement of France, a country driven by envy of America, in the eyes of unilateralists, and a misguided notion that it can regain its lost global importance—weakens America's ability to act. Unilateralists hold that America is better off taking initiatives on its own so that hesitant allies cannot hold it back. And they believe that America should retain its sovereignty by avoiding international treaties and covenants. Unilateralists have opposed American adherence to the nuclear weapons test ban treaty, the land mines treaty, the Kyoto environmental accord, and the International Criminal Court. Unilateralists favored America's abrogation of the 1972 U.S.–Soviet Anti-Ballistic Missile Treaty.

The unilateralist position involved a contradiction, of which its adherents were aware but believed was worth taking. On the one hand, unilateralists wanted other countries to play by a clear set of rules, while on the other hand, the United States kept itself free from such rules. Characteristically, status quo powers, those that want to preserve the present order of things from which they derive advantage, favor international agreements. American multilateralists generally adopt this position. Unilateralists, on the other hand, believing that America can continue to increase its global power, consider that entering into such covenants involves trade-offs that are not in the American interest.

THE EMPIRE DEBATE, though not called by that name, roils American politics in the lead-up to the 2008 presidential election. It is a debate about how large an empire can be defended by the United States and afforded by its taxpayers. It is, as well, a debate about the extent to which America can go it alone, with or without allies. Just over a century ago, the rulers of the British Empire were wrestling about whether they could continue on a course they called "splendid isolation," or whether they needed to form permanent military alliances. Two thousand years ago, the leaders of the Roman Empire had to decide how much of Germany they could hold onto, given the intractable and wild disposition of the German tribes. Such debates have taken place in the great empires of the past. The ability of leaders to understand their situation, free from illusions, played a great part in determining how effectively they coped with challenges.

PART 2
HOW
EMPIRES
RISE AND FALL

The Empire in History

No historian can name the first empire to have existed. That empire, and dozens of others that succeeded it, are lost simply because we lack written or other records. We can surmise that the first empires or proto-empires appeared simultaneously with slavery. It is a chicken-and-egg question to ask which came first. They were essential to each other. Together, slavery and empire were the underpinnings for the emergence of civilization.

Empires first emerged when humans became able, through new techniques, to do more than merely provide for their own survival. This was the tragic and significant moment when it became profitable for conquerors to enslave, rather than simply to kill, their conquered foes. Empires were erected on the basis of the first rudimentary division of labor. It was Marx and Engels who first mentioned the link between slavery, empire, and the onset of civilization. Their explanation was as elegant as it was unwelcome. It demonstrated that before the existence of labor that had the means to produce a surplus, there would have been no point to slavery. Once a surplus could be produced, humanity crossed a great threshold. Gaining control of the labor of others was the indispensable way for those in a position of power to avoid menial toil. It was the road to luxury, riches, and greater power. Perhaps most important of all, it created an entirely new commodity—time for the fortunate few to be freed from toiling for mere survival so they could devote themselves to other pursuits. Those pursuits included making war, inventing new methods for constructing dwellings, and discovering novel ways to harvest crops and rear animals. As well, the newly created space and time opened the way to the arts, to the study of human and nonhuman nature, to debauchery, decadence, and the other refinements of civilization. Initially, it seems, slavery and empire were invented independently in a number of different places and times. Undoubtedly, some of those early imperial ventures did not succeed and people reverted to more primitive ways. At last, though, the leap forward was well and truly made.

It may come as a surprise to some that Engels wrote glowingly of the invention of slavery. In a famous passage, he concluded that "we are compelled to say—however contradictory and heretical it may sound—that the introduction of slavery under the conditions of that time was a great step forward." Engels reasoned that slavery "was an advance even for the slaves; the prisoners of war, from whom the mass of the slaves were recruited, now at least kept their lives, instead of being killed as they had been before, or even roasted, as at a still earlier period."[1]

It should not surprise us that the link between slavery and empire was an unwelcome insight. For the most part, the history of the species has been written by and on behalf of the privileged. The idea that wealth, the arts, sciences, and literature rest on the exploitation of the vast majority of the human race is a truth that has always been shunned. The rulers of empires, in common with the ruling classes within societies, have always been at pains to get out their side of the story. Broadly put, they have made the case that the road to material progress has necessitated human inequality, that inequality is the basis on which liberty and enlightenment rest. Thus it is the destiny of the primitive to be ruled by those who are culturally and technically superior. Indeed, the defenders of empires and ruling classes insist, the subjugation of primitive people is the means to their ultimate liberation.

The first type of empire we encounter, even when it rose to considerable heights as a civilization as in the case of Rome, is the slave empire. The first substantial slave empires, which came into existence thousands of years before Rome, arose in the great river valleys, which were conducive to agriculture and thus to the emergence of a division of labor in which some people, a lucky few, were able to live off the surplus wealth produced by others.

The second type of empire to take the historical stage was the mercantile empire. Wealth was generated through trade on advantageous terms between the metropolis and its colonies and dependencies. Frequently, little distinction was made between trade and plunder in early mercantilism. Pirates and traders were often interchangeable characters. The Venetian Empire, which emerged during the Dark Ages of the West after the fall of Rome, is an early case of this type of empire. Later, Portugal established a far-flung mercantile empire. Following Portugal was the

Spanish Empire, which for a considerable time made Spain the greatest global power.

The third historical type of empire was capitalist. Its heyday was the period from about 1870 to the outbreak of the First World War in 1914. During these few decades, about one-quarter of the world's land surface was seized or redistributed by eight advanced countries. For well over a century, debates have raged about what drove the great capitalist powers in their competitive grab for empire. Why in the space of a few decades did Britain, France, Germany, Italy, Belgium, Holland, Russia, and even the United States and Japan decide to avail themselves of colonies in Asia and Africa? Who profited from such empires?

Today's American Empire represents a new stage in the history of empires. To the three earlier stages—servile, mercantilist, and capitalist—we can add a fourth. Let's call it "global," by which we mean not only the unprecedented geographical sway of the American Empire, but its strategy of attempting to impose a system of rules for the whole world. This fourth stage imperialism, the American Empire, should not be confused with the neo-colonialism of the period following the break-up of the old European empires in the decades following the Second World War. Making use of the institutional structure first established at Bretton Woods in 1944, and building on those structures, the United States has concentrated on establishing a system that is most congenial to the norms of American capitalism.

The American Empire rests on a central contradiction. Rather than depending on the military occupation and annexation of foreign territories, it exercises control over states that are, to one degree or another, sovereign. Nominally sovereign states administer vast regions of the world in which the Americans have been able to impose their economic rules, military dominance, and cultural sway. This, of course, forces us to define the word "sovereign." In our era, many states, most in fact, are sovereign in theory, while operating within the norms of the American-centered global order. Their leaders may make decisions about their country's social and economic programs, but they are constrained by the overall power relations within the American-centered system. Those who govern these states operate largely in the realm of administration. On crucial matters such as flows of capital, relations of labor and capital, and rights of property, such states are constrained in the choices they can make. Those states that do not conform are labeled "rogue states" and are often on Washington's hit list for regime change. Then there are giants, like China, that operate within the American system in the way they run their economy and respect the rights of foreign investors but are also competitors and potential challengers that can be said to exercise much more sovereign power than most states.

One of the features of empires past and present is their need to proclaim their legitimacy and their merit to those in their own heartland and to those they dominate. When there is a marked degree of inequality, as is the case in empires, there is a more pronounced need to strive for legitimacy than is the case in more egalitarian settings. It is remarkable how often the same kinds of arguments have been made over the course of millennia to justify empires in different historical settings.

The most crude rationalization for imperial rule is that the conquerors are racially superior and have won the right to rule through force of arms. This is the most venerable of justifications, although it has been couched in terms that suit the ideas and culture of the times. In the earliest unrecorded empires conquest itself may have sufficed to prove that a particular tribe or leader was fit to rule. Even in these proto-empires it can be inferred that the will of particular gods could be invoked to establish legitimacy for the rulers.

The most hateful and crude of modern uses of the doctrine was that promulgated by the Nazis. Hitler's claim that the Germans had the right to rule others was based on pseudo-scientific "evidence" of Aryan racial superiority. The pseudo-science, of course, had its origins in the genuine science of Darwin's theory of evolution. From Darwin's depiction of survival of the fittest among species, it was not a long metaphorical step to concoct a struggle to the death among humanity's racial subgroups. The nineteenth-century forebears of Nazi ideologists were fond of studying the sizes and shapes of the heads of men and women to buttress their conclusion that northern Europeans were the pick of the crop.

When Hitler put into terrifying practice the ravings of the beer halls of Vienna and Munich, the Germans created a short-lived empire with a genocidal conception of the proper relations between the conquerors and the conquered. Given Germany's relatively modest population and resources and its geographical position in a crowded landscape surrounded by potential foes, Hitler's ideology was fatally flawed because it helped cement the alliance that ultimately crushed the Third Reich. In his last testament, dictated in his bunker beneath the ruins of Berlin in April 1945, Hitler turned on the Germans, declaring that they had shown themselves wanting in the supreme struggle for survival.

In modern times, the claim of racial superiority was by no means unique to the Nazis. The claim was advanced to underpin other European empires and the early American Empire. For late nineteenth-century Europeans and Americans, it seemed to be the dictate of nature itself that white men should rule peoples whose skins were black, brown, or yellow.

Racial and cultural justifications for conquests easily overlapped. Nineteenth-century Europeans and Americans possessed the advantages of industrial technology, the key to military supremacy. In an age that prized the idea of progress, industrial prowess itself became a justification for empire. To late nineteenth- and early twentieth-century Europeans and Americans, the cultural superiority of their countries was axiomatic. Science, technology, and physical might and the attribute that was cavalierly assumed to go with these, rationality, were all thought to belong to the imperialist nations of the West and to the white race.

Publicists and politicians who made the case for the British Empire claimed that Britons were spreading civilization to the far corners of the earth, enlightening peoples who were without science, reason, or culture. Far from being the product of conquest or of exploitation, imperialism was presented as a selfless gift from the strong to the weak, from the cultured to the benighted.

The purest form this took, of course, was the missionary movements, whose role was to propagate the Christian faith, in one form or another, to non-Christian peoples in Asia and in Africa. Missionaries had their own, often quite selfless, goals when they took the faith into places like western China, where they frequently spent decades running their missions. Missionaries often learned the languages of the people among whom they lived and some even became experts on their cultures. There was, however, an indelible assumption that the Christian faith they brought with them was the one true path to salvation.

Although missionaries might deplore the profiteers, the military, and the administrators who were a part of the imperial enterprise, the missionaries themselves were a component of it and played a crucial role in helping legitimate imperialism among the righteous, well-meaning middle classes in the imperial heartlands.

No empire can be sustained on the basis of force alone, although force is an indispensable feature of imperial rule. Winning the acceptance, however reluctant, of those ruled and of the people at large in the dominant society is a feature of every successful imperial venture. Indeed, as a general rule, as empires become more advanced in the techniques at their disposal, they rely ever more on seeking legitimacy for their rule.

The Roman, British, and American empires all found ways to legitimate their rule, each with quite different technologies available to them. In cities and administrative centers throughout their empire, the Romans spawned replicas of the society of Rome itself, each with its own hierarchy. The values of these satellites were closely attuned to those of Rome. The architecture of Rome, the celebration of Roman triumphs, and the worship of the emperor were all features of life in centers such as Bath in Roman Britain. The ability of the Romans to transform the outlook of the mass of local populations was limited. Nearly two millennia later, the British also concentrated on local elites as the key to establishing imperial legitimacy. Like the Romans, the British recruited locals into units of their military.

Only the Americans, with the full range of advanced technology at their disposal, have been able to undertake a drive to legitimate their dominance, not only through cultivating and educating the local elites, but by winning the hearts and minds of the population at large through the power of American popular culture. On movie, television, and computer screens, American cultural products have captured a global audience to a degree that completely eclipses the sway of earlier imperial cultures. American popular music can be heard in the streets of the world's cities; the annual Academy Awards ceremony in Los Angeles is watched by billions around the world.

Empires use the techniques of "soft power"—persuasion, propaganda, cultural and religious influences—to gain acceptance for their rule. But empires also require "hard power," the capacity to ensure domination through the use of force and, of equal importance, to create the perception that force can and will be used. In the earliest period of ancient Egypt, for instance, royal commemorative art was deployed as a way to illustrate who had power and who did not. "The king and his officials are shown in the special dress of their offices," writes Boston University historian Kathryn Bard, "while their conquered enemies wear next to nothing. A hierarchy of social classes is also evident, from the large-sized king, who is followed by his smaller sandal-bearer, to his even smaller officials, to the smallest figures of conquered enemies, farmers, and servants. The king is frequently depicted trampling on his enemies."[2] If intimidation was in use as early as 3000 B.C. in Egypt, it has not gone out of style today. On the first night of its assault on Baghdad in March 2003, the U.S. military unveiled a technique it called "shock and awe." The theory was that the foes of America would be so overpowered by the murderous pyrotechnics of the aerial assault that those who survived it would be enfeebled in its wake.

Both kinds of power, soft and hard, that have been deployed by the United States need to stand the test of scrutiny both at home and abroad to be effective. In *The Case for Goliath*, Michael Mandelbaum, the Christian A. Herter Professor of Foreign Policy at The Johns Hopkins University School of Advanced International Studies in Washington, DC, asserts that the world is much better off because of the governing role America plays in global affairs. "The plausible alternative" to the "American role as the functional alternative of the world's government," he writes, "is not considerably better global governance but considerably less of it, and the consequences of less government are not likely to be pleasant. For that reason, the verdict of other governments is, on the whole, in favor of the American role. Although they sometimes speak as if they would prefer that the United States shrink its global presence dramatically, they do not act as if that is what they really want." "About other countries' approach to the American role as the world's government," he concludes, "three things can be safely predicted: They will not pay for it; they will continue to criticize it; and they will miss it when it is gone."[3]

Egypt: The Secret of Longevity

The first region of the world to develop a recognizable civilization, distinct from the earlier patterns of life in neolithic times, was southern Mesopotamia, in the river valleys of the Tigris and Euphrates rivers. The richness of the soil, enhanced by a drainage system that brought deposits from further inland and by the effects of annual flooding, gave this region special advantages for the development of agriculture that could produce a yield well beyond the needs of the producers. This surplus was the key to the development of towns. But the floods and marshy conditions that made high-yield agriculture possible also imperiled the river valleys and pressured inhabitants to protect and raise low-lying land by banking it and building canals to drain away excess water. Collective action and plenty of labor were needed to address these problems. Mobilizing labor and determining who would get the benefits of the agricultural surplus were the engines that propelled the development of rudimentary states. Mud walls were constructed to protect towns from floods and enemies. The differentiation of roles between the mass of the population and warriors and elites, which was the key to development, occurred in these highly suitable conditions.

The Sumerian civilization that emerged in the region endured from about 3300 to 2000 B.C. The Sumerians are credited with the invention of writing in the form of pictograms on clay tablets, called cuneiform. Writing was used to keep a record of the commerce and trade that were also hallmarks of Sumerian achievement. During their long history, the Sumerians were involved in frequent struggles with neighboring peoples. Around 2000 B.C., an invasion of their territory by outsiders spelled the end of their distinctive culture. Following an era of struggle, around 1800 B.C., the first Babylonian Empire emerged, ruling a greater territory than the Sumerians had.

Paralleling the emergence of civilization in Mesopotamia was the rise in Egypt of the first major empire of which we have a substantial record. Because of the enormous legacy of ancient Egypt in the form of pyramids, monuments, and artistic achievements, the world has been captivated by the works of this culture ever since. As in the case of Mesopotamia it was the fertility of a great river valley that promoted the emergence of Egyptian civilization. The lands on either side of the Nile were the vital corridor of life in Egypt. The annual flooding of the river was the source of the richness of the soil, the resource that drove all else. Unlike Mesopotamia, where city-states emerged before greater states were established, during the fourth millennium B.C., Egypt appears to have moved swiftly from pre-civilization to the existence of two states that ruled the territory, one in the north and one in the south. Then around 3200 B.C., a great king in the south, called Menes, conquered northern Egypt and united the whole of the country in a single kingdom.

It may be that the rise of the two kingdoms and then the single kingdom were triggered by an environmental transformation that dramatically changed the conditions of life in the region. From about 4400 B.C. onwards, the sections of the Sahara Desert adjacent to the Nile Valley, where human habitation had previously been possible, became more and more arid. As the climate became drier, a development that has continued to our own day, settlements became ever more precarious. Encroaching desert drove settlers down from the land they had occupied into the Nile Valley, inevitably provoking a struggle for the life-giving soil of that fertile area. Population pressure, it has been surmised, was likely an important factor in forcing the development of a more centralized, imperial regime. "Scholars suppose a period of warfare," military historian John Keegan has written, "between the chiefs of population centres along the valley, as they struggled for control of the migrants from the extending desert's fringe. . . . The local big men lost their authority to a single ruler."[1]

The civilization that arose in the valley of the Nile is noteworthy, not least for its immense longevity. It was to endure, despite great conflicts and crises, for roughly three thousand years, a period 50 percent longer than the duration of Christianity to the present day. Experts have long debated ways of dividing the eras within this span of time. A relatively simple scheme is suitable for our purposes, beginning with what can be called the Protodynastic period from 3000 to 2686 B.C. Then followed the Old Kingdom, 2686 to 2160 B.C.; the First Intermediate period, 2160 to 2055 B.C.; the Middle Kingdom, 2055 to 1650 B.C.; the Second Intermediate period, 1650 to 1550 B.C.; and the New Kingdom, 1550 to 1069 B.C. At this point, Egypt experienced a series of crises generated from outside the country. The civilization survived this chaotic period into the Greek and Roman eras that followed until Egypt was annexed as a Roman province in 30 B.C.

The kings in the period of the Old Kingdom were absolute rulers of the land. As time passed, the king was worshipped as the descendant of the gods and later as a god in his own right. The worship of the king, and later the pharaoh, as god incarnate placed him in the awesome role of mediator between the actual world and the forces of the unworldly. Egyptian culture and belief were centered on this aspect of the role of rulers, and from this developed the building of mighty monuments and pyramids to rulers as the sites for their entombment.

The supreme rulers stood at the apex of a civilization; the base was made up of the peasantry, who formed the immense majority of the population. Egyptian peasants were not slaves, but they could be conscripted as laborers to participate in the construction of the vast public works that were to be the resting places of the monarchs. It required immense, centralized organizational power to mobilize tens of thousands of laborers, and in some cases, thousands of soldiers, to cut huge pieces of stone to be moved into place in the construction of the pyramids. Primitive construction techniques, levers and sleds, and the preparation of enormous ramps of earth along which stones were moved into place, were all that were available to the Egyptians for these unprecedented achievements.

Above the level of the peasantry was a middle tier composed of thousands of scribes who worked in the large government bureaucracy keeping track of decisions in the affairs of state. Those who worked in this civil service made use of hieroglyphic writing, an Egyptian invention. More difficult to master than Sumerian cuneiform, Egyptian calligraphy made use of little pictures. This system of writing evolved as early as 3000 B.C. and was still in use at the end of the fifth century A.D. From that time until 1822, when a French scholar deciphered the famous Rosetta Stone—which had been unearthed by a French military expedition to Egypt in 1799—Egyptian calligraphy was incomprehensible. The ability of later scholars to understand the meaning of Egyptian calligraphy was crucial to our wider insight into the nature and workings of Egyptian society. In addition to nobles and scribes were Egypt's large number of skilled craftsmen, including goldsmiths and coppersmiths. Ancient Egypt was noteworthy as well for its pioneering studies of medicine, and the drugs and potions used by the Egyptians left a legacy for posterity.

The top tier of Egyptian society comprised members of the nobility, from whose ranks were drawn the highest officials and provincial governors.

As in the case of Mesopotamia, the production of a large surplus of food was essential to the rise of a civilization in which an increasing number of people were freed from the need to devote themselves to food production. Egypt's chief crops were vegetables, barley, and emmer, grown in rich soil whose productivity was increased by vast irrigation projects organized by the state. Poultry, fish, and game rounded out the Egyptian diet.

The cult of the Egyptian rulers continued after their deaths, with the monuments and pyramids that housed their corpses. The monuments of ancient Egypt continue to fascinate artists, theorizers, and mountebanks, who find in them inspiration for contemporary art, for speculation about Egyptian knowledge of astronomy, and for fantasies about the extraterrestrial origins of the pyramids. One can only imagine the impact that monuments of stone dozens of meters in height and in length must have had on the people who lived among them at the time they were constructed. The solidity of the structures signaled a reach for certainty and eternity that legitimized the regimes of the pharaohs and underscored their hegemony.

Because Egyptian civilization endured for so long, it can be wrongly imagined that little evolution took place in Egyptian society and in the structure of the Egyptian state. While changes were exceedingly slow in our terms, crises and transformations did occur. The Egyptian state in the epoch of the Old Kingdom was initially a highly centralized affair. The king and his court were installed in the capital and were surrounded not only by elite society, but by those who possessed the administrative expertise that was essential to keep the state running. The apparatus of state religion, preoccupied with the cult of the king, was also centered in and around the capital. While the royal emissaries who were placed in charge of areas of the Nile Valley had to deal with affairs in their fiefdoms, they retained their attachment to the capital, to the royal court, and to high society. During this era, the accoutrements of elite society were little seen outside the immediate vicinity of the capital.

This pattern of centralization weakened toward the end of the Old Kingdom. Beginning in the Fifth Dynasty and fully implemented by the end of the Sixth, a new decentralized system shifted power to the regions. Provincial administrators were appointed to manage a single district in which they settled permanently. These administrators were often succeeded by members of their own families. Instead of economic surpluses flowing to the capital to be redistributed according to the priorities of the royal administration, a portion of the surplus was retained by the local administrations. With members of the social elite permanently in place as provincial administrators, power struggles between the center and the periphery ensued.[2]

Evidence that the movement of administrators to the regions was accompanied by a shift in power and wealth comes from the monumental tombs that have been found in regional centers throughout Egypt and that have been dated from the late Old Kingdom or the early First Intermediate period. The tombs were much more artfully decorated than in earlier times with ornaments and gems that bespoke the shift in wealth.[3]

The outlook and bravura of one local administrator, Ankhtifi, is recorded in his autobiographical account inscribed on pillars of rock at his burial site, located thirty kilometers south of Thebes. "I am the beginning and the end of mankind," the account reads, "since nobody like myself existed before nor will he exist . . . I surpassed the feats of the ancestors, and coming generations will not be able to equal me in any of my feats within this million of years."

"I gave bread to the hungry and clothing to the naked," his memoir records in a shift to his good works. "I anointed those who had no cosmetic oil; I gave sandals to the barefooted; I gave a wife to him who had no wife."

"All of Upper Egypt was dying of hunger and people were eating their children," he reports in an account of bad harvests and civil strife, "but

I did not allow anybody to die of hunger in this nome (province) . . . I am the hero without equal."[4]

A new and potent reassertion of authority from the center inaugurated the Middle Kingdom beginning around 2000 B.C. Under the reign of Amenemhet I, the regime, with its capital at Thebes, was able to reunify the country. During the Middle Kingdom, the cult of the pharaoh evolved so that the ruler was depicted not merely as god, but as the descendant of gods and the ancestor of gods to come. These claims can be seen as a response to the troubles and disorder of the First Intermediate period and as an attempt to create a sense of eternal and timeless order, a reassurance for the future. Enduring for about 250 years, the Middle Kingdom succumbed in the end to internal political upheaval. During the Second Intermediate period that followed, Egypt was subjected to invasion by the Hyksos, likely an Asian people, who possessed iron-fitted chariots, a formidable weapon that gave them a military edge. For a time, Egyptian rulers paid tribute to these invaders, who managed to establish themselves in the Nile Delta. While the invaders appear to have kept Egyptian bureaucrats and customs in place, they did not assimilate and were eventually expelled from Egypt after 1570 B.C. The newly reinvigorated Egyptian regime proceeded to send its armies into the strongholds of the Hyksos and occupied much of Palestine and Syria.

What made Egypt an imperial power in the true sense of the word were its forays into the territories of others. During the subsequent New Kingdom, the Egyptians, outfitting their armies with Asian-style chariots, managed to push their conquests as far as the Euphrates River. The greatest extent of Egyptian occupation of foreign territory came during the Eighteenth Dynasty, when Egyptian forces were established not only on the Euphrates but far to the south of Egypt in Nubia (located in today's southern Egypt and Sudan) between the fourth and fifth cataracts of the Nile. Monuments from the time celebrated the arrival in Egypt of tributes and slaves from conquered lands. Under the New Kingdom, an increase in the quantity and quality of artistic output matched the renewed power of the Egyptian state. Egyptian art drew the line sharply between domestic and foreign. Enemies, whether Asian or Nubian, were reviled and depicted in demeaning postures, often as bound captives. On stone palettes and temple pylons, the king was shown executing or humiliating foreigners. Images of captives were even used on the sandals and footstools of royalty, so that Egyptian kings could literally walk on their foes. On the seal of the necropolis of the Valley of Kings, nine bound captives are depicted with a jackal hovering above them.[5]

Fortifications mounted by the Egyptians against foreign predators give us a sense of what territory was regarded as Egyptian or non-Egyptian. Episodic invasions of Palestinian and Syrian territory and thrusts even further afield took the Egyptians well beyond their own land. Scholars are divided on how long and to what extent Egypt occupied territory in Palestine. There is evidence of economic relations between Egypt and Palestine, and it is thought that military pressure could have been a feature of the relationship.[6] There is solid evidence for sustained Egyptian occupations of the country's immediate hinterland. The Egyptians pushed southwards beyond the first cataract of the Nile, hundreds of kilometers, into the territory of Nubia at various times between 3000 and 1200 B.C. Economic motives, including the quest for slave labor, predominated in the initial Egyptian penetration into Nubia. During the Middle Kingdom, the Twelfth Dynasty pharaohs used military force to occupy the lands at least as far south as the third cataract of the Nile. Elaborate fortresses were constructed at this point, outfitted to sustain substantial garrisons and massive granaries. This suggests that the purpose of these bases was far more ambitious than frontier control. The bases seem to have been a point of departure from which sustained and frequent forays could be mounted much further south into Africa.[7]

The links between Egypt and neighboring societies are attested by the presence among Egyptian artifacts of materials that could not have come from the Nile Valley. Turquoise was obtained from Sinai; silver from Anatolia or the northern shores of the Mediterranean; copper from Nubia, Sinai, and the Eastern Desert; and gold from the Eastern Desert and Nubia. In addition, highly prized woods such as cedar, juniper, and ebony were imported from western Asia and from as far south as tropical Africa. The Egyptians sustained commercial links far to the south beyond Lower and Upper Nubia into the territory of the Kingdom of Punt. From this East African region, the Egyptians obtained gold, fine woods, ivory, slaves, and wild animals such as monkeys and baboons.[8]

How did the conquest of regions south of Egypt and the conduct of commerce with the outside world fit into the functioning of the Egyptian state? "By the time the full national administrative apparatus was operating, in the Middle and New Kingdoms," writes historian Ian Shaw, "there were large sections of royal bureaucracy and military power dedicated solely to the process of obtaining taxes and conscripted labor from the provinces of Egypt. This efficient national economic system formed the ideal basis for the process of exacting tribute (inu) and spoils from the lands outside Egypt's borders. Both ideologically and economically, the acts of conquering and ruling were inseparable from the idea of absorbing new wealth into the estates of the king and the major religious cults."[9]

What is striking is the extraordinary longevity of the Egyptian Empire, possibly the longest-lived empire in history. One of the reasons Egypt's imperial sway lasted so long is that Egypt was advantageously isolated geographically from potential foes. The Egyptian state was surrounded on the east and the west by desert and on the north by the sea. On the western rim of the Nile Valley lay the Sahara Desert, a formidable barrier to the passage of armies even in modern times; it provided a secure frontier for the ancient Egyptians.

On the eastern side of the Nile Valley, a wide and largely impassable ribbon of desert about 160 kilometers wide lay along the shore of the Red Sea. Secured against attack along its lengthy flanks, the Egyptian state was open to invasion only from the south and the north. The rulers of Egypt took energetic steps to shut off potential incursions from both of these directions. A series of forts in the south were erected to keep out attackers from the Sudan. In the Nile Delta, which fronts on the Mediterranean, forts were also constructed. As a hedge against attack from the north, the Egyptians moved their capital south from its original location in Memphis to Thebes. Evidence of the splendid advantage of isolation is to be found in the fact that techniques of Egyptian warfare remained primitive for a very long period in comparison with those employed in adjacent civilizations in the same epoch. Long after other armies were equipped with bronze-tipped spears, Egyptian warriors fought with spears tipped with sharpened shards of flint. Less-developed weapons were not a sign of cultural backwardness since the Egyptians had already made great strides in irrigation techniques to allow farmers to grow crops along the Nile, which alternated between annual floods and dry periods. Moreover, the spectacular monumental architecture that has been a wonder of the world was already present in Egypt. Relatively primitive weapons were an indication that Egyptian rulers had not yet felt the pressure to adopt more lethal weaponry.

The remoteness of the Nile Valley protected Egypt from outside invasion for long periods of time. One of the first major civilizations to come into existence in the world, Egypt was physically separate from Mesopotamia, another early civilization, from which challenges could have come. In this respect, the most ancient of major empires shared an advantage with the empire that dominates the world in our own time. Geographical isolation was a key to the rise of the American Empire. Located in the western hemisphere, beyond the reach of most potential challengers, the United States benefited for many decades from having weak neighbors—Canada and Mexico. This left America in an ideal position to expand across the continent and to construct a powerful state on which to sustain its future empire. The American state emerged, of course, in an age of much more advanced transportation and weaponry than had been available to the Egyptians.

Following the end of the New Kingdom, Egypt was inexorably drawn into the movements of people and the struggles for power that erupted in the broader region of the eastern Mediterranean. Its enormously long epoch of relative isolation from other societies came to an end. During the four-century era known as the Third Intermediate period from 1069 to 664 B.C., local centers of power came to the fore at the expense of a strong central government. Large numbers of Nubians from the south and Libyans from the west migrated into Egypt, permanently altering the country's demographic makeup. Invasions from these quarters subjected Egypt to periods of foreign rule. Generals were able to vie for power with kings during the era. As a result of foreign invasion and the loss of central authority, Egypt's capacity to project power outside its borders was sharply diminished. The following age, known by Egyptologists as the Late period, 664 to 332 B.C., witnessed a revival of central authority, but this was followed by periods of foreign invasion and ascendancy. Outside pressures came from the Libyans, the Nubians, and then the Persians in 525 B.C.

The initial Persian conquest of the country was resisted by a briefly successful revolt, but a few years later Persian control was reinstated. Persian control, as was to be the case with many other empires in other parts of the world, was exercised by a Persian satrap. This member of the Persian aristocracy ran the central administration through a staff whose language was Aramaic. To communicate with the lower levels of the bureaucracy a group of Egyptian translators was employed.[10] Over two thousand years later, the British ran the Egyptian state in similar fashion without formally annexing the country. As a dependent state in the Persian Empire, Egypt was called upon to assist Persian operations in the ultimately unsuccessful campaign to subdue the Greeks. While the Egyptians contributed financially and supplied warships (triremes), the obligations were not excessively heavy. The Persians showed their understanding of the need to come to terms with the traditions of the Egyptians by portraying the Great King as pharaoh. He was nonetheless a distant monarch, and tensions were evident between the local population and the Persian rulers. That tension resulted finally in a successful uprising against Persian control and the restoration of Egyptian independence in 404 B.C. The next six decades, until 341 B.C., represented the last era of Egyptian self-rule during the period of pharaonic civilization.[11]

The Persians made several attempts to recover Egypt, finally succeeding by 341 B.C. This new chapter of Persian rule was accompanied by the plundering of temples and a systematic effort to denude Egyptian cities of their defenses. The Persian regime, while not unlike the system of rule prior to 404 B.C., was noteworthy for both its periodic harshness and its administrative incompetence.[12]

During the final years of Persian control, a new power was rising, one that would permanently alter the Mediterranean and western Asia. Alexander the Great, king of Macedon, was conquering the lands bordering on the Aegean Sea and the whole of the Persian Empire, driving into Afghanistan and the corner of India before turning back to the west and seizing Egypt in 332 B.C. The end of Persian rule was welcomed by the Egyptians. Alexander was crowned in Memphis, thereby conferring on him the role of an Egyptian pharaoh. When Alexander died in Babylon in 323 B.C., his vast empire quickly fell into pieces, with his successors warring over their respective shares. The Hellenistic world that had been established by Alexander was subsequently to be dominated by three great states: Macedon, the original base of Alexander's power; the Seleucid Empire, anchored in Syria and Mesopotamia; and the empire of the Ptolemies, based in Egypt and Cyrenaica.[13]

The Ptolemaic state was anchored in two cultures that coexisted uneasily, the Egyptian culture of the overwhelming majority of the Egyptian population and the Hellenistic culture of the ruling elites. These elites were bent on fighting for control of the Aegean and its Greek states and cities in a struggle with Macedon. The capital city of the Ptolemaic regime was Alexandria, founded by Alexander, which became the urban jewel of the Hellenistic world.

Over the long term, the Ptolemaic Empire stagnated, with the loss of most of its foreign possessions and as a result of political instability in Egypt itself. Egypt's fate, along with that of the rest of the Mediterranean world, was to be determined by the rise of the new superpower in its midst, Rome. The story of the affair between Egypt's Queen Cleopatra and Roman general Mark Antony has captivated the world ever since. In 31 B.C., the lovers were defeated in the battle of Actium, and a year later, the victor, Octavian, who changed his name to Augustus in 27 B.C., visited Egypt for the only time in his life. The Roman period, during which Egypt was to become the granary of the empire, takes us beyond the story that concerns us here—the career of Egypt as an empire in its own right.

To what can we attribute the Egyptian Empire's longevity? Certainly geographic isolation, especially in the earliest period, was a crucial factor. As one of the first major states to evolve in the world, Egypt stood alongside the civilizations of Mesopotamia in breaking out of the neolithic past. No later empires, at least in this crowded part of the world, were ever to enjoy the advantage of establishing an empire where none had existed before. In addition to its relative isolation from outside attack, Egyptian civilization had the immense advantage of the rich soil of the Nile Valley. This indispensable asset was the key to its ability to generate the surplus on which to establish a complex division of labor and a powerful state. That powerful state was the engine that mobilized, funded, and supplied the armies for the push outside Egypt's borders, especially the long-term drive to the south.

An interesting feature of the Egyptian Empire was its relative lack of military advantage over its foes. While the Egyptians certainly had the numbers and the means to create and sustain armies, they were slow to develop sophisticated weapons and did so only in response to outside pressures. The absence of a compelling drive to acquire iron weapons and chariots can be attributed to the relative freedom of the country from the danger of invasion by those who possessed such weapons. Military supremacy has generally been one of the indispensable assets of would-be empires. The Egyptian case reminds us that this must be understood in relative terms. Supremacy over those an empire chooses to subdue is essential, but that is a relative matter. It does not mean that an empire must be militarily more proficient than any other country.

The other great key to the longevity of the Egyptian Empire was its ability to construct an enduring legitimacy for itself. The pioneering Canadian political economist Harold Innis, in his groundbreaking study *Empire and Communications*, studied the relationship between methods of communication and the longevity and spatial extent of states. He conjectured that stone tablets, as a medium of record and a method for announcing government edicts, promoted the long-term duration of a state, in comparison with other lighter, less durable, forms, such as papyrus, paper, and, in our time, electronic media. Whether the analysis stands up, the Egyptian state did manage to make itself durable and to create for itself an aura of timelessness. The very notion of change is the enemy of empire because it fosters the idea that the arrangements by which one people dominates another and by which great inequalities are sustained are open to question. The possibility of change is the acid that eats away at imperial rule. The rulers of Egypt and their advisers understood this, at least implicitly. Theirs was an ideology that contained no room for any possibility of change. In its highest form, the pharaonic culture rested on the notion that the pharaoh was a god, descended from gods and the ancestor of gods to come. This was an eternal order, beyond question. The elaborate funerary cults and arrangements that are the most spectacular legacy of ancient Egypt were conceived as ways to dramatize and convey the message of an eternal system. The pyramids were, in their time, a formidable medium of communication. They communicated certainty and authority arguably much more effectively than the nuclear weapons, military bases, and naval fleets of today's dominant power.

The Athenian Empire: Reducing Allies to Subjects

At the height of their brilliant civilization, the Athenians built an empire that was not especially noteworthy for its extent and certainly not for its durability. It has haunted the collective imagination of humanity for over two millennia because of the questions the Athenians raised about the state and the individual, citizenship and slavery, allies and a dominant power, and colonies and empire.

Athens combined slavery and class division with notions of direct democracy. And it combined a fierce sense of its own independence as a city-state with pride in its commercial and military dominance over other Greek cities. The alliance it constructed with other city-states, an alliance in which it was first among equals, changed over time into an empire in which Athens collected tribute from other cities to help underwrite the expenses of its own military. Can an empire also be a center where liberty flourishes and where the empire makes a contribution to its satellites as well as to its heartland? This question, very much alive in the twenty-first century, was first raised in the Athenian Empire.

Athenian hegemony over much of the Greek world emerged after the Greeks—principally, the Athenians and the Spartans—had successfully resisted the military assault of the Persians. Following their victories on land at Cithaeron and at sea at Mycale in 479 B.C., the Greeks were rid of the invader in Greece proper. To guard against any future Persian military threat, and to push ahead with the liberation of Greek cities on Aegean islands and on the Asian mainland, many Greek cities and islands placed themselves under the leadership of Athens and formed the Confederacy of Delos. The league's treasury and meeting place were located on the sacred island of Delos, the ancient center of Ionian worship.

The members of the confederacy were sea states; they made a compact to mount a united defense in which each would contribute ships to a common fleet. Most of the member states were small and far from wealthy. Many of them could afford to contribute only one or two ships, and others could only contribute to building a portion of a ship. It was recognized, as well, that an effective navy could hardly be created with such a motley array of ships. It was agreed, therefore, that the member states would fall into two categories. A small number of large states, with Athens by far the largest, would contribute ships, and most of the states, including some large ones, would contribute money to the building and upkeep of the fleet. Contributions were based on the size and resources of each member state.

The special role of the Athenians in the confederacy was made clear by the fact that the contributions of member states were collected by a body of ten Athenians who were known as "treasurers of the Greeks." Each member state had a single vote. In practice, the Athenians had little difficulty getting their way on important matters. The small states, especially those that were most vulnerable to future Persian attacks, were strongly inclined to defer to Athenian leadership. This meant that Athens faced few real challenges even from the larger states in the confederacy. The confederacy has often been compared to the North Atlantic Treaty Organization, a military alliance made up of many member states but consistently dominated by the super-power among them, the United States.

During the decades following the establishment of the Confederacy of Delos, the Athenians threw themselves into their role as a great naval power. In the war against Persia, the city of Athens had been sacked, with many of its temples despoiled. To underline the strategy of defending Athens by sea, more than by land, the Athenians decided to connect their old city around the Acropolis to Piraeus, the Athenian port eight kilometers away, by building the Long Walls, fortifications to protect both. The Long Walls gave Athens and its port a single defensive position. It was, though, a cumbersome strategy, since the walls were expensive to build and maintain and difficult to defend. The Athenians, in opting for the walls, had eschewed two alternative possible strategies: to maintain land-based fortresses to protect Athens from attack or to give up on Athens and move the whole of the city to the port of Piraeus, which could more easily be safeguarded by a powerful navy.

During this era, Athens was a major commercial state, the hub from which large-scale, sea-based commerce flourished, as well as an important manufacturing center. A large number of resident aliens, or metics, ulti-mately as many as ten thousand, were allowed to settle in Athens to practice their crafts, to engage in manufacturing or in commerce. During times of war, a property tax was established, and these noncitizens were taxed at a higher rate.

Like other Greek states, the population was composed of both slaves and free citizens. Slaves in Greek city-states came from two sources: those who had been taken captive in military operations and those obtained through the slave trade throughout the Greek world, which supplied needed labor for an expanding economy, a source of increasing importance to Athens during the city's era of greatest power.

In the days when Athens had depended principally on mounting an army to defend itself, free Athenian males had been subject to military service and required to provide their own weapons. Later, with the adoption of a naval strategy, wealthy Athenians were burdened with the task of fitting, launching, and maintaining warships. The state was responsible for providing the hull and some of the rigging. The rest, including the training of the oarsmen of these triremes, was the chore of the wealthy. Each trireme had 170 oarsmen, who could be foreigners, slaves, or the lowest class of Athenian citizens. Rounding out the complement, each ship had an additional crew of twenty men to oversee the trireme, including those whose job was to call out the time to the oarsmen. Ten soldiers were also deployed with each ship.

It did not take very many years for Athens to achieve a position of coercive dominance within the confederacy. Athens was widening its naval grip on the Aegean Sea, establishing posts not only on the far corners of the sea, but at intermediate stations of strategic value as well. For instance, in 474–73 B.C., the Athenians seized and annexed the rocky island of Scyrus, formerly in the hands of pirates. The people of the island were taken into slavery and Scyrus was repopulated with settlers from Athens.[1] Two years later, the confederacy, until then a voluntary alliance of states, forced the city of Carystus, which had stayed outside of the alliance, to join against the will of its citizens. In 469 B.C., when the member city of Naxos decided to secede, the ships of the confederacy blockaded the recalcitrant city and forced it back into the alliance.[2] Of ominous import for the future of the confederacy, the citizens of both Carystus and Naxos were deprived of self-rule and instead became subjects of Athens.

Four years after the subjugation of Naxos, the commercial interests of Athens clashed with those of Thasos, a substantial member state in the confederacy that possessed a naval fleet of its own. Tension over who was to dominate trade in Thrace and a dispute over control of a gold mine provoked Thasos to revolt against Athenian domination. A projected major alliance to support the cause of Thasos—to include Macedonia, Thrace, and even Sparta—fell apart. The Athenians prevailed, subduing the rebellious state, pulling down its walled fortifications, and seizing its warships. Thasos was forced to concede defeat on the question of the gold mine and on outstanding commercial disputes and further agreed to pay the tribute demanded by the Athenians.[3]

The Athenians took similar steps to subdue noncompliant states in numerous other cases for which we do not have a detailed record. The consequence was that instead of two classes of members—those who contributed ships and those who contributed money but remained independent—there was now a third and growing category: subject states that were required to pay tribute.[4] Athenian policies were aimed at moving states in the confederacy to a lower rung on the hierarchy. The Athenians preferred to have states contribute money rather than ships to the confederacy because this meant a direct transfer of resources to the Athenian navy itself, which heightened the power of the city within the alliance. It did not take many years for the number of states contributing ships to be reduced to three in addition to Athens itself: the wealthy island states of Lesbos, Chios, and Samos. The Athenians also preferred to transfer states from the second to the bottom rung on the ladder, that of subject status. In the cases of states that revolted against Athenian domination, a lowering of status was the inevitable consequence. When new states joined, under varying degrees of coercion, they too were not allowed to retain independence and were shunted into the third category of membership in the league.

The imperial character of the relationship between the Athenians and the subject states can be seen in the fact that the actual position of each state was determined by an agreement dictated by Athens. The specific terms of the agreements varied from case to case. As well, it was the general practice of the Athenians to impose a variation of their own constitution on the subject states. As was the case with the Athenian system of government, these constitutions were invariably democratic in character. A part of the governing arrangements for the city of Erythrae, drawn up between 463 and 454 B.C., has survived for posterity, preserved on a stone. The degree of autonomy granted by the Athenians differed from city to city. In the cases where a tributary state was most closely tied to Athens, an Athenian garrison and Athenian civil officers were stationed on its territory. All of the tributary states, whatever their degrees of autonomy, were required to provide soldiers to the confederacy when war broke out. The requirement that states provide soldiers deviated from the original arrangements of the Confederacy of Delos. It is reasonable to conclude that the Athenians were content when this dictated change provoked revolts. The suppression of revolts allowed Athens to strip their former allies of their autonomy. When this process was complete, all of the member states, with the exceptions of Lesbos, Chios, and Samos, seem to have been subject to the requirement to provide soldiers.

As Athens's power appreciated, the formality of holding consultative meetings at Delos was discontinued and the treasury of the confederacy was transferred to Athens in 454–53 B.C. The term "alliance" continued to be used after this time, although the Confederacy of Delos had ceased to exist. In common speech, however, men did not hesitate to use the word "empire" to describe the relationship between Athens and the subject states.[5] To symbolize the demise of the confederacy and the reality of an Athenian Empire, the tribute money collected from the member states was placed under the protection of the goddess of the Acropolis, and in return for this service a small proportion of the annual sum was paid into the goddess's own treasury.

At its peak, the Athenian Empire was dominant throughout the Aegean Sea. Two hundred and sixty of the cities that belonged to it are known to us from the record of the tributes they paid. Every four years, the amounts to be paid by each member city were readjusted, with the total amount collected remaining constant at 460 talents. This sum was raised for a few years in response to unusually high needs, but in general, as new states became members, the tribute for member states declined accordingly. Member states that believed their assessment was too high had the right to appeal the level of their payment to an Athenian court.

Underlining the imperial character of the relationship, disputes between Athens and any of the subject cities were adjudicated in Athens. Similarly, if a citizen of a subject city was accused of treason against the empire, his trial was held in Athens. In some of its relationships with cities in the empire, the Athenians claimed jurisdiction over other types of cases as well. Citizens of the city of Chalcis, for instance, who were accused of crimes that carried the penalties of death, banishment, or loss of civic rights, had their cases heard in Athens. Other legal situations were decided more equitably. For example, lawsuits arising out of claims of breach of contract between Athenians and citizens of other cities in the empire were heard in the city of the defendant, which opened up the opportunity for courts in subject cities to find against Athenians, something they may not have been loath to do.[6]

The Athenian Empire was to be a short-lived affair, enduring for only half a century after the demise of the Confederacy of Delos. Among the reasons for the empire's decline, the question of legitimacy was critical. Despite the luster of Athens's commercial and cultural accomplishments and the role it played in pushing back the Persian invaders, the Athenian Empire was a standing affront to the citizens of the subject cities. The city-states of the Greek world prized their sovereignty and independence, and regarded any arrangement that robbed them of autonomy as negative. The citizens of Greek city-states could be convinced to form an alliance in a time of common danger and to place themselves under the leadership of the strongest among them in such an emergency. That, indeed, was the basis for the formation of the Confederacy of Delos. The rise of an Athenian Empire was quite another matter. However light the tether of imperial rule, however much the subject states shared in common with the Athenians in their general outlook, the unequal arrangements of the empire flew in the face of what citizens and elites believed was right. In the case of the Athenian Empire, the absence of legitimacy was a major reason why this empire lasted so briefly.

The demise of the Athenian Empire resulted from a deep division within the Greek world, between Athens and its vassal states on one side and Sparta and the states aligned with it on the other. While Athens and Sparta had cooperated uneasily against the Persian invaders, the emergence of Athenian hegemony rankled in Sparta. Some pictured the division as one between the culture of Ionian Greeks, whose exemplar was Athens, and Dorian Greeks, whose champion was Sparta. Whatever the truth in this explanation, the friction between the two powers was about the old question that was so often at stake in such struggles—which one was to predominate?

The two cities exemplified dramatically different social orders. While the societies of both Athens and Sparta relied on slave labor, the Spartan social order was a cauldron in which a conservative, militaristic social elite was perennially on guard against the danger of a revolt of the underclass, the helots, whose miserable conditions of life drove them, at any opportunity, to turn on their oppressors. At the head of the Spartan government was a council of elders, five magistrates who were called "ephors," and two hereditary kings who were responsible for certain military tasks. This oligarchic regime was ultimately responsible to the assembly of Spartiates, which numbered about five thousand men in the early fifth century. The source of the Spartan system was a large aristocracy, whose membership originated in a warrior class. While Athens launched itself on a brilliant commercial career, Sparta remained staunchly agricultural, allowing no commercial class to emerge. Spartan boys were trained from a very young age to accept deprivation and discomfort to prepare them for the hard life in the military that lay ahead of them. Sparta was not unlike a perpetual military camp, constantly on guard against revolt from below. The social tension at the heart of Spartan existence was one reason the Spartans were always chary of allowing their army to venture too far from home.

Sparta's domestic customs were, at the very least, odd. Among males, it was the norm to dine at communal messes. At a Spartan marriage the bride's hair was cropped short and she was attired as a boy. The ceremony was followed by the simulated rape of the bride, who then did not live with her husband. He continued to reside with his male companions in a military mess and to take his meals with them. Spartan society was characterized by a martial egalitarianism among citizens, and excess or luxury was frowned upon.

In 464 B.C., the town of Sparta was severely damaged by a powerful earthquake. In the aftermath of this natural disaster, Messenian serfs took advantage of the disarray to rebel against their masters. Initially things went well for the rebels, who managed to wipe out a force of three hundred Spartans in a pitched battle. Driven into a fortress in Messenia, the helots managed for several years to hold out against Spartan soldiers and formations from a number of Greek cities, including Athens. Solidarity among elites in ancient cities against slave rebellions, even among cities that were potential foes, was a widely recognized code. The Athenians sent four thousand hoplites (well-armed citizen soldiers) to serve in the combined effort to defeat the helots. But perhaps concerned about the influence the Athenians might have on their own soldiers, the Spartans informed the Athenian commander that the services of his soldiers were not needed.

The diplomatic rebuke of the Athenians had the effect of widening the wedge between the two cities and discrediting the conservative politicians in Athens who had tried to maintain good relations with Sparta. This opened the door to further democratic reforms in Athens and, in the longer term, to the war with Sparta that would spell the end of the Athenian Empire.[7]

The democratization agenda was driven by Pericles, who was to dominate Athenian politics for several decades. The Council of Areopagus, the Athenian governing body, whose members were drawn only from the wealthiest classes, had its powers significantly reduced. For instance, the power of the body to punish government officials for violations of the law and to supervise the administration, acting as a watchdog to ensure that laws were being followed, was abrogated. These responsibilities were transferred to more popularly based institutions: the Council of Five Hundred, the Assembly, and the popular law courts. High office was also opened to the poorest free citizens. Membership in the Council of Five Hundred was to be chosen entirely by lot from all the eligible citizens, and those who served were to receive payment. Judges were also to be paid for their service. Payment for holders of public office was especially popular among the mass of the Athenian population and helped cement the power of Pericles.[8]

Athenian foreign policy also turned sharply against Sparta and its allies during this period. Commercial rivalry helped provoke an Athenian war against Corinth, Epidaurus, and Aegina. While these cities were allies of Sparta, Sparta remained in the background, at war with Athens, but not willing to pursue the war with any vigor. This lengthy and sporadic war continued for fifteen years and was followed by another fifteen years of tense peace.

In 431 B.C., the Peloponnesian War broke out, with Athens and its subject states on one side and Sparta and its allies on the other. This was the conflict that ultimately led to the passing of the great age of classical Greece. It was the struggle of a naval-based power—Athens, and its subject cities throughout the Aegean—against the land-based power of Sparta, whose key allies were Boetia, Corinth, and, less dependably, Macedon. Under the leadership of Pericles, who died two years into the war, which lasted with pauses until 404 B.C., the Athenians did not try to defend their countryside against the Spartans, who mounted annual occupations of it. Instead the people of Athens withdrew during these assaults inside the city and the port of Piraeus, surrounded by the walled fortifications that linked the two. For sustenance, the Athenians relied on their navy and the importation of grain to feed themselves. This hostile deadlock lasted until 421 B.C., when a temporary peace was brokered, to be followed by a resumption of the war. The Athenians then gambled all on a risky venture: they launched a naval assault on the wealthy Greek city of Syracuse, a colony of Corinth that was located in Sicily. Had the gambit worked, the Athenians would have enriched themselves at the same time as they cut off grain supplies for their foes. The booty reaped in Syracuse could have enabled the Athenians to further expand their fleet, allowing them to break the deadlock in the struggle against Sparta. Instead of decisive victory, the Athenian expedition met with catastrophic defeat. The Athenian fleet was destroyed, along with half the city's army.

This turn of affairs galvanized Athens's enemies and led to internal dissension and an attempted coup at home. The Spartans seized the moment and concluded a secret deal with the Persians, agreeing that the Greek cities on the Asian mainland could again fall under the control of Persia. With Persian aid, the Spartans were able to assemble a fleet of their own that could both offer release from Athenian dominance to its subject cities and sustain a naval blockade of Athens itself. In the end, the starvation of the Athenians, as a result of the blockade, forced the city to make peace in 404 B.C., a peace that included the dismantling of the Long Walls, which had been so important to Athenian strategy.

Defeat in the Peloponnesian War spelled the end of the great age of the Athenian Empire. History is rarely neat and tidy, however. Following the defeat of Athens, Sparta and Persia had a falling-out as the Spartans tried to prevent the Persians from resuming control over the Greek cities on the Asian mainland. Under these circumstances, Athens was able to launch a new navy and to rebuild its Long Walls. In 387 B.C., the Spartans and the Persians, both wanting to prevent the reassertion of Athenian power, reached a new agreement.

The Athenian and the Greek saga took an entirely new turn with the rise of Macedonia and the conquests of Alexander the Great, which spread Hellenistic civilization over a wide part of western Asia and the Mediterranean. For our purposes, though, the story of the Athenian Empire ends with the defeat of Athens in the Peloponnesian War.

In vastly different historical settings and parts of the world, other empires have had to grapple with the issues that confronted the Athenians—how to deal with allies that were less powerful than themselves and when to convert allies into subjects.

The transformation of the Confederacy of Delos into the Athenian Empire has often been compared to the relations between the United States and its allies. For the most part, the Athenians did not annex the states that became subject to their dominance and did not extend their citizenship to the free citizens of these city-states. In spirit, if not in military and economic might, the Athenian Empire was the truest ancestor of the American Empire. Here after all was an empire that existed almost 2,500 years ago that dominated subject states while imposing democratic constitutions on them. The contradictions are telling. They seem as though they were drawn straight from the actions of the United States in Iraq and Afghanistan.

While the short duration of the Athenian Empire had many causes— among them limited resources and a powerful coalition of foes—not least was the problem of legitimacy. Athens became an imperial power despite the fact that its political culture was intrinsically anti-imperialist in important ways. Athens combined the ownership of slaves with democratic rights for its citizens, an uneasy combination as both the cases of Rome and the United States were to demonstrate—in Rome through the demise of democracy and in the United States through the abolition of slavery. Despite the dissonance created by slavery, at the height of its imperial power, the political culture of Athens placed a high value on the rights of individual citizens to play a role in determining public policy and in holding public office. In addition, Athenian direct democracy—the right of citizens to assemble to make decisions rather than to elect legislators to do it for them—was ideally designed for a city-state of limited size. Built into the Athenian approach to statecraft, therefore, was the idea of self-determination for both individual citizens and the city-state. By its very nature, this notion placed a severe limit on how large the Athenian polity could grow before its system became unworkable. The Romans were to solve this problem only by stripping citizenship of most of the political rights that went with it.

Because the Athenians did not evolve an imperial culture that reduced citizenship to a largely symbolic category and because they insisted on exporting their political culture to the dependent states in their empire, the messages the Athenian Empire transmitted, both at home and abroad, were decidedly mixed.

The American case today is different from that of Athens in a host of ways. The United States is a vast continental power that for a long time enjoyed a high degree of geographical isolation from serious foes. Athens, on the other hand, was a small state located in a volatile neighborhood, encircled by potential foes. Moreover, American statecraft, although it began with a strong element of direct democracy in the form of the New England town meeting, quickly evolved into representative democracy and federalism, ideally suited for what was to grow into an immensely populated country straddling a continent. That said, the twin ideals of citizens' rights and national self-determination are embedded at the very heart of American political culture. That is why it has been unthinkable in popular American discourse for politicians and most analysts to even accept the notion of an American Empire. An empire in denial about itself as it transmits notions of national self-determination to those that fall under its sway is a highly contradictory beast indeed. The Athenian case would suggest that the American Empire will either have to be short-lived or, as in the case of Rome, have to pass through a period of intense political and cultural crisis and emerge as an imperial state that has banished the anti-imperial ideals on which it was originally based.

China: An Affair of State

Alone among the great imperial powers, China succeeded in building a vast empire that simultaneously developed into an enormous nation.

The first empires to emerge in the world were of two kinds, slave empires and peasant empires, some of them simultaneously exhibiting the features of both. In "servile" empires, the labor force was accumulated and replenished through continuing conquests in search of fresh pools of slave labor. A variation on this type of empire was the "peasant" empire. The most noteworthy case of the peasant empire was the Chinese Empire, in which a highly refined bureaucracy and ruling authority collected rents and taxes from the peasants, in return providing some measure of security and, at times, irrigation. In this kind of empire the labor force was made up not of slaves, but of a virtually limitless supply of peasants tied to the land. The secret of Chinese success was the creation of a state that did not cost the society too much and that was effective at carrying out its central tasks. If ever there was a state that was a successful Hobbesian Leviathan, an absolute authority that insisted on its right to oversee all social relationships, it was the Chinese Empire.

In the Chinese Empire, citizens could achieve power and wealth by climbing the ladder of the state bureaucracy. The model was threatened many times by the rise of wealthy landowners who sought power for themselves. When landlords consolidated their holdings and drove small peasants off the land, they threatened the imperial system with political fragmentation. Unchecked, wealthy landlords could behave like the fractious nobility in medieval Europe. Over the course of history, the Chinese Empire was broken up and reconstituted a number of times. Unlike Europe, which was permanently divided into a large number of states, China managed to survive as a single, giant entity. The overwhelming historical accomplishment of the Chinese Empire was to preside over the consolidation of a Chinese nation. Although the country is not without internal strains, such as Beijing's notorious occupation of Tibet, the success of the empire in nurturing the nation is without parallel.

Following two centuries of what is called the age of the Warring States—an era of struggles among feuding principalities and kingdoms dominated by the upper tier of the nobility—the first Chinese imperial state was established in 221 B.C. It was created by Prince Cheng of Ch'in following his military victory over his foes. Having unified the Chinese lands under his control, the prince took the title of "august sovereign" (*huang-ti*), in future to be the title of Chinese emperors. History was to know him, however, as the "First Emperor" (*shih huang-ti*). This first imperial dynasty was short-lived: a civil war brought down the regime, to be replaced by the Han dynasty, whose history can be divided into two periods. The First Han dynasty prevailed from 206 B.C. to A.D. 9, followed by the Later Han dynasty from A.D. 25 to 220.[1] The civil war notwithstanding, the imperial regimes were mounted on the military strength of the small farmers, which was used to break the power of the nobility. The empire was created through the direct social and military link between the peasantry and the imperial state. What the brief period of the Ch'in dynasty had achieved, the Han dynasty brought to fruition. China became an empire, unifying the Chinese lands and exerting itself in expansionary moves against the peoples of the steppes, who had posed, and would continue to pose, threats to the regime. What was of epochal importance in the initial Chinese imperial regimes was the realization of the idea of China as a civilization with a unity of identity that was to endure in the future.

The First Emperor, acting on the help of his legal adviser, initiated a series of reforms that centralized power and rationalized and extended the administrative capacity of the state. The regime initially divided the territory of the empire into thirty-six, and then forty-eight, units. It standardized the currency with the creation of a circular copper coin with a square hole in the center, a type of coin that lasted until the twentieth century. Weights and measures and the gauge of cartwheels were standardized, and attempts were made to establish standard characters to replace the variations in writing that existed from region to region. To ensure that the imperial victory was not overturned by a resurgence of the power of the nobles, fortifications that they had erected on the frontiers of kingdoms to defend them against their neighbors were demolished and the possession of arms was banned.

Major public works and new defense fortifications were launched. Imperial roads, towns, and post houses were constructed and canals built to provide irrigation for farmers. To house the emperor, a massive palace was constructed in the capital of Hsien-yang, on the left bank of the Wei River. Along the northern frontier, the emperor decreed that a Great Wall was to be built to block invasions by the Hsiung-nu, a nomadic people of cattle herders on the steppes. In 213 B.C., the imperial government sent a force of 100,000 men to attack the northern nomads. In addition, the regime pushed its area of effective control south with attacks on peoples in South China and Vietnam.[2]

The vigor and ambition of the regime, however, provoked the growth of powerful opposition movements. Despite the measures taken to rein in their power, the nobility remained a force to be reckoned with. As well, the emperor alienated scholars when his regime banned all books with the exception of those on medicine, farming, and divination. In 213 B.C., the regime undertook the measure for which it is best known, the mass burning of books. This notorious event was followed by the execution at the capital of four hundred opponents of the imperial government. Following the First Emperor's death, insurrections were launched against his son, the Second Emperor.

At the head of the expanding forces of rebellion was a minor government official who did not come from a prestigious family. Liu Pang succeeded in mobilizing an army and in 206 B.C., the year from which the Han Empire was to be dated, defeated the imperial army in the valley of the Wei. Four years later, having eliminated the emperor, Liu Pang took the imperial title for himself and moved the capital to Ch'ang-an (present-day Sian). To his comrades in the insurrection, he bestowed titles of nobility and land.[3]

Having led the rebellion, the new emperor installed a regime that, in essential respects, was like that of its fallen foe. The system rested on the direct relationship between the peasantry and the state, overseen by the bureaucracy and the military. To make the system work, the empire required an accurate census and the payment of a head tax levied on each subject (including minors) to be paid in coin. Yearly stints of forced labor and periods of military service were also enforced by the state.

There was a broad resemblance between Chinese society in the era of the Warring States and the decentralized feudalism of Europe during the Middle Ages. The oscillation of power relations in China followed a predictable pattern: when the central government was strong, the local nobles, with their regional centers of power, were brought under the control of a centralized state that can be compared in very general terms to the absolute royal regime in early modern France; when the central government lost authority, the nobles rebounded in their power and the regime was much more like that in feudal Europe. Naturally, these comparisons are broad and do not deny the enormous cultural, economic, and technological differences between China and Europe.

To prevent the resurgence of the noble families, the regime undertook the large-scale, forced migration of members of aristocratic families, along with criminals and civil servants, to territories the government wanted to open up to economic development. Such transfers spawned new communities in the north in areas prone to invasions from the peoples of the steppes. The new communities were dependent on the support of the state during their establishment and were much less likely to become centers of resistance to the imperial regime. Transfers of population were also used to dominate or outnumber a local population that was culturally distinct and not easily integrated into the imperial system. During the Han dynasty, the relocation of several million people resulted in the long-term transfer of Chinese civilization to the peripheries of the empire.

As in the case of the Roman Empire, which overlapped historically with the Han dynasty, the peasantry formed the main source of wealth generation. However, the difference in the way the surplus was extracted from the peasantry for the benefit of the upper classes was crucial. In the case of Rome, it was slaves, for the most part, who produced the surplus that went directly to the great landowners and aristocracy who dominated the Roman state. In the case of the Han Empire, the peasants paid taxes directly to the state. In the Chinese system, the route to great wealth was via the state, which appropriated the surplus from the peasants to provide for the income of officeholders, from the lowest members of the bureaucracy all the way to the emperor himself.

In principle, and to some extent in practice, the Chinese state was run as a meritocracy, with competitive exams determining who would gain access to the civil service. The examinations tested applicants' mastery of

Confucianism, a body of thought that served as the ethical basis for the Chinese administration for a long period of time. Confucian orthodoxy was a force for conservatism that helped unify the servants of the state so that they preserved a common outlook even during periods of transition from one dynasty to another or when foreign invaders overran the country. This ideology gave civil servants, who were regarded as scholars, a status similar to that of the clergy in medieval Europe. The Chinese bureaucracy could only exist in a country in which a common sense of identity was developing, but there is no question that the bureaucracy reinforced the development of that sense of identity. (Perspective is required in assessing the role of the Chinese bureaucracy. In the eighteenth century, it is estimated that 30,000 bureaucrats were employed by the Chinese states, a number large for the time, but one that is far below that needed in any modern state.)

From its inception, the Han Empire was expansionary, undertaking a drive not only northward into the territory of the steppe peoples, but south as well, beyond the Yangtze River. The empire pushed its authority into southeast Asia, and in the northeast it expanded into Manchuria and brought much of the Korean peninsula under its sway. Military expansion was accompanied, even driven, by increased economic output and commerce with other realms. One of the novel features of the empire's relationship with its neighbors was the practice of bestowing gifts on them. Silks were the customary gifts, and the scale of this gift-giving went far beyond nominal tokens. It was a strategy of the imperial regime to bestow gifts on an enormous scale, so as to establish a dependency in neighboring states, to reduce their commitment to alternative regimes, and even to corrupt their rulers to undermine their capacity for resistance.

During this historical epoch, the famous "silk route" was established. Silks from China reached India and Parthian territory (the Parthian Empire at times included parts of modern Iraq, all of Iran, and parts of Afghanistan and Pakistan) to be sold in the eastern reaches of the Roman Empire. This trade facilitated contact between two civilizations, both at a peak of their power and both imbued with the idea that their empire was the center of the world. Although these two universes touched each other, their ideologies and practices remained unchanged. The high point for this commerce came in the first and second centuries A.D. Silk reached the

Roman Empire from the east, and woolen cloths and frescoes of Greco-Syrian design reached China from the west. Greek merchants played an important role in the direct overland trade route as well as the route that linked China and the eastern Mediterranean through India. In A.D. 97, the Han dynasty sent an envoy, Kan Ying, to make contact with the great empire of the west. The Parthians, who stood in the way of direct contacts between Rome and the Han Empire, did not prevent Kan Ying from reaching the Mediterranean. In his report to his own government, he noted the flourishing cities of the Roman Empire, the milestones on its roads, and the robustness of its commerce.[4]

Although the Han dynasty was succeeded by other regimes, both internal and external, the traditions and practices of the administrative elite remained intact and retained its core values over the course of changing dynasties and empires.

The Han dynasty was followed by the T'ang dynasty, A.D. 618 to 907, and then the Sung dynasty, A.D. 960 to 1126. From A.D. 1234 to 1368, the Mongols, who invaded from the steppes north of the Great Wall, established their dominance in China. In the early years of the thirteenth century, China was divided between a Sung regime in the south and the Chin Empire in the north, with their capital in Peking. By 1234, the Chin Empire collapsed under the combined assault of the Sung from the south and the Mongols from the north. In 1279, the last southern Sung emperor committed suicide as his regime collapsed and the Mongols gained control of all of China. By the mid-fourteenth century, anti-Mongol insurrections arose in many parts of China. In 1368, the Ming dynasty was proclaimed and Peking was liberated from Mongol control. Until 1644, the Ming dynasty prevailed until it was succeeded by the Manchu or Ch'ing dynasty. By the time the last dynasty sank into oblivion in 1912, to be replaced by the short-lived republican regime of Sun Yat-sen, China had suffered the effects of more than a century of incursions by the industrialized imperialist powers of the day, outfitted with their superior military power.

Throughout the nineteenth century and with growing intensity, the great imperial powers saw China, with its vast population—361 million inhabitants according to the census of 1812—and its great commercial potential, as an enormous target for their own expansion. For long historical periods, Chinese development had clearly been in advance of that in other parts of the world. By the second century B.C., paper had been invented in China, followed by a rudimentary printing process before A.D. 700. Movable type was in use in China by the eleventh century A.D., allowing for the publication of books in large numbers, centuries before this was possible in Europe. Gunpowder was also invented in China. One scholar has concluded that by the eleventh century A.D., the Chinese were producing as much iron as all of Europe produced in early modern times.[5] Indeed, the Chinese had unearthed the secret of casting iron fifteen hundred years before the Europeans did. Breakthroughs in the mass production of textiles and the use of new rice varieties that allowed for two crops on well-irrigated land led to productivity increases and what can be described as a process of industrialization during the era of the Sung dynasty (A.D. 960–1279). During the same period, Europe was frozen in the backwardness of feudalism. Also during the Sung era, Chinese navigators were equipped with the magnetic compass. In the fifteenth century, when the Europeans were on the verge of making their epochal ocean voyages, China had its own great ships that visited the Persian Gulf and East Africa. In the eighteenth century, the Chinese cities of Canton and Peking were more populous than any in Europe.

Although Chinese development clearly outstripped that of Europe, it was the Europeans who succeeded in establishing overseas empires, powered in large part by the labor of African slaves, and who made the breakthrough to a sustained industrial revolution that provided them with military superiority. Just as the European imperial powers used that superiority to colonize the Americas, Africa, and India, they had their eyes set on China, which loomed as the biggest prize of all.

By 1816, the British East India Company was determined to open up the Chinese market to the importation of opium. In the Opium Wars that followed, China was subjected to further external pressure. In 1842, under the terms of the Treaty of Nanking, Hong Kong was leased to Britain, and Canton, Shanghai, Amoy, Foochow, and Ningpo were opened to opium imports. Other foreign powers followed in Britain's wake to carve out extraterritorial rights for their citizens and special spheres of authority for themselves. In 1897, Germany gained control of the Ch'ing-tao area in Shantung; the following year, the British acquired the Wei-hai region also in Shantung; and the Russians acquired Ta-lien and Lu-shun in Liao-tung. In 1899, the French gained control of the Chan-chiang region in western Kwangtung.[6]

The drive of the imperialist powers into China met with periodic waves of resistance. In 1900, in the course of the Boxer Rebellion, insurgents occupied Peking and besieged the embassies of the foreign powers. In response, the European great powers, who were vying with each other in deadly competition to divide up the world, buried their differences and dispatched a joint military mission to the Chinese capital to suppress the revolt.

In 1910, Japan and Russia agreed on a division of northeastern China. The following year, the Russians acquired control of Outer Mongolia. During the first decades of the Chinese Republic, Japan became the chief menace to Chinese sovereignty. In 1919, at their Peace Conference in Paris, the victors of the First World War handed over Germany's Chinese holdings to Japan. In the decade that led up to the Second World War, Japan launched a concerted and murderous assault on China, beginning with the invasion of Manchuria in 1931. In 1937, the Japanese occupied China's major cities.

During the next few years, the Japanese invasion of China blended with the outbreak of war in Europe to create a truly global conflict. The Japanese attack on Pearl Harbor on December 7, 1941, was followed a few days later by Nazi Germany's declaration of war against the United States. China's resistance to the Japanese was complicated by the country's own internal struggle that had been waged between the Nationalists under the leadership of Chiang Kai-shek and the Communists, whose drive for power was directed by Mao Zedong. The end of the Second World War did not stop the Chinese conflict, which raged until 1949 with the victory of the Communists, the proclamation of the People's Republic on October 1, and the flight of the Nationalists to Taiwan.

With the conclusion of the civil war, China's long and immensely painful era of domination and repeated invasions by foreign powers came to an end. As China emerged from its travails as a united country (with the important exception of Taiwan), the entire course of Chinese history was once more cast into view. The latest era of conflict had much in common with earlier periods. Over the course of the past six decades, China has emerged into a new era of unity and power.

Over the long course of its history, China achieved what no other empire had ever accomplished: the forging of an immense nation-state from an imperial foundation. China benefited from its relative isolation from other civilizations over long periods of time. The great achievement of the Chinese state and bureaucracy was to oversee the creation of a nation from cultures at least as diverse as those of Europe. This process continued over several millennia. Twenty-first-century China is far from being a homogeneous nation. Nonetheless, this country with a population of well over one billion people is both a nation and an empire, with the potential to challenge the United States for global supremacy in coming decades.

Rome: Military Supremacy

The Roman Empire has left a legacy in which the idea of the universal state looms both as a nightmare and as a beacon of solidity.

In the West, Rome has served as an inspiration, with its symbols and styles eagerly adopted to demonstrate the power of the state. The eagle, emblem of the Roman legions, was copied by the eagle of the German Empire, the two-headed eagle of the Austro-Hungarian Empire, the Napoleonic eagle, and the eagle of America, which holds both olive branches and arrows in its talons. Similarly, Roman architecture became the model for those wanting to denote power and longevity in their capital cities—the Palais Bourbon in Paris and the Capitol in Washington, with its countless imitations in U.S. state capitals. Both the Arc de Triomphe in Paris and the Brandenburg Gate in Berlin are obviously patterned after Roman triumphal arches, as are the numerous arches in many other cities. And, of course, the name Caesar, redolent with authority, has been copied by the Germans with their kaiser and the Russians with their czar.

Rome's long-lasting imperial success rested on two factors—sustained military superiority and the acquisition of fresh sources of slave labor through wars of conquest. For centuries, scarcely a year passed without the Romans going to war against some adversary. When the *New York Times* editorialized in the autumn of 2002 that the Pentagon's new global strategic overview was transparently aimed at global domination, the editorial complained that America's military strategists had adopted an outlook much like that of the commanders of Rome's legions.

Rome began its career as a small city-state in 753 B.C. As the city launched expansionary wars and forged alliances, first in central Italy, Rome retained its city-state character. Although Rome started out as a monarchy, it became an aristocratic republic in 509 B.C., ruled by patrician landowners, who later were forced to share some of their political power with poorer citizens, the so-called plebeians. Decisive power, however, remained in the hands of the upper classes throughout the life of the republic.

It took centuries for Rome to conquer central Italy, and then the whole of the peninsula, before it entered the era of life-and-death struggles against the other great powers of the day: the Carthaginians and the Macedonians. From the start, Rome used its ample citizen manpower to carry out its conquests. With conquests came slaves, and with slaves came an expanded labor force that vastly increased the wealth and profits of Roman patrician landlords. The completion of the Roman conquest of the Italian peninsula made the Republic a formidable power.

Across the Mediterranean, on the coast of North Africa, lay Carthage, a very different kind of great power. Unlike land-based Rome with its agricultural economy, Carthage was a seagoing state, with a powerful navy and with commercial interests from Spain to the eastern Mediterranean. The issue over which Rome and Carthage first went to war concerned the city of Messina on the island of Sicily. Carthage had interests in western Sicily, and the Romans also coveted the island, which lay across a narrow strait from the toe of Italy. An accidental local conflict drew the two major powers into the first Punic War, which broke out in 264 B.C. and lasted twenty-three years. In 218 B.C., the second war with Carthage erupted. That war brought Rome to the edge of collapse with defeats at the hands of Hannibal, the brilliant Carthaginian military commander, at Lake Trasimene and Cannae. For years Hannibal's army dominated Italy, with the Romans locked behind the walls of their city and reduced to fighting a long, guerilla-style war. At last, in 202 B.C., Scipio Africanus defeated Hannibal at Zama in North Africa, bringing the second Punic War to a conclusion. With victory in the western Mediterranean, Rome went to war against the Macedonians, achieving victory over Philip V in 197 B.C. and defeating the Macedonians in Persia in 168 B.C. Then came the final struggle against Carthage from 149 to 146 B.C., which ended with the victorious Romans razing their defeated enemy's city to the ground. In 146 B.C., both North Africa and Macedon and Greece became Roman provinces. In the space of 120 years, less than the length of time it took Britain to win its struggles against France in the eighteenth and early nineteenth centuries, Rome became the master of the Mediterranean.

States that become imperialist powers are inexorably transformed by the experience. The Roman Republic had grown into a giant with vast imperial holdings. The fact of empire results in shifts in the internal balance of authority among elites in a society, as well as the balance between the rulers and the people. Rome's increasing sway over much of the Mediterranean fatally upset the Roman state and its governing arrangements in the first century B.C. It created a cohort of victorious generals whose command over their legions gave them the capacity to seize power from Rome's elected institutions, principally the Senate. This led to decades of political turmoil and civil war and ultimately the demise of the Roman Republic. Those struggles ended in 27 B.C., when the victor Octavian took the name Augustus and the republic became the empire. During the transition from republic to empire, there was scarcely any awareness among Rome's thinkers and political leaders that the republic was headed for oblivion, to be replaced by a new imperial regime. Indeed, Augustus, the first emperor, shrewdly cloaked his state in the garb of a restored republic.

Is America sleepwalking through a similar transition today? An argument that defenders of the American Empire regularly make is that because the United States is a democracy in which the rule of law and human rights are unshakably embedded, it can be counted on to promote these practices and values in the countries it dominates. What these observers rarely consider is the corroding effect that empire can have on American democracy. As in the case of Rome, the existence of an American Empire has been altering the nature of the American state and the balance of power among its ruling elites and between its ruling elites and the American people. In the United States the interests, corporate and military, that engorge themselves and grow stronger as a consequence of empire hollow away the body and the sinews of American democracy. When President Dwight D. Eisenhower gave his farewell address in 1961 to warn of the rise of a "military-industrial complex" in the United States, the phenomenon was just beginning. Since then the linkage between corporations that profit from the military, such as Halliburton and Boeing, and those in power has grown enormously. At the heart of the American imperial exercise, as was the case with the Romans, is the existence of a military machine superior in its armaments, strategy, and organization to any it could conceivably fight.

The military machine Rome established to fend off its deadly foes and to conquer the world of the Mediterranean was noteworthy both for its bloody ferocity and for the painstaking bureaucratic care with which it was trained, armed, supplied, and renewed. It was this combination of qualities that made the Roman army the model for the armies of the world to follow. "So ferocious were the Romans of the later first millennium BC," writes the distinguished British military historian John Keegan, "that, in broad historical perspective, their behavior bears comparison only with that of the Mongols or Timurids 1500 years later. Like the Mongols, they took resistance, particularly that of besieged cities, as a pretext justifying wholesale slaughter of the defeated."[1] Keegan cites the fearsome example of the Roman siege of the city of New Carthage in Spain in 209 B.C. during the second Punic War. Having won his victory, the Roman commander Scipio Africanus instructed his men to hold back on their looting until they had killed everyone they encountered inside the walls of the fallen city. In their wanton slaughter of men, women, and children in cities they had taken, the Romans even hacked dogs and other animals to pieces.[2]

"Few others are known to have displayed such an extreme degree of ferocity in war while reaching a high level of political culture," concludes classical historian William Harris. "Roman imperialism was in large part the result of quite rational behavior on the part of the Romans, but it also had dark and irrational roots. One of the most striking features of Roman warfare is its regularity—almost every year the Romans went out and did massive violence to someone—and this regularity gives the phenomenon a pathological character."[3]

Fierceness in the waging of war has characterized the successful rise of imperial powers. Today's great imperial power, the United States, has never shirked when it has been necessary to dispatch both enemy armies and civilian populations that have stood in its way. In his acclaimed analysis of American foreign policy, historian Walter Russell Mead acknowledges the brutal manner in which the United States has waged its wars:

It isn't fashionable to say so, but the United States of America is the most dangerous military power in the history of the world. Since World War II, the United States has continued to employ devastating force against both civil and military targets. . . . The United States dropped almost three times as much explosive tonnage in the Vietnam War as it used in World War II.... Some 365,000 Vietnamese civilians are believed to have died as a result of the war during the period of American involvement. That is a ratio of 8 Vietnamese civilian deaths for every American killed in the war. . . .

The United States over its history has consistently summoned the will and the means to compel its enemies to yield to its demands. Attacks on civilian targets and the infliction of heavy casualties on enemy civilians have consistently played a vital part in American war strategies.[4]

What made the Roman military formidable over the long term—the same could be said of the American military—is that in addition to its willingness to inflict enormous casualties on civilians and opposing forces, it was a highly organized machine. Initially, when Rome was no more than a small city-state, its military approach was similar to that of the Greeks, in which citizens were required to arm themselves and to fight when necessary without being paid. The Greeks, it is true, frequently failed to live up to their ideal of a citizen army when Greek cities hired mercenaries to fight their battles. But often enough Greek citizen soldiers, most of whom were farmers who owned small pieces of land, assembled to fight when their territory was threatened by an opposing army, often composed of men like them who were taking time off from tending their own fields.

The Greek approach to warfare, initially adopted by the Romans, involved extremely violent, face-to-face, pitched battles designed to secure a decisive outcome that would allow part-time citizen warriors to return to their fields as soon as possible. The Greeks fought in a phalanx formation usually eight rows deep, in which they were packed shoulder to shoulder. Citizen soldiers were expected to provide their own bronze helmets, breastplates, and shin protectors.

By the fourth century B.C., the Roman army had abandoned many features of Greek warfare. For one thing, the Romans moved away from the tightly ranked phalanx in favor of a more open formation; they also gave up the heavy armor that was a feature of the phalanx. Instead, they went into battle with a light oblong shield fashioned out of hooped iron and much lighter body armor than before. Over time, they replaced the thrusting spear with a javelin, the pilum, which could be thrown, after which they would fight sword in hand. These changes allowed for much greater maneuverability. Small units, called maniples, could be deployed flexibly in a battle. Maniples were units within the legions, the basic division into which the Roman army was organized. Also by the fourth century B.C., the Romans gave up the idea that citizen soldiers should arm themselves and come, when necessary, to the defense of the state. Instead, the Romans created a professional force, whose recruiting base was the large class of landowners who were less and less able to make a living on the land in an age of increasingly powerful landholders. These professionals earned a daily stipend.[5]

The Roman army was so uniformly reliable because at its core was a body of trained professionals who passed on traditions, lore, methods, tactical wisdom, and esprit de corps. "The Roman centurions, long-service unit-leaders drawn from the best of the enlisted ranks," Keegan writes, "formed the first body of professional fighting officers known to history."[6] More than a thousand years after the demise of the Roman Empire in the West, rising European states still used the Roman army, with its professional corps, as the model for the construction of their national military establishments.

At the end of the reign of Augustus, the Roman army, divided almost equally between the legions and the auxiliaries, was composed of between 250,000 and 300,000 men.[7] This was a modest force, considering that it was charged with the task of securing lengthy frontiers. Most of the forces were garrisoned along the Rhine and the Danube, in the regions where the greatest threat of incursions existed. The rest of the empire was held, in the absence of a specific crisis, by very small forces. As can be seen from these figures, the Romans were able to carve out and sustain an immense realm with a military force that was not so large as to cripple the treasury. That was true until the troubles of the third century A.D. erupted and the empire entered a long period of barbarian invasions and internal attempts by sections of the army to depose emperors and impose their favorites.

Empires are never built without warfare. All imperial systems have had to raise robust military forces that can sustain the empire without provoking crises of taxation and government finance. Rome managed this difficult balancing act for centuries. Imperial expansion fueled Rome's rise because it resulted in a continuous supply of new, cheap slave labor.

Moreover, cheap labor on the estates of the great aristocrats enormously increased the value of land and drove small landowners off their holdings and into the army. From the Roman point of view, this virtuous cycle of new additions of slave labor and a continuing supply of manpower to carry out more conquests that netted yet more slaves drove the imperial machine forward. "The Roman propertied classes were vastly enriched by this whole process," writes historian Ellen Meiksins Wood, "from expropriation of peasants at home, appropriation of great wealth from imperial revenues and, above all, from land. . . . The Roman 'elite' was arguably more dependent on the acquisition of land than any other ruling class had ever been before."[8]

The broad territorial outline of the Roman Empire was clearly evident at the time of Augustus's death in A.D. 14. Over the next century, further significant additions were made. Both Caesar and Augustus had concluded that it was not worth the effort for Rome to conquer Britain, and that policy was followed by the immediate successors of Augustus. However, in A.D. 43, motivated by the prospect of bountiful riches, the emperor Claudius dispatched a force of fifty thousand men across the English Channel to Kent. The emperor himself participated in the campaign that followed. Following easy initial victories, Claudius returned to Rome to celebrate the triumph. In the following years as the Romans extended their initial base in eastern England, the conquerors met with serious resistance in places. When this was overcome, bloody suppression was meted out to those who had stood in the way of the conquest.[9] Several decades after the initial seizures of territory in southern England, the Romans sought strategically defensible frontiers in Britain that would allow them to hold the English lowlands with as little effort as possible. Roman forces scoured the hills and valleys of Wales to end resistance there and pushed north into Scotland.[10] During the reign of Hadrian—the emperor paid a personal visit to Britain—the Romans abandoned some of their northernmost holdings and sought to give finality and solidity to their northern boundary through the construction of an east-west wall across the neck of the island, one hundred and seventeen kilometers in length. Between A.D. 122 and 127 construction took place on Hadrian's famous wall, a barrier made of solid masonry that extended from the estuary of the Solway to the estuary of the Tyne.[11] As was the case with the Great Wall of China, Hadrian's Wall (and the subsequent variations made to it) was not entirely successful in insulating Roman Britain from incursions across the line. Such walls have been as much graphic statements of political intent as they have been actual military barriers.

In addition to the conquest of most of Britain, during the century after Augustus, the Romans acquired a piece of territory in southern Germany that straightened out the line of their holdings along the Rhine and the Danube. They also gained a foothold along the western coast of the Black Sea in present-day Bulgaria and Romania. From the southeastern coast of the Black Sea, the Romans acquired territory all the way to the Caspian Sea, adding the provinces of Cappadocia, Armenia, Assyria, and Mesopotamia. They widened their holdings in Arabia and acquired Mauretania, the westernmost stretch of North Africa all the way to the Straits of Gibraltar.

ONE QUESTION THAT ARISES from this brief history of Rome is why that great civilization, successful in so many things for so long, did not take the leap forward to the beginnings of an industrial revolution that was not to come in Europe until the seventeenth and eighteenth centuries. After all, the Romans had developed a vast system of road and water transportation that would not be equaled until early modern times. Moreover, the Roman Empire established the largest single market the West was to see until the nineteenth century. Rome had developed many of the key features of the transition to capitalism—with a huge market in grain, wine, olive oil, and other commodities, with a financial system that was presided over by major businessmen. In addition, much of the science and mathematics needed for the leap to industrialization had already been developed by the Greeks. For example, Hero of Alexandria produced, as a plaything, a functioning steam engine that operated on the turbine model.[12] Here in the hands of the most advanced ancient civilization was the key invention that opened the door to industrialism many centuries later. Why did the Romans not seize the labor-saving potential in this and other techniques? Why did Rome's avaricious capitalists not see the gains they could make against their competitors through the use of such technology? The most convincing answer to this crucial question is that the system of slave labor remained so pervasive throughout the history of the Roman Empire that there was no pressing need to develop labor-saving technology. In his seminal book written in the late 1950s, British analyst John Strachey concluded that it was "above all the dead weight of slavery itself, fed by imperialism, which made the forward leap represented by industrialization and capitalist relations of production impossible."[13]

Given its technical, social, political, and economic development, why did Rome fail to advance beyond the levels achieved at the point where the republic transformed itself into the empire? In their search for answers to this question, historians are quick to point out that the second century A.D. was an age of stability and well-being that was not equaled or exceeded until at least the time of the Renaissance. "If a man were called upon," wrote Edward Gibbon in his classic history, "to fix the period in the history of the world, during which the condition of the human race was most happy and prosperous, he would, without hesitation, name that which elapsed from the death of Domitian to the accession of Commodus."[14] Commenting on this passage, Bertrand Russell entered a caveat about this supposed golden age: "The evil of slavery involved immense suffering, and was sapping the vigour of the ancient world. . . . The economic system was very bad; Italy was going out of cultivation, and the population of Rome depended on the free distribution of grain from the provinces. . . . Men looked to the past for what was best; the future, they felt, would be at best a weariness, and at worst a horror."[15]

The disintegration of the Roman Empire had its roots in the excesses of imperial rule. The expansion of Rome's rule across the whole of the Mediterranean wiped out the independent small farmer class in Italy that had been the backbone of the Roman army during the era of imperial conquest. Enriched in the process were the great landowners, who availed themselves of the vast new pool of slave labor made available as a result of the conquests. Rome's yeoman class, driven off the land, moved in huge numbers to the cities, Rome in particular, where they joined an urban proletariat that enjoyed free grain from the provinces and had its senses titillated by the bread and circuses provided by the wealthy, not least the gladiatorial extravaganzas at the Coliseum.

Meanwhile, despite its sophistication in some ways, the capitalism that grew up in Rome rested on the institution of slavery and the inequalities that resulted from imperial conquests. The Roman technique of imperial rule was based not on establishing a bureaucracy to rule over the whole empire, such as existed in China, but rather on the reproduction in the provinces of the social and ruling structures of Rome itself. The Roman rulers set up local land-owning aristocracies that depended on local slaves for their labor force. For the merchant class in Rome, huge profits were made shipping and selling products from one part of the empire to another and using their power to shape the terms of trade grotesquely in their favor. This system resembled the mercantilism of later empires such as that of the Venetians more than it did the capitalism of more recent times.

AS THE ROMAN FREE LABOR CLASS lost its vigor, living as it did in the city, on food handouts, Rome turned to the barbarians to defend imperial borders. Recruiting the barbarians, first into Roman units, and later wholesale into units made up of barbarians, bought time for the empire, but signaled the perilous condition into which it was sinking. In the days of the later empire, the armies of Rome discovered what Rome's leading chieftains had learned in the era of the collapse of the republic: that they held in their hands the power to make and unmake emperors. The story of imperial units abandoning their posts on the frontiers and marching on Rome to topple an emperor and put another in his place became all too common. Meanwhile Rome was losing its ability to raise the tax revenue to keep the imperial legions in place. A system that had once depended on local tax collectors to raise money to meet a quota set from the center became increasingly coercive. The later empire was becoming a police state in which people were ordered to remain where they were, inheriting their form of employment from their parents. Taxes became increasingly onerous where the system still functioned. To escape these burdens, people fled from the centers where Roman power remained intact. A great civilization was in its terminal throes. Slavery had served as the labor base for the great empire, and the empire could not find a way past slavery.

Rome thrived when it was able to acquire new territories from which vast riches could be derived for the wealthy classes. After the first century A.D., however, territorial expansion ceased and the burdens of the system accumulated over time. "The mode of administration, and the system of private property on which it was based, meant that the Empire tended toward fragmentation from the start," writes Ellen Meiksins Wood:

> And in the end that tendency prevailed. The imperial bureaucracy grew, above all for the purpose of extracting more taxes—as always, largely to maintain the Empire's military power. . . . With no significant new conquests after the first century A.D., the Roman army was over-stretched in keeping control of the existing empire, which the burdensome bureaucracy and the tax-hungry state grew in order to sustain the army. The burden this imposed on Rome's imperial subjects simply hastened the decline. The so-called "barbarian" invasions were less a cause than an effect of Rome's disintegration. By the time these incursions became a fatal threat and not just an annoyance, a crumbling state had long since become an intolerable burden to peasants and a dispensable nuisance to landlords.[16]

The most famous explanation for the decline and fall of the Roman Empire is Gibbon's claim that it was the consequence of the emergence of Christianity, with its emphasis on the world to come rather than this world. Gibbon's history was a stark warning written by a man with a secular sensibility about the danger of religious zealotry. In his view, the immense Roman world, with its capacity to govern the whole of the Mediterranean and to make of it an arena for trade and commerce, was subjected to the acid effects of the rise of a religion within its midst that deprived it of the means to sustain itself. The task of the Roman state in Gibbon's view was also to provide a weight in opposition to decentralist forces that threatened to tear the empire to pieces. Christianity tipped the scales too far toward disorder, Gibbon believed.

Founded on the might of its military, the Roman Empire collapsed when its military was no longer up to the task. In the twenty-first century, the United States relies heavily on the superiority of its military to sustain its empire. The ability to maintain a strong military over a long period of time depends on economic strength, a tax system that can be counted on to deliver sufficient resources to the military, and a state and political culture unswervingly devoted to keeping the military up to par. In the first period of its rise, the Roman Republic was able to rely on the strength of its citizen manpower to provide an ample military. As the republic expanded, the Romans extended their citizenship throughout central, and eventually the whole of, Italy, which meant that the military was never short of dedicated, reliable soldiers. In the struggle against Carthage, which relied on paid mercenaries, the citizen army of Rome was a priceless asset. Only such a military could rally from a defeat as serious as that at Cannae to win ultimate victory. A mercenary force, on the other hand, could fight well while the going was good, only to melt away in the face of lengthy adversity. Eventually, the Romans shifted their military from a conscript to a volunteer force, just as the United States has done in recent decades.

The professional army was the backbone of the Roman Empire for centuries and was indispensable to its capacity to hold onto the territories it ruled. Indeed, as the empire entered its long period of decay and decline, the army became an end in itself, the means to sustain rule and the method by which the tribute to finance the army was enforced. When an empire becomes little more than a feeding ground for an army, and its other economic and social purposes have vanished, it is in terminal decline. This process may take a long time or it may proceed rapidly depending on other circumstances. There is a close relationship between the economic output of an empire and its capacity to sustain a major military force. As Rome declined, the military became a dead weight much in the same way as the Soviet military became a dead weight on the Soviet Union. While the U.S. military eats up a much smaller proportion of American economic output than was the case in the Soviet Union, the United States is much more dependent on its military as the key foundation of its imperial power than it was in the period following the Second World War. In 1945, U.S. economic output was equivalent to half the economic output of the world. In the early years of the twenty-first century, the United States produces about 20 percent of global economic output, still a high proportion but dramatically reduced from the dominance enjoyed six decades ago.

When the Roman world collapsed Europe was thrown into a long twilight in which civilization itself seemed to have ended. A way forward would come again only after many centuries of retreat.

Spain: The First World Empire

In the autumn of 1491, the Spanish army was encamped at Santa Fe, a new town built by Queen Isabella and King Ferdinand, the wife and husband who ruled the kingdoms of Castile and Aragon. Ten kilometers to the east, nearly a thousand meters above sea level, was the splendid city of Granada, the last center of Muslim power on the Iberian Peninsula. In the offing was the collision between a nascent imperial power and one that had long been in decline. The tall minarets and palaces of Granada were visible to the soldiers in the Spanish camp. Soon the mosques in the city would be converted into churches, the Christian attackers fervently hoped and believed. Besieged Granada was all that was left of a Muslim empire that had once included lands in much of Spain, all the way to the Pyrenees and beyond.[1] The fervor of the Christian drive to win all Spain back from Muslim rule fueled a larger passion that would take the Spaniards across the seas in the creation of an empire that literally circled the globe.

In November 1491, the leading elements of society in Granada, including nobles, commoners, learned men, and knights, assembled to consider the plight of their city. Those who met took the message to the emir, their ruler, that Granada was in no condition to offer serious resistance. There was not enough food, there were few fighting men available, and very little assistance had reached them from their fellow Muslims in North Africa. The alternative was to seek liberal terms for the protection of the property and religious rights of the residents in return for the peaceful surrender of the city. The emir agreed with his advisers and opened talks with King Ferdinand. Generous terms were agreed to, and on January 1, 1492, the city surrendered and Spanish troops took over the following day. King Ferdinand and Queen Isabella entered four days after that. The surrender of the last Muslim power in western Europe was feted across the continent with the Pope celebrating an open-air mass in Rome to mark the victory.[2]

The extraordinary year, 1492, was noteworthy not only for the surrender of Granada and the first voyage of Christopher Columbus to America, but for the fateful decision taken by the monarchs of Castile and Aragon to demand that the remaining Jews in their kingdoms either convert to Christianity or depart from Spain. Leading members of the Jewish community offered substantial sums of money to dissuade Ferdinand and Isabella, but the policy was implemented. Estimates vary on how many Jews converted, putting the figure at no fewer than fifty thousand and no more than one hundred thousand. Similarly, between fifty thousand and one hundred thousand Jews chose to depart, leaving their homes for exile, primarily in Morocco and Portugal. The expulsion of practicing Jews rang down the curtain on the rich culture of the Sephardic Jews of Spain.[3]

Though religious zeal played a part, the Spanish Empire and the other imperial realms carved out by European powers during the transition from feudalism to capitalism were chiefly motivated by another kind of passion—a drive for profits for investors and booty and wealth for the imperial adventurers themselves. The Spanish Empire, the greatest of the early mercantilist empires, began its expansion in the fifteenth century, prior to Columbus's first expedition to America. The empire had its start in the islands off the coast of Africa, especially the Canaries. While Portugal colonized the Azores and Madeira, it was the Spaniards who colonized the Canaries. For the Spaniards, the Canaries were a source of native labor and a site to which African slaves could be transported to work on sugar plantations. Along with gold and silver, sugar was the most valued staple of the Spanish mercantilist empire. Those who gained the lion's share of the profits were Genoese as well as Spanish capitalists.

Helping establish the state that served as the base for the Spanish Empire was the marriage in 1469 of Princess Isabella, claimant to the crown of Castile, and Prince Ferdinand of Aragon. The marriage established a dynastic union between Castile and Aragon, the two principal monarchies in Spain, and had the advantage of bringing to a close a long period of civil war among Spaniards. Castile, much the larger of the two kingdoms, had its capital in Madrid, while Aragon, located in the eastern portion of Spain, had its capital in Barcelona. Few would have regarded these two kingdoms, with their small populations, as the anchor around which a world power would emerge.

Underlying the explosive growth of the Spanish Empire were crucial technological achievements. The development in the fifteenth century, first in Portugal then in Spain, of the all-weather sailing vessel with three masts—the caravels and galleons—marked an advance over the vessels that were deployed in other parts of the world. These new ships, capable of undertaking immense voyages, and of mounting cannons on their decks, were superior to the galleys that were used in the Mediterranean, Black, and Baltic seas, as well as to the Arab dhows, and the Chinese junks.[4] These sailing vessels gave the Portuguese and Spaniards, and the Europeans who later followed in their wake, the capacity to venture any-where on the oceans of the world without fear of attack from vessels of other civilizations. The vessels made it possible for the Spaniards to pick the time and location of their incursions into the lands of other peoples and provided them with the means to transport armies, slaves, and the booty of empire.

While the Spaniards had some of the assets needed to launch an empire, they lacked others. Short of skilled manpower and financial prowess, the Spanish Empire depended on its willingness to recruit people and services from abroad. The Spaniards availed themselves of the talents not only of Italian financiers, but also of German technicians and Dutch traders. Portuguese, Basque, Chinese, Flemish, West African, and British participants made the Spanish Empire a global enterprise. (The British Empire got its not very glorious start when Captain Henry Morgan raided Spanish ports and ships to enrich himself and his associates with gold and silver.)

The American Empire has been immensely successful in pursuing a similar strategy of attracting the talents of people from many back-grounds and countries. American universities have recruited many of the best and the brightest from around the world to study, teach, and pursue research within their walls. American multinational corporations and global corporate law firms hire able recruits from a huge number of countries.

In the Americas, the Spaniards initially employed the mercantilist practices they had developed in the Canaries. Within a few decades, how-ever, they switched to the establishment of colonies, hacked out through rivers of blood by the conquistadores, and settled by immigrants from Europe. The Spanish Empire began as a mercantile venture, but then it reverted to the earlier servile type of imperialism. The Spaniards, it is true, did not import huge numbers of slaves into Spain itself from their American imperial holdings. Instead, they deployed their slaves in New World mines and reaped the profits in the form of gold and silver shipped back to Spain. When the number of slaves in their American colonies was inadequate to the task their masters had set for them, the Spaniards established an enormous slave trade to ship additional labor from Africa to their mines and plantations in the New World. The wealth the Spaniards acquired from their American empire gave them the means to create Europe's most powerful military force of the day, a force strong enough to threaten the rest of the continent.

A crucial element of the Spanish conquests in the New World was that they were achieved not by the armies of the Spanish crown, but by a kind of "private enterprise." The conquistadores were freebooters, who set themselves up as enterprises and went in search of conquest from which they could earn profits from which dividends were paid to the investors who had provided the capital. The conquerors deployed terror weapons—their firearms and cannons, and their horses, unknown in the New World—to overawe the societies they shattered. The Spaniards used divide-and-conquer strategies in their campaigns. While the number of Spaniards deployed was often quite small, alliances with native populations against their traditional enemies meant that the conquerors were normally supported in the field by native warrior allies. Diseases that had been brought to the New World by the Spaniards ravaged the native societies that were being assaulted. At times, the freebooters had to deal with other mercenaries who were trying to stake out a claim to the territory they coveted. In some cases, this led to armed battles among the Spaniards themselves.

In their overthrow of the Aztec and Inca empires, the Spaniards used all these methods, relying most of all on their alliances with the subject peoples of the empires and on their ability to make use of their own superior seagoing vessels to attack at times and places of their choice and to put the enemy at a strategic disadvantage. Not only were native warriors key to the success of the conquerors, so too were natives, often slaves, who transported the supplies of the Spaniards, kept them fed, and assisted them with their knowledge of the terrain. Many of the expeditions were led by men who had been granted what was called an *encomienda* by the Spanish crown. This arrangement gave the recipient the legal right to demand tribute and labor from the natives. In return, the encomenderos undertook to win natives to Christianity and to serve and defend the crown.[5]

A spectacular, if characteristic, example of the bravado of the conquistadores was the decapitation of the Aztec Empire by Hernando Cortés and his four hundred soldiers and sixteen horsemen, a force equipped with a few artillery pieces. In the early months of 1519, Cortés and his meager complement sailed from Cuba and landed in the Yucatán. The expedition spent a couple of months moving up the coast. On April 21, 1519, Cortés's fleet landed at San Juan de Ulua, where the Spaniards were immediately greeted by two large canoes manned by Mexica Indians, who paddled out to their ships. These native envoys said their lord served Montezuma, the Aztec emperor. The natives had heard reports of the new arrivals in their territory. Their initial response was to welcome them lavishly. On shore, Cortés and his men received copious gifts of gold and jewels.[6]

Cortés and his force spent months in their progress across Mexico, forging alliances with some tribes and savagely attacking others. Both elements of this approach were critical to final success. The supreme power center in the Aztec Empire was the city of Tenochtitlan, which had a population of more than a quarter of a million people. To overpower this center, Cortés made an alliance with the Tlaxcalans, who were initially hostile to the Spaniards but came over to their side when they saw that the European invaders were not at all friendly toward Montezuma. The Tlaxcalans proved indispensable in dealing with another people who were close allies of Montezuma and the Mexicas, the Cholulans. At first hoping to win over the Cholulans, Cortés concluded that he was being lulled into a trap, and instead he sprang his own trap. Making a pretense of preparing to depart, the Spaniards invited the Cholulan warriors into a large courtyard and then ambushed them, killing the unarmed Cholulans with spears. Into the fray came thousands of Tlaxcalans, who butchered their traditional foes. In five hours of fighting, it is likely that more than three thousand Cholulans were killed.[7]

The effect of the massacre was to instill a great fear in the peoples of the whole region. Cortés spent a few days arranging a peace between the defeated Cholulans and the Tlaxcalans. Having won over key peoples to his side, he advanced toward the increasingly isolated capital, Tenochtitlan. The procession was like nothing that had been seen before in this part of the world. At its head were the Spaniards, including Cortés, with under five hundred men, supported by about one thousand natives who served as guides and porters. Behind them were the native allies, including the Tlaxcalans, who came ready for battle. When this strange force entered the great city, Cortés and his men were met by Montezuma, who gave a speech of greeting.[8]

Things then settled into an uneasy calm. Cortés and his force remained in the city for six months and exercised effective control over Montezuma. But given their paltry numbers, they were highly vulnerable to attack. Leaders of the Mexica who had remained quiescent became furious when Cortés ordered that their statues be destroyed. At this point, Montezuma informed Cortés that a fleet of Spanish ships, dispatched from Cuba, had landed at Vera Cruz and that the commander of that force was under orders to arrest Cortés.

Cortés responded quickly to this disconcerting news and led most of his men out of Tenochtitlan to meet the newly arrived Spanish force. In a short battle, he defeated the newcomers, seriously wounding their commander, and won over to his banner most of those who had been sent to arrest him. News then reached Cortés that the small party he had left behind in the capital to guard Montezuma was facing rising unrest within the city. When Cortés, reinforced by the additional cohort of Spaniards, reached the city, a full-scale revolt was underway. Determined to throw out the Spaniards, chiefs of the Mexica elected a new emperor to replace Montezuma, who had effectively become a vassal of Cortés. In the ensuing violence, Montezuma was killed.

The Spaniards were forced to flee from the city. About eight hundred of Cortés's men were killed in the rout, as well as more than one thousand of his Tlaxcalan allies. Resting and regrouping in the city of Tlaxcala, Cortés and his remaining force prepared for the next round against the capital of the Mexicas, a preparation that took them eight months.[9] Cortés used the time to rebuild his force, with men and supplies arriving from Spain, Cuba, and Jamaica. With the aid of the Tlaxcalans, he undermined the Mexica Empire, winning over its cities, so that by May 1521, he launched the siege of the completely isolated capital of Tenochtitlan. While Cortés had only about nine hundred Spaniards with him for the assault, he now was able to put in the field an enormous native army as well. The beleaguered capital, which was also coping with an outbreak of smallpox, held out for three and a half months. Tens of thousands died in the city, which at last fell into the hands of Cortés. The great Aztec Empire had been toppled.

Cortés's motives were clear from the start. In Cuba, he declared, "I came here to get rich, not to till the soil like a peasant." After he had over- thrown the Aztec Empire, he became the largest landowner in the Americas, and thousands of indigenous laborers tilled the soil for him.[10]

A decade after the fall of Tenochtitlan, Spaniards based in the newly established town of Panama in the strategic Isthmus of Panama assembled the means to undertake forays down the Pacific coast of South America. These expeditions were to bring the Spaniards into conflict with the Inca Empire.

From the twelfth century on, the Inca tribe had extended its rule over an enormous portion of South America, eventually extending from the southern reaches of contemporary Colombia to central Chile. Inland the empire stretched across the Andes Mountains into the great Amazon forest. The empire was structured so as to superimpose an Incan elite over local elites that remained in place. This feature, despite the enormous dif- ference in the technologies of the two systems, is similar to the structure of the American Empire, in which an American elite and global system operates through states that have their own elites.

At the time of the intrusion of the Spaniards into Incan territory, the empire was internally divided as a result of a conflict between two claimants to the title of supreme Inca. One claimant held power in the south, in the Incan capital of Cusco, while the other claimant had his power base in the north, in the city of Cajamarca. As had been the case with the Spanish assault on the Aztecs, internal divisions opened the way for the outsiders to take on the Incas. In the autumn of 1532, Atahualpa, the northern rival for the throne, sent envoys to greet the small party of Spaniards, only sixty horsemen and one hundred foot soldiers, who had entered the territory of the Incas under the command of Francisco Pizarro. At the time, Atahualpa did not feel threatened by the small size of the Spanish force. Just then, he was prevailing in his conflict within the empire. One of his commanders had recently defeated the forces of the rival claimant and had succeeded in capturing him.

What followed was one of the most remarkably one-sided military triumphs in history. Unlike Cortés, who had developed crucial alliances with the native enemies of the emperor, Pizarro forged no such alliances. He and his men were a tiny force, marching into the heartland of the Incas, who vastly outnumbered them. On November 15, 1532, Pizarro's force marched into the city of Cajamarca. Atahualpa, who was camped outside the city with a huge army, was completely aware of the movements of the Spanish intruders. The following day, the Inca leader entered the city. He was carried aloft into the ceremonial square where he came face to face with Pizarro. Atahualpa was directly surrounded by eighty of his nobles, and his entourage included several thousand of his people.

Aware of the hopelessness of his position in any real fight, Pizarro arranged to spring a trap on the Inca leader. He had hid his men around the square so that at the critical moment he could use terror and surprise to achieve his end. An Indian interpreter translated the message of the Spaniards to Atahualpa, which included the words of a Dominican friar who urged the supreme Inca to accept the teachings of the one true God. When a breviary was presented to Atahualpa, he hurled it to the ground. The friar, furious at this disrespect, ran back to Pizarro, who raised a cloth to signal his men that the moment had come to attack. One cannon was brought into view and was fired directly into the heart of the Inca throng. Panicked by this unknown weapon, the Incas were attacked by the Spanish soldiers who had hidden in the buildings around the square. The Spaniards fired arquebuses into the mass before them. As the crowd fled, with hundreds trampled to death, Pizarro and a few of his men sprang forward and seized Atahualpa, taking him prisoner.[11]

With Atahualpa as their captive, Pizarro discovered a way to rob the Incan Empire of a vast treasure. He promised to release the leader unharmed provided the Incans paid a stupendous ransom to win his liberation. The prisoner was kept in a room that was twenty-two feet long, seventeen feet wide, and nine feet high. He would be freed when the

Incans had handed over gold and other treasure, sufficient to completely fill the volume of this room. From all across the Incan Empire, the treasure was assembled and shipped to Cajamarca. It came in the form of cups, plates, jewelry, artifacts, and tiles from temples. The treasure was no less than the repository of the artistic labor of the peoples of the region over preceding centuries. The Spaniards, however, had no interest whatsoever in that invaluable artistic legacy. Straightaway, they melted down the treasure, reducing it to 13,420 pounds of gold and 26,000 pounds of silver.[12]

Having collected this booty, Pizarro and his men proceeded to put Atahualpa to death, as though he were nothing more than a common criminal. The Incan leader was garroted and his body was burned to charred ashes. The conquistadores shipped the treasure back to Spain, setting aside one-fifth of the take for the Spanish crown. By the end of 1533, the first of the four ships bearing the ransom and the tale that went with it entered the harbor at Seville. The fabulous riches and the prospect for much more inspired would-be adventurers and financiers in Spain and elsewhere in Europe to follow in Pizarro's footsteps.[13]

Pizarro's exploits displayed empire in its most extreme form as a venture undertaken by a civilization that had no regard for the rights, values, and accomplishments of the civilization that had fallen under its sway. Not even elementary honesty, supposedly a part of the Spanish religious code, came into play in this episode.

Despite the presence of the Dominican friar in his entourage, Pizarro's expedition was motivated, above all, by plunder and profit. Such expeditions were financed to bring back riches for those who had bankrolled them. Religion was used by the Spaniards, on this and other occasions, to provide a thin cover of legitimacy for their depredations. The claim of the Spaniards to have the right to invade the territory of other peoples was that the Pope, the representative of God on earth, had divided the western hemisphere between Spain and Portugal and that, therefore, the native peoples of the hemisphere must submit to this authority. Documents were thus often read aloud to native peoples and their leaders proclaiming the authority of Spain, acting under the direction of the Pope. Often those hearing the message had no idea what was being said.

In the Cortés and Pizarro expeditions, the nature of the Spanish Empire was revealed. It combined elements of both the mercantile and servile types of empire. The raising of capital to undertake private missions in a quest for plunder was quintessentially mercantile, having much in common with the operations of the Venetian Empire and the later British Empire. When the Spaniards resorted to slavery, both through the enslavement of native populations in America and through the African slave trade, they went beyond short-term plunder in favor of the long-term exploitation of slave labor to extract gold and silver and to grow sugar cane on plantations—all to earn a profit for investors.

Permanent settlements were established by the Spaniards in the conquered territories. These towns were the focal points for the administrative apparatus that governed the adjacent territory, where mining ventures and plantations made use of the forced labor of the indigenous population. In theory, the encomienda system recognized the Indians as owners of the land they already farmed. Adjacent land was another matter, however. On this land, the encomandero could establish his own plantation. In addition, Indian ownership of land, notional as that was in practice, did not extend to minerals below the surface.

Slavery in the Spanish Empire was highly controversial almost from the beginning. From time to time, the crown attempted to limit slavery or even to ban it altogether, sometimes in response to pressure from elements in the church. In practice, however, little was done to put a stop to slavery. The sheer cruelty of the Spaniards in the Americas had been noted by other Europeans by the early decades of the sixteenth century. And there is no reason to substantially reassess the conclusion that the cruelties in Spain's American empire were virtually without limit. That said, the greatest devastation as a result of the Spanish presence in the New World was brought about not through butchery and brutal working conditions, although there was plenty of both, but by the diseases imported to the western hemisphere from Europe. As many as twenty million people were wiped out. On many of the Caribbean islands, and on large swaths of the mainland, the native population perished completely.

From an administrative standpoint, the Spanish Empire was always something of a shambles, confounded by overlapping structures and ever-present contradictions. Not only were conquests carried out by private adventurers who had been licensed for the purpose, and who quite often found themselves in struggles against each other, but there was a long-term battle for power between the crown and the Spanish settlers in the New World. The crown attempted to prevent settlers from moving onto land held by natives, but the appetite of the settlers for access to profitable land was insatiable, and for the authorities in Spain this was a long-term and losing battle. The desire of settlers for the right to encroach on native land contributed enormously to the tensions between settlers in the thirteen colonies and the British government in the lead-up to the American Revolution. Similarly, it played a large role in alienating Spanish settlers in the New World from Spain.

Theory and practice were very different in the Spanish Empire. Regulations and rules set down in Spain were regularly ignored in practice in the colonies, which meant that behavior varied chaotically from place to place.

Empire brought with it the idea that power assembled on such a scale must have a divine purpose, a notion common to a number of empires, not least the American Empire in our own time. Tommaso Campanella, a Dominican friar from south of Naples, a territory ruled by the Spaniards, was tortured and jailed beginning in 1599 for supposedly plotting to overthrow Spanish rule. Remarkably, he believed that the Spanish monarchy could be a force for good in the world and, as it ruled an ever-greater portion of the earth, could help achieve universal peace and prosperity. "This monarchy of Spain, which encircles the world," he wrote, "is that of the Messiah, and thus shows itself to be the heir of the universe."[14]

In the sixteenth century, as the Spanish Empire was being consolidated in America, the crown took steps to rationalize its holdings in Europe, to transform what had been a hodgepodge of dynastic holdings into a functioning whole. The Castilian monarchy that presided over the empire had established its authority in Spain and in other parts of Europe on the basis of dynastic alliances. Within Europe, therefore, the holdings of the Castilian crown were separate states, rather than territories within an integrated administrative and state system. Castile, the home territory of the monarchy, was relatively poor, and with a population of only five million people, it was far from able to match the potential manpower of more populous regions of Europe, such as France, Italy, and Germany, regions that were still far from being nations. To make a success of the empire, the Castilian crown relied on bullion from America and the manpower and expertise of much of Europe. Within Europe, the Castilian monarchy began to exercise control over the whole of Spain as a consequence of a dynastic alliance with Aragon. Outside Spain, the crown had holdings in Italy and in the Netherlands, holdings that were also administered locally. Even in the case of the colonies, administrative control from Castile was haphazard.

In addition to the importance of the conquests in the New World to the emerging Spanish Empire were the marriage alliances arranged by Ferdinand in Europe. The dynastic alliances were to give future Spanish monarchs control over additional states and provinces in Europe. Following the death of Ferdinand in 1516, the inheritor of the thrones of Castile and Aragon was Ferdinand's grandson, the archduke Charles of Hapsburg. (Although Charles was declared ruler of these Spanish kingdoms in 1516, his mother remained legally the Queen of Castile until her death.) Charles was the inheritor of a vast array of realms, making him the ruler of a larger portion of Europe than any other monarch. He was ruler of the Hapsburg territories, including Austria, which lay inside the Holy Roman Empire, and Hungary, which lay outside it. He ruled the Italian states of Naples and Sicily, and, in addition, the Netherlands, the whole of the Spanish peninsula, and the territories in Spain's American empire. In 1520, Charles was declared to be the emperor of the Holy Roman Empire.[15]

After a life of traveling from realm to realm throughout his enormous holdings, Charles abdicated the throne in 1556. The result was the division of the realms he controlled. Philip II inherited the Spanish and American territories, as well as some of Charles's other European holdings. The Hapsburg realms of Austria and Spain, however, did not go to Philip. The division of Charles's inheritance did ameliorate the concern that had been growing in Europe that his vast power could lead to a Hapsburg hegemony throughout the continent. Philip's inheritance served as the base on which the Spaniards constructed their empire from that date forth.

In 1519, Ferdinand Magellan, a Portuguese, led the Spanish expedition that resulted in the first circumnavigation of the globe. Despite the loss of most of the members of the expedition, including Magellan himself, the venture demonstrated to Spaniards the potential for carving out a sphere for themselves in Asia. In these undertakings, as in the Americas, their chief competitors were the Portuguese. In the Americas a treaty signed in 1494, overseen by the papacy, divided the New World between the two powers of the Iberian Peninsula (a division that was not recognized by later imperial powers including the Dutch, the English, and the French). In Asia, where the Portuguese had enjoyed a head start, a similar effort was made to divide the region between the two powers, but the line of demarcation was a matter of dispute from the beginning.

As a consequence of their penetration of the region, the Spanish established themselves in the Philippine archipelago, with their headquarters at Manila on the island of Luzon. Although Spanish maps were to display the Philippines as a part of the Spanish Empire, this was always something of a conceit. Much of the archipelago, where most of the population was Islamic, remained effectively outside any but notional Spanish suzerainty. The Spaniards did control Manila, but even the mountainous regions of Luzon were not effectively administered by the Spanish. Because of the enormous distance of the Philippines from Spain, the Spanish enclave in Manila received provisions from Mexico and at first was administered as a dependency of the viceroyalty of New Spain. Soon, though, the colony was run autonomously, rather than from the Americas. The Spanish colony in the Philippines never became economically self-sustaining and prosperous in the way the empire in the Americas had. Indeed, the Spanish arrival in the islands did not dramatically transform the local economy. Although the Spaniards introduced cattle to Luzon, the land was not as suited for large-scale ranching as was Mexico, and the principal crop of the island remained rice. While the Americas had provided bullion and highly profitable export crops for the Spaniards, this was not the case with the Philippine colony. Indeed, on a regular basis, the Spanish administration in Manila received a direct subsidy from Mexico, in the form of a transfer of silver in Spanish galleons, and this subsidy continued until the nineteenth century.[16]

While the Spaniards did not set up highly profitable operations in the Philippines, the colony did become a huge success as an entrepôt that connected East Asia to Europe. Few Spaniards settled in Manila—most who did were from New Spain, and many of these were criminals or vagrants who had been dispatched there by the authorities—but thousands of Chinese did locate there, establishing export businesses. Fine Chinese silk products were exported from Manila to New Spain and from there to Europe. In addition to silk, which caused a sensation among buyers in Mexico and Spain, the exports of Chinese merchants included porcelain, chinaware, gold jewelry, and woolen shawls. A smaller Japanese community was also established in Manila, and an important trade link developed between Japan and Manila. In effect, the Spanish imperial holding in the Philippines became an outpost for the major Asian powers, China and Japan, and existed more at their pleasure than as a consequence of the might of the Spanish military. The Spanish military post in Manila always constituted a minor complement, capable of putting on a show of force in the other islands in the Philippines from time to time but not capable of turning aside any serious external challenge.

Relations between the Chinese community and the Spanish authorities turned violent on a number of occasions. Insurrections were launched from the Chinese community in Manila, and there were bloody massacres of Chinese residents by the Spaniards. In 1603, a Chinese insurrection resulted in the killing of nearly half the city's Spanish population. In that conflict, it is estimated that the Spanish, with the help of Filipinos, who harbored their own resentments against the Chinese community, killed 23,000 Chinese residents. Serious outbreaks of violence and the widespread killing of Chinese residents of Manila occurred as well in 1639 and 1662.[17]

A remarkable feature of the Manila outpost of the Spanish Empire was the immense challenge of the journey from Luzon to Mexico in the galleons of the day. The huge distance and the vagaries of the winds meant that the journey from Manila to Acapulco normally took about six months, sometimes as much as nine months, with no ports of call along the way. The journey westward from Mexico to the Philippines took a little less time. The preferred route took the galleons close to a line along the fortieth parallel of north latitude. For over two centuries, the galleons took this journey, never encountering the Hawaiian Islands located at about twenty degrees north latitude. Many of those making the trip perished at sea, and many ships were lost during these arduous journeys, which continued to be made until 1815. Despite the unimaginable hardships, the link between Manila and Mexico was the lifeline of the Spanish Empire across the Pacific and a crucial trading link between East Asia and the West.

If its Asian outposts made the Spanish Empire genuinely global, it was the wealth that flowed out of America that solidified Spain's position as an imperial power. The two greatest centers of silver production in Spanish America were in Potosi (Bolivia) and in Zacatecas (Mexico). In the early years, the production of silver was meager, but when the Spaniards, borrowing from German ideas on the subject, learned how to separate silver from waste through the use of mercury, production took off. It is scarcely an exaggeration to say that the Spanish Empire was built on a foundation of silver. At an altitude of 13,000 feet, located in a frigid range of mountains, Potosi soared in population from 14,000 in 1547 to close to 160,000 in 1650. Most of the population, not surprisingly, was made up of indigenous laborers who worked in the mines, drafted to do so by the Spaniards and paid a small wage. Epidemics and miserable working conditions resulted in a very high death rate. Between 1550 and 1800, the mines in Spanish America produced over 80 percent of the world's silver and 70 percent of the world's gold.[18]

In 1630, a friar who visited the Spanish mine at Potosi concluded that the impact of the silver produced there was far-reaching. He wrote that "Potosi lives in order to serve the imposing aspirations of Spain: it serves to chastise the Turk, humble the Moor, make Flanders tremble and terrify England."[19]

The bullion and the crops that flowed in from the Americas played a role in the undoing of Spanish power over the long term, however. Most of the profits from the American empire of the Spaniards flowed to financiers in other parts of Europe, to Italians, to the Dutch, and to the Germans and Swiss. The consequence was to promote a general increase in economic activity in Europe, concentrated on the rise of cities. Royal treasuries benefited, and the countries that challenged the Spaniards in the next phase of mercantilism were helped along the road to the creation of their own empires. The Spanish advantage, derived from the far-sightedness of the kingdoms of Castile and Aragon at the end of the fifteenth century, and the capacity to enlist adventurers and investments from many parts of Europe, gave Spain a lead in deploying the new ocean-going vessels of the age. The advantage was crucial in erecting the great European empire of the day. It was, however, an advantage that would not last.

Spain itself remained, for the most part, a poor country, through which the riches of empire passed to others and from which thousands left to work in the military, administrative, and commercial operations of the far-flung empire. Although Spaniards were, in their days of imperial glory, the most traveled of Europeans, to be encountered in many parts of Europe, the New World, and Asia, Spain itself seemed resistant to the countries it dominated. Foreigners found Spain a strangely backward country whose population was often unfriendly to outsiders. In the 1660s, when Francis Willughby visited Castile, he reported that people were "uncivil to strangers, asking them, 'What do you come into our Countrey for? We doe not go into yours.'"[20]

One way the Spanish Empire resembled its imperial successors, such as the United States, was in the inability of Spaniards to acquaint themselves with languages other than their own, Castilian. Despite the fact that the Spanish Empire was, in its heyday, the greatest in the world, with bases of power in the Philippines, Europe, and America, there was little taste in Spain itself for mastering other languages or coming to know, in any intimate fashion, the cultures that the Spanish dominated. Like Americans in our time, the Spanish became famous for their arrogance and their narrowness of culture. The curious fact of Spain's shortage of officials who could speak tongues other than Castilian meant that the empire was forced to rely on foreigners to act as diplomats and to play the role of intermediaries between Spain and its empire, as well as the rest of the world.

The Spanish Empire was heavily dependent on the acumen and the financial resources of capitalists in other parts of Europe. Genoese financiers played a critical role in underwriting Spain's enterprises in the New World. Because of Spanish regulations that did not initially allow the export of specie (gold and silver), these investors were obliged to realize their profits in Castile, where they then invested their capital locally and, in the process, took over a large proportion of the Castilian wool trade and other industries. When the ban on exports of specie from Spain was dropped in the mid-1560s, European financiers pulled out of the Spanish economy and turned their attentions to the more lucrative international money market.[21]

Despite the fact that so much of the wealth that flowed to Spain from the far reaches of the empire flowed out again just as quickly to foreign financiers, the great Spanish port of Seville became an emporium for the produce of the world. Ships from Canada, South America, Mexico, Cuba, Japan, and Italy visited the port. The commerce of the Spanish Empire was truly global, with African slaves shipped to Mexico, the silver of Mexico to China, and Chinese silks to Spain.[22]

In the closing decades of the seventeenth century, which were the last decades of the Hapsburg monarchy in Spain, foreigners saw the Spaniards as presiding over an empire that was visibly in decline. More than ever, the profits of the empire were pouring into France, England, and Genoa, among other places. In November 1700, the last Spanish Hapsburg king died. Not long before his death, Charles II named Philip Duke of Anjou, the grandson of Louis XIV of France, as his successor. Crowned Philip V, the new king opened a new era of Bourbon rule in Spain, bringing the ailing empire into close alignment with France, which was then the rising power of continental Europe.

The threat to the balance of power in Europe posed by a Bourbon king in Spain provoked the formation of a powerful counter-alliance whose principal members were England, Austria, and the United Provinces (the Netherlands). The goal of the anti-Bourbon coalition was to unseat the Bourbon monarch of Spain and to replace him with a Hapsburg. In May 1702, the members of the coalition declared war on France and Spain and were joined a year later by Portugal. The French discovered to their horror that the Spanish military, both on sea and on land, was a far cry from the forces it had mustered in the glory days of the empire. To turn things around, the French sent a contingent of officials to Madrid whose task it was to completely overhaul the administration of the empire, both in Spain and in the lands the Spaniards ruled. Those who had been in charge were roughly pushed aside, thrown out of their jobs and sometimes imprisoned.

To counter the onslaught of the coalition powers, Spain was forced to rely on the French to mount a defense of the Iberian Peninsula. The once-proud Spanish fleet was no match for the British, who seized Gibraltar and occupied the Spanish cities on the Mediterranean coast, most important among them Barcelona.[23]

In 1707, in the decisive battle of Almansa, French-led forces routed an Anglo-Portuguese army, opening the way for the clearing of enemy armies out of Spain and the retention of the Spanish crown by its Bourbon monarch.[24] While Philip V retained control of Spain in the Treaty of Utrecht of 1713 (minus Gibraltar, which was kept by the British), Spain was stripped of its other European holdings in Italy and in the southern Netherlands. The war had the effect of ending the great era of the Spanish Empire. It opened the way for the central power struggle of the eighteenth and early nineteenth centuries between the two principal powers of the epoch, Britain and France.

One of the consequences of their empire for the Spaniards was to incur the enmity and wrath of many other peoples, an outcome not uncommon for the imperialists who came before and after them, and one that has deeply affected the Americans in our time. Marcos de Isaba, a soldier who served Philip II, wrote bitterly in the 1580s about the feelings foreigners had developed about Spaniards as a consequence of their imperial pre-eminence:

> These nations outside Spain that are subjects, friends or allies of His Majesty, are by nature inconstant, unreliable, restive and seditious. The greatness of our king and the blessed name of Spaniard have few friends. In the past Spaniards were well loved by all peoples, but for the last ninety years we are hated and detested and all because of the wars. Envy is a worm that does not rest, it is the cause of the resentment and hatred shown to us by Turks, Arabs, Jews, French, Italians, Germans, Czechs, English and Scots, who are all enemies of Spaniards. Even in the New World there is hatred and detestation for the valorous arms of this nation.[25]

Similarly, in 1570, a Spanish official based in Milan wrote: "I don't know what there is in the nation and empire of Spain that none of the peoples of the world subject to it bears it any affection."[26]

In the final years of its existence, with its days as a world power long in the past, the Spaniards tried to appeal to the common ties that ought to exist between Spain and its American colonies. Threatened by the rise of Napoleon in Europe and by the threat of rebellions in America by peoples who wanted to follow the United States along the road to self-government, Spanish authorities tried to reform the empire to give those who lived in it a greater stake in its survival. In 1809, when the Spaniards were fighting against French armies in their homeland, the Junta Central, the governing body in Spain, wrote to the city officials in Bogotá to appeal to their sense of common identity: "There exists a union between the two hemispheres, between the Spaniards of Europe and America, a union that can never be destroyed, because it is grounded upon the most solid bases that tie men together: a common origin, the same language, laws, customs, religion, honour, sentiments, relations and interests. These are the ties that unite us."[27]

The following year an effort was made to change the structure of the empire to establish a Cortés (governing assembly) in which not only Spaniards from the metropolitan homeland would be represented, but also residents in the American territories and the Philippines.[28] It was too late in the day, however, for any such grand makeover.

IT IS A CHARACTERISTIC OF EMPIRES under stress, or in decline, that their rulers attempt to broaden their base to achieve stability. A century after the Spaniards tried to enlist overseas compatriots on behalf of the empire, when the British were under similar pressure from competing powers, imperial federationists floated the idea of establishing an imperial parliament that would sit in London. The idea was that Canadians, Australians, New Zealanders, and South Africans would sit in the parliament alongside the English, Scots, Welsh, and Irish. A problem that relegated this notion to nothing more than speech-making on grand occasions was the fact that 80 percent of the population of the British Empire resided in India. The thought that sooner or later Indians would end up electing a majority of the members to an imperial parliament consigned this idea to the dustbin. The Romans tried to achieve stability by enlisting German units into their legions and extending citizenship to those who served in these units. The Americans are now experimenting with granting citizenship to foreign volunteers in the U.S. armed forces. And the French, in a desperate and failing bid to hold onto Algeria, tried extending citizenship to the population of that country.

Within a couple of decades, most of the countries of Spanish America would fight for and achieve their independence. What was left after that would be lost in the Spanish–American War of 1898. The legacy of the Spanish Empire, of course, was enormous, most visible in the existence of hundreds of millions of Spanish-speaking peoples in the Americas and the fact that Spanish is one of the world's most widely spoken languages.

The empire itself had subjugated the peoples of the western hemisphere, from whom vast wealth was plundered. Conceived as a mercantile empire, whose goal was profits for those who invested in its ventures, the Spanish Empire changed into an enterprise that carried millions of Africans to the New World as slaves. It was also an empire of colonization, transplanting a large population of Spaniards to the Americas. While the wealth of the empire passed through Spain, enriching a few there, those who profited most from this multinational venture were usually not Spaniards, but bankers and investors elsewhere in Europe.

The Spanish Empire displayed an enigmatic combination of features, reflecting as it did the moment of its birth, a time when capitalism was emerging and when the remnants of feudalism were still strong. It was the proverbial elephant, which, examined by a group of blind men, could be described in a multiplicity of ways. Spain's American empire was encased within the shell of feudal forms. The private expeditions that carried out conquests were licensed for the purpose by the Spanish crown, according to feudal hierarchical norms, with the king at the top of the pyramid, and his vassals, in theory, acting according to royal will. In reality, the conquistadores were private operators who were underwritten by financiers. This was an expression of the mercantile capitalism that predominated in Europe from the end of the fifteenth century until the end of the eighteenth century. The system, unlike later capitalism, which relied largely on the surplus produced by wage labor, produced profits for investors through plunder, slave labor, and terms of trade that were rigged in favor of monopolists. The first phase of the Spanish Empire in America was almost exclusively devoted to plunder. The conquistadores invaded a territory and stole the riches of the people who lived there. The fact that these invaders carried out exploration of territories not known to

Europeans, were underwritten by the most respected bankers on the continent, and came with the blessings of the papacy and the Church cannot disguise the fact that they engaged in pure theft.

During the second phase of the Spanish Empire in the Americas, plunder was replaced by slave labor as the means to profit. This was a primitive capitalism in which the cost of labor was held to an absolute minimum—slaves were fed barely enough to survive, and when many died, they were replaced by slaves brought in from Africa. Slaves extracted silver and gold from mines and produced crops for export on great plantations, the principal one being sugar. The export of these products to Europe was carried out under the aegis of the Spanish crown. The exporters were monopolists who did not compete with each other when it came to price as was to be the case with the next phase in the history of capitalism. This was to be a crucial feature, not only of the mercantile capitalism of the Spaniards and the Portuguese, but of their later competitors, the Dutch, the English, and the French. In Europe itself, the Spanish presence was sustained through dynastic alliances that gave Spain, for a considerable period, influence in many parts of the continent. What made this more than a mere matter of temporary dynastic advantage was the role that bullion from the Americas played in consolidating Spanish power in Europe. Silver and gold from America gave the Spanish crown the means to hire soldiers from all over Europe. Most of the soldiers who fought for Spain during the period of its ascendancy were not Spaniards. Thus the wealth derived from the colonial empire gave Spain a powerful position in Europe for more than two centuries.

Hugh Thomas, the esteemed historian of the Spanish world, states that those who created the Spanish Empire were motivated by more than gold. As was the case with other empires over the millennia, the empire builders were certain of the moral righteousness of their cause: "Most of them [the conquistadores] believed that the long-term benefit of their discoveries would be the acceptance by the natives of Christianity, with the cultural consequences that that implied. They believed, as the Spanish Crown put the matter in 1504, that they were 'ennobling' the new lands with Christians. They made their conquests with a clear conscience, certain that they were taking with them civilization."[29]

The British Empire: Cultural Superiority

Take up the White Man's Burden
Send forth the best ye breed
Go bind your sons in exile
To serve your captives' need;
To wait in heavy harness
On fluttered folk and wild
Your new-caught, sullen peoples,
Half devil and half child.

Take up the White Man's Burden
And reap his old reward:
The blame of those ye better,
The hate of those ye guard. . . .
— RUDYARD KIPLING,
"THE WHITE MAN'S BURDEN," 1899

Rudyard Kipling, the greatest of imperial poets, managed in these verses to make it seem that rulers of empires make sacrifices while the ruled are sullen ingrates. Those at the center of empires always find ways to express their sense of superiority over others. Some have done it with haughty disdain for those they have ruled. For their part, the British managed to radiate a sense of serene paternalism that no other imperial rulers have quite managed to carry off.

Throughout the ages, the rationale for imperial rule has rested on the claim that one country represents the forces of good doing battle against the forces of evil. In the final analysis, that was the basis for George W. Bush's invasion of Iraq in 2003, just as it was the rationale for the British invasion of Bengal in the 1750s. (Lord Clive's conquest of Bengal was sold to the British people as revenge for the massacre of Britons in the Black Hole of Calcutta—Britain's eighteenth-century version of 9/11.)

Another common rationale used to justify empire is that a particular people or state is highly civilized and is therefore duty bound to bring others who are less enlightened under their influence to teach them the ways of civilization. Closely related to this notion is the recurrent idea that some peoples are naturally suited to self-government and democracy while others are not, and that it is the right of the former peoples to rule the latter. The British, and not just Rudyard Kipling, were fond of making this case to bolster their claim that they ruled an ethical empire. In 1882, the Regius Professor of History at Oxford made this assessment of the Irish: "The Celts of Ireland are as yet unfit for parliamentary government. . . . Left to themselves, without what they call English misrule, they would almost certainly be . . . the willing slaves of some hereditary despot, the representative of their old coshering chiefs, with a priesthood as absolutist and as obscurantist as the Druids."

As the struggle for Home Rule in Ireland became a festering issue in British politics in the late nineteenth century, the opponents of self-determination for the Irish turned to ethnic slurs when they made their case. The Irish were depicted as "naughty children" or as "voluble, ineffective—not trustworthy in business." Others saw them as being as "unstable as water" and described Ireland as "a backwater spawned over by obscene reptiles."[1]

Similar slurs were employed by the British defenders of empire against the population of India, especially during the last century of British rule in the subcontinent. The great uprising of Indians against British rule in 1857 was known by the British as the "Indian Mutiny" because it began among sepoys in the Army of Bengal. The term connoted an act of unspeakable treachery by people who were benefiting from the wisdom of British administration and military training. British newspapers provided their readers with lurid accounts of the uprising, which featured brown heathens killing captives, massacring babies, and raping white women. That there were atrocities is undeniable, but the evidence suggests that few of the Indians who took women captive raped them. That did not stop the spread of lies that fed the racial loathing of the British for dark-skinned men who supposedly relished the idea of violating white women.

The rebellion was put down with great ferocity. Some Muslim rebels were sewn into pigskins before being hanged, a deliberate way of dishonoring their religion and inflicting on them a terrible death. Other mutineers were fired out of the mouths of cannons. In the aftermath of the rebellion, the East India Company lost its last governing functions, which were taken over entirely by the British government. If anything, the racial hatred that was a feature of British rule in India deepened after the rebellion, and it was commonplace for the British stationed there in the army or the administration to despise the Indians. In the lives of luxury they enjoyed in India, the British separated themselves almost completely from those they ruled, leaving the disciplining of the population almost entirely to their Indian underlings. It was in the decades following the great rebellion that the British developed a mindset that combined loathing for the native population with the conviction that they were carrying out a noble work on behalf of a lesser people.

At the same time, the British were not unaware of the vast benefits that flowed to them from India. Particularly following the opening of the Suez Canal in 1869, which greatly shortened the passage to India by making the voyage around the Cape of Good Hope unnecessary, British trade with India expanded dramatically. At a time when Britain was facing challenges from the United States and Germany, the world's new industrial powers, trade with India was immensely profitable. In 1855, British exports to India were worth 23 million pounds; by 1910, British exports were up appreciably to 137 million pounds and by the latter date, Britain's trade surplus with India was 51 million pounds.[2]

On top of that, Indians' taxes covered the entire cost of administering their country, including its large army, and netted the British an additional 10 million pounds a year in interest payments by 1900. Forty percent of Indian tax revenues went to the upkeep of the military by the end of the nineteenth century. India's large army, with its complement of three thousand British officers, proved a highly useful source of manpower for British imperial expeditions that fought in China in 1839, 1856, and 1859; in Persia in 1856; in Abyssinia in 1867; in Egypt in 1882; in Nyasaland in 1893; in the Sudan in 1896; and in the two world wars.[3]

Lord Curzon, who was viceroy of India in 1901, admitted frankly: "As long as we rule India, we are the greatest power in the world. If we lose it, we shall drop straightway to a third-rate power."[4]

One of the keys to making sense of the empires of the past two centuries is not to obsess too much over the difference between informal and formal imperialism. Analyses of British imperialism have often foundered on making too much of the distinction between those parts of the world dominated by British capital and those regions of the globe over which the Union Jack flew. In truth, British governments preferred the route of informal empire—that is, the non-annexation of a territory—provided that British commercial and strategic interests could thereby be upheld. When such arrangements failed, the British state was prepared to act with military occupations or annexations.

The drive to protect investors and to enhance the opportunities for entrepreneurs was uppermost in the thinking of the British government in a number of its key acquisitions in the late nineteenth century. It was to prevent financial default by the khedive of Egypt on the holdings of British and other investors that Britain staged its military takeover of Egypt in 1882. And what motivated the British seizure of South Africa and therefore caused the Boer War at the end of the nineteenth century was the vast opportunity for profits from the gold and diamond mines of the territory. For mining magnate Cecil Rhodes and other moguls, this was a territory worth placing under the Union Jack. In the case of Egypt, the British government was acting on behalf of rentiers and in the case of South Africa, Britain was standing up for the interests of great entrepreneurs.

IT WAS SIR JOHN SEELEY in the early 1880s who offered the famous observation that Britain acquired its empire "in a fit of absence of mind." None of the empires we have spoken of were launched with foresight about where the imperial adventure would lead. Only much later, when an empire is at its height or even in decline, do poets and other imperial advocates come up with a rationale for its existence.

In the middle of the seventeenth century, few observers would have predicted that the islands off the northwest coast of Europe would become the center of the greatest empire in the world, that from these islands adventurers, conquerors, capitalists, and missionaries would sail forth and paint the world with the colors of Britain. At the start, the English quest for empire was modeled on the great empire of the day, that of Spain. Envy of Spain spawned scavenging raids whose purpose was to pick up crumbs from Spain's bountiful larder. In 1663, Henry Morgan, the Welsh buccaneer, carried out a daring assault on the Spanish outpost of Grenada,[5] and this exploit in the Caribbean showed that the British were aware of the profits of empire, if as yet uncertain about how to forge a profitable empire of their own.

By the time Morgan had set out to plunder Spanish gold, the British presence in North America was already solidly established, and the British had conquered Ireland. Various motives underlay the founding of the British colonies in America, profitable commerce and the quest for religious freedom topping the list. The two archetypal colonies in the new British North American Empire were Virginia and Massachusetts, the first a commercial venture tied to tobacco and slavery, the second a new home for English Puritans seeking a place apart in which to build their promised land. The character of early Massachusetts was made clear in an order passed by its General Court to the effect that no one could settle in the colony until his religious orthodoxy had been recognized by the magistrates.[6] In Virginia, meanwhile, a version of gentlemanly England was being reproduced, so that by the end of the seventeenth century a landed gentry class, increasingly dependent on black slave labor, dominated the colony.

Britain's great internal struggles of the seventeenth century, which included the Civil War, the execution of King Charles I, and the dictatorship of Oliver Cromwell, ended with the Glorious Revolution of 1688, which struck a new balance between Parliament and monarchy, landed gentry and commerce. What emerged was the post-feudal Britain that forged an empire the like of which the world had never seen. Over the course of the following century, the British Empire expanded enormously in North America, India, and the West Indies. A vast and wide-ranging struggle with France was crucial to the rise of the British Empire, and that struggle continued during and following the American Revolution and through the Napoleonic era to 1815. During the eighteenth century, through to 1815, Britain was a heavily militarized society for the time, with a very high proportion of the gross domestic product (GDP) financing the fighting of wars and servicing the debt that arose as a consequence of military spending. Indeed,

the most rapidly growing sector of the British economy in the eighteenth century was government and defense, rather than agriculture
and industry.[7] In 1700, the British national debt amounted to 14 million
pounds. It rose to 78 million pounds in 1748, 133 million pounds in
1763, 245 million pounds in 1783, reaching 700 million pounds in 1815.
During periods of peacetime, interest payments on the national debt
accounted for more than 50 percent of public expenditures. In the years
immediately following Waterloo, interest payments on the national debt
soared to over 80 percent of public outlays.[8]

Managing the spending and investing in the holding of the debt played
a great role in promoting the rise of the financial services sector in
London. A compelling argument can be made that a critical factor in
Britain's success in its long series of wars against France was the country's
much stronger system of public finance, which allowed the regime to
raise vast sums of money, enabling Britain to serve as the paymaster of the
coalitions against France, particularly during the Napoleonic Wars.
Britain's tax revenues and its rate of taxation were higher than those of
France during the period. The stresses of such large government outlays
for the military and debt servicing were immense. At times, these stresses
threatened the regime with serious political opposition. In France, however, where the same crisis of public finance was faced much less successfully, one of the causes of the French Revolution and of the overthrow
of the Bourbon monarchy was the inability of the regime to cope
adequately with the problem.

After 1815, British military spending, and with it government spending as a whole, declined dramatically. Over time, the debt was paid down
so that the proportion of the GDP going to the military and debt servicing dropped significantly. For Britain, this was the "peace dividend" that
came with the defeat of Napoleon. As the British case illustrates, it has
always been much more costly to acquire hegemony and empire than to
sustain them. The willingness of privileged classes to submit to high rates
of taxation to underwrite a military machine with the capacity to defend
and expand an empire is a crucial matter. The record shows that Roman
elites were prepared to pay the necessary price for long periods of time,
although in the latter decades of the empire, their unwillingness to pay
was an important cause of imperial collapse. In the eighteenth century,

the British ruling classes solved this issue of taxation, an issue that drove the French monarchy and aristocracy to its ruin. In our day, the American elites have shown themselves highly unwilling to submit to high rates of taxation, with the consequence that as the United States fights to define its imperial sphere, the country is in a fiscally perilous condition with the national debt and the indebtedness of Americans to other countries skyrocketing.

Over the course of the wars with France until 1815, the proportion of British exports going to markets in continental Europe declined markedly in favor of overseas markets. While continental Europe's share as a destination of British exports was 82 percent at the beginning of the eighteenth century, this had declined to 40 percent by the early 1770s. Meanwhile, the share of British imports from the continent fell from 68 percent of the total to 47 percent during the same years. During the period 1713–17 to 1803–7, the continental European share of Britain's trade plunged from 74 to 33 percent.[9]

As British society shifted slowly from an agrarian and financial ruling class to a ruling class in which industrialists played their role, Britain continued to expand its overseas holdings in Australia, New Zealand, Africa, and a myriad of islands and coaling (refueling) stations on the world's oceans, the stepping stones of Britain's mastery of the seas.

The British Empire plainly illustrates the proposition that while colonies and subject territories are transformed by their imperial rulers, the ruling society is also transformed. Just as the Roman Republic became a victim of the Roman Empire, so too were efforts to advance the interests of industrialists and the working class retarded by the power of those who benefited from control of the empire. As a consequence of empire, vestigial social relationships from the age of the great landowning nobility survived long into the period of industrial capitalism. It was not that British society remained feudal; far from it. What happened is that Britain's road to capitalism was unique, involving an early revolution, albeit one far less sweeping than the French Revolution, and an alliance between great landowners and financiers that created a state capable of carving out a global empire.

What has been called British "gentlemanly capitalism," a particular amalgam of interests, was the locus of British imperial ventures for three centuries from the late seventeenth to the late twentieth century. These elements included the remnants of the old landed class, top civil servants, financiers, and rentier money interests (Britain's famed coupon clippers). The critical link was that between land and finance, a link that held up well past the middle of the nineteenth century when domestic agriculture was in decline. The settlement of 1688, which established a power-sharing arrangement between the monarchy and Parliament, brought the great landed magnates to the height of their power. By the end of the eighteenth century, four to five thousand great landholders possessed 75 percent of the country's agricultural land.[10] These magnates had decisively won the battle of the enclosures against the small peasants, who were driven off the land, many of them forced to emigrate to North America. Alongside the landed gentry was a rising and powerful coterie of financial interests, centered in the city of London. Even though Britain became the world's first industrialized country—the "workshop of the world" as it was called—industrialists never won power in the management of the British state the way the great landowners and financial interests had. The set of service industries that grew up around the management of finance, including insurance, became the center of the British economy as it moved slowly away from agriculture, especially as a consequence of free trade in the mid-nineteenth century. The resultant gap, between the manufacturing north and the financial services of the south, proved to be an enduring one. And it was empire and the outlets it provided for this financial sector and for the sons of the aristocrats that gave this structure of power its continuing lease on life.

Historians P.J. Cain and A.G. Hopkins, in their groundbreaking study, *British Imperialism 1688–2000*, have traced the evolution of gentlemanly capitalism, showing the extent to which it was influenced by the existence of the British Empire. They divide their analysis into two historical periods: before and after 1850.

The first period begins with the Glorious Revolution of 1688. Nineteenth-century reformers referred contemptuously to this as the age of "old corruption." Cain and Hopkins write that the system "was dominated by the landed interest, the aristocrats and country gentry . . . in association with a junior partner, the moneyed interest, which gained prominence after the financial revolution of the 1690s. Patronage and speculation were endemic to the system; but they were also consistent with the emergence of an effective military-fiscal state."

Close ties between the old landowning interests and the new financial powers, centered in London, "produced a strong and stable government, managed from London, which was capable of financing the defense of the realm and winning political loyalties without penalizing wealth-holders or crushing the largely disenfranchised tax paying public."[11]

"After 1850, when our second period begins," the authors conclude, "the composition of the gentlemanly order experienced a change which reflected the growing influence of finance and associated service occupations, and the steady decline of the agrarian interest." In the second half of the nineteenth century, therefore, the roles were reversed—the London financiers became the senior partners, and the landowners, whose wealth was in decline, were the junior partners. Intermarriage between the two groups allowed landowners to marry money and permitted financiers to acquire titles.[12]

In the nineteenth century, author James Mill, father of the more famous John Stuart Mill, called the British colonies "a vast system of outdoor relief for the upper classes." This famous comment has held as a partial explanation for Britain's drive to empire. However, the empire enriched and not only empowered the landed magnates, the great financial interests, the top civil servants, and the military; it also widened the scope for the religious and humanitarian forces in Britain, who played no small part in the enterprise of empire. Here the analogy with the American Empire of our day is striking. Missionaries and humanitarians, who thought themselves, quite justly, as very different from the more obvious beneficiaries of empire in Britain's ruling classes, sailed forth in large numbers to stamp their mark on colonized peoples. It was the missionaries and the humanitarians who gave the British Empire its liberal, human face, much the way American culture and today's proselytizers on behalf of imperial missions to rescue peoples from tyranny and chaos provide the American Empire with its humane patina. This was the British version of the soft power that is such a vaunted part of the authority America's Empire now wields. The champions of the British Empire made self-righteous claims on its behalf, just like those who do battle on behalf of the American Empire in our time. In the British case, the self-righteousness had a high-minded, religious edge to it, while promoters of America's cause clothe themselves in the garb of the common man.

The British success in holding off the challenge of France in the eighteenth century and through the Napoleonic Wars to final victory at Waterloo engendered a fierce nationalism in the kingdom. In the Victorian Age, Britons gloried in the maps that painted large parts of the world imperial red. The British Empire helped create and sustain the alliance between the landed gentry and the financial interests of the city. The result was a class-divided society in which the English exposed their place in the hierarchy as soon as they opened their mouths. Pride in the empire and the unifying power of the cult of the monarchy helped overcome the divisions that were engendered by gentlemanly capitalism.

The Second British Empire was a different creature than its mercantile predecessor. Two revolutions transformed it—the Industrial Revolution and the revolution in economic thinking—the second intimately related to the first. The First British Empire ended with the American Revolution, which broke out in 1776, the year Adam Smith published his *Wealth of Nations*, a treatise that was to resonate, in large measure, because of the industrialization that was underway in Britain. The Industrial Revolution, which took half a century to transform Britain and make it the "workshop of the world," gave force to the argument that mercantilism must give way to the new economic doctrines of what came to be called classical economics. Mercantilism was based on the theory that trade between nations was a form of war by other means. Much of the profit of the mercantilist age came from plunder, piracy, slavery, and terms of trade that were stacked in favor of one party against another. Adam Smith and the classical economists invented the theory of comparative advantage, the idea that a trading relationship can be advantageous to both parties involved, because each party can be effective at producing the goods it is selling, so that both parties can benefit from the exchange.

By the 1830s, having completed the first Industrial Revolution, and with no serious military threats facing the country, the British establishment was prepared to embrace the new thinking. Over the next two decades, Britain transformed its parliamentary system, making it much more representative than had been the system of patronage and "rotten boroughs" that was the legacy of the eighteenth century, the age of the great landowners. Financiers and industrialists would have a greater share of power. Fundamental to the change was the elimination of the Corn Laws and the Navigation Acts, the last remaining elements of mercantilism. Gone was protectionism, and in its place the British embraced free trade, not only for the countries that were formally a part of their empire but for the whole world. Gone was imperial preference for the products of the British North American colonies (and for those Americans who shipped their merchandise through British North America to avail themselves of the preference).

At the helm of the most competitive country in the world, the British ruling class had come around to the idea that they should buy their raw materials and food from the cheapest possible sources and sell into whatever markets they could pry open for their industrial exports, the leading one being cotton. Why buy from protected and more expensive sources, when free trade could only benefit them, since British industry had the edge on the rest of the world? they asked rhetorically. The consequence of the shift was that the power of the great landowners was reduced, while that of the financiers and industrialists was enhanced. The sociopolitical alliance that held sway in the country was that between finance and the landed aristocrats, this time with the landowners as the junior partners. In the mid-nineteenth century, the British Empire, both formally and informally, achieved its zenith. As the world's leading hegemonic power, Britain was the world's most important lender of capital. This was the age when the Bank of England, the "Old Lady of Threadneedle Street," managed the terms of credit for projects around the world, many of them railway construction ventures. British hegemony had its effect on the building of the Canadian Pacific Railway and similar projects in the United States, South America, Asia, Europe, and the Near East.

How did empire fit into Britain's embrace of free trade and its rejection of mercantilism? For the liberal "little Englanders" (as those who believed in a limited empire were called) of the day, there was much enthusiasm for ditching the formal empire. But by the 1870s, this idea lost its cachet and the empire came back into favor, personified by Benjamin Disraeli, the great leader of the Conservative Party. There were two reasons for the reversal. First, in the closing decades of the nineteenth century, the leading industrial countries were unleashing a second industrial revolution, this one centered not on cotton, but on steel, chemicals, electronics, and later the automotive industry. Britain was losing its industrial pre-eminence to the United States and Germany and faced challenges as well from France, Japan, and even Russia. The days when Britain could dominate South America as a part of its informal empire as much as it could dominate India, over which the Union Jack flew, were quickly passing. Under competitive pressure, the advantages of formal empire began to reappear. Second, there had always been enormous benefits to the empire for members of the British aristocracy. In the nineteenth century, thousands of scions of the great families were given posts administering the vast empire and serving as senior officers in its armed forces. The empire, despite the fervor for free trade, remained highly profitable for those who won high posts and for the special interests that profited mightily from the spoils of imperial rule.

Faced with the competition from the new industrial powers, British imperialism reverted in the late nineteenth century to an emphasis on the older forms of empire. As French, Belgians, Germans, Japanese, and even Americans rushed to get their hands on territory they could colonize, modeling themselves after the British in this endeavor, the British, too, gobbled up as much of Africa as they could in the frantic imperialism of the belle époque. Much has been written about whether the British Empire was actually a profitable venture or a costly white elephant. The question, as in the case of other empires, is somewhat beside the point. In the British case, while taxpayers may have paid out more to sustain the empire than Britain got in return, special economic interests made huge profits. For them, the British Empire was a highly worthwhile venture. And since it was the ruling classes who made the case for empire, the overall balance was not something that was seriously considered, except by critics such as J.A. Hobson in his famous book, *Imperialism*. For instance, the South African War, or Boer War, in 1899, was a war fought, in large measure, to safeguard the mineral interests of Cecil Rhodes. For Rhodes and others like him, this was a war worth fighting, even though it was ruinously expensive for the British treasury.

Queen Victoria's Diamond Jubilee, the celebration of the sixty years she had spent on the throne, was the grandest of all gala events, a signal to the British people, the peoples of the empire, and to the world of the solidity of British rule, the magnificent realm on which the sun never set. On a bright June day in 1897, troops from all over the world marched through London in their many-colored uniforms. It appeared that all the world was in attendance. A third of the world's people and a quarter of the world's land mass lived under the Union Jack. And yet there was a frantic quality about the Jubilee. While most of the world was prepared to acknowledge that Britain was the greatest power in the world, the greatest empire that ever was, the empire was about to be sorely tested.

By the time of the Diamond Jubilee, Europe was divided into two armed camps. After the Prussian victory in the war against France in 1871, German Chancellor Otto von Bismarck was determined to keep the German Empire at the center of Europe and to prevent another major war. To achieve both goals, he had to keep the French isolated and the British unworried. Bismarck's European system rested on a military alliance with Austria-Hungary, the Dual Alliance of 1879, later expanded to include Italy, and on a reinsurance deal with Russia (the unlikely name for this understanding), to prevent the Russians from forming an alliance with France. Bismarck's strategy contained a dangerous contradiction. His alliance with Austria-Hungary was directed against Russia and yet his reinsurance treaty with Russia was arranged to reassure the Russians so that they would not go elsewhere to find friends. To prevent the British from becoming fearful that Germany was growing too powerful, Bismarck was prepared to limit his ambitions to Europe itself. He regarded it as a cardinal error to challenge British supremacy on the seas. It was the mark of Bismarck's genius that he was able to contain German appetites and to keep the different elements of his European system intact despite the inherent contradictions.

When the young, hot-headed, and impetuous William II succeeded his father as kaiser, he soon tired of Bismarck's tortuous diplomacy and of his unwillingness to contemplate a more grandly ambitious foreign policy for Germany. Bismarck was pushed out of office in 1890, and within a few years his European system lay in ruins. In 1892, the Russian czar did the unthinkable when he agreed to a military alliance with Republican France, thereby ending the isolation of France that had been the goal of all Bismarck's alliances and counter-arrangements.

Having driven Russia into the arms of France, the government of William II pursued a so-called world policy, which set Germany on a course of confrontation with the British. The Germans decided to build a great navy whose only long-term goal was to challenge the supremacy of the Royal Navy. It was one thing for the British to remain calm in the face of the rise of two competing military alliances on the continent. After all, they balanced each other off, which meant that neither would achieve hegemony. And it had been the perennial goal of the British to ensure that no single power dominated Europe. But Germany's challenge to the Royal Navy was quite another matter. This struck at the instrument that had kept the British Isles free from invasion and which had allowed the island kingdom to sustain its global empire.

The last decades of the nineteenth century have been called an era of "splendid isolation" for the British Empire. The phrase oversimplifies since the British remained active throughout the period in forging arrangements among the powers outside Europe, but it was true enough as far as Europe itself was concerned. In this respect, the British policy of the age bears some resemblance to the unilateralism of the United States in its imperial policies in the first years of the twenty-first century. The British felt strong enough to sustain their hegemony without the aid of allies who could become an encumbrance. Just as George W. Bush and his advisers were only prepared to contemplate alliances on their own terms, the British did not want to be drawn into arrangements where they would have to tailor their policies to suit others.

The resemblance between the British at the end of the nineteenth century and the Americans a century later goes beyond a preference for splendid isolation. Just as our day has been called an age of globalization, the epoch at the end of the nineteenth century can equally be depicted as one in which the forces of globalization were in the ascendancy. Britain was the world's great creditor power and the Bank of England effectively set lending rates for most of the world. Wedded to its policy of free trade, the British fought against high-tariff, protectionist policies on the part of industrial rivals. While the British campaign for free trade met with stubborn resistance at times from the Americans, Germans, French, and Italians, the British managed to preside over what was a wide-open market for a long list of products. The proportions of the economies of major nations devoted to trade were not to be equaled again until our own day. Frontiers in the late nineteenth century were relatively easy to cross, indeed easier for the most part than they are today.

It was the challenge to British hegemony, the world wars, and the advent of communism and fascism that destroyed the era of globalization that appeared to be so firmly entrenched at the end of the nineteenth century. But just as today's version of globalization is intimately linked to the fate of the American Empire, the globalization of the belle époque was inseparable from the Pax Britannica.

The intellectual who most famously got this all wrong in the early twentieth century was Norman Angell. In his book, *The Great Illusion*, published in 1910, he argued that the economies of nations had become so intertwined that war would be ruinous for all, the winners as well as the losers. The message of his book, which instantly became a bestseller and was translated into many languages, was that war was an atavistic remnant of the human past and that in the rational present, in which economic calculus was paramount, the nations of the world would not be so boneheaded as to launch a crippling war. Angell graced many platforms to make his case to the cognoscenti and was thought to be a great sage.

Indeed, Angell was not the first to make the case that war was outdated. In the mid-nineteenth century, the little Englanders, men like Richard Cobden and John Bright, who formed the Anti-Corn Law League to fight the remnants of mercantilism, had made a similar argument to justify free trade. With a fervor that bordered on religiosity, they argued that free trade would tie nations together, cementing a mutual interest that would make them more prosperous and less inclined to go to war against one another.

In the days of the collapsing Soviet Empire Francis Fukuyama's *End of History* hypothesis again presented Norman Angell's case to the world. According to Fukuyama, liberal capitalism had triumphed over its Communist and fascist challengers, leaving most of the major issues of history resolved. There was now one broad road ahead for humanity, with only the details to be worked out. The problems of the human future, it seemed, had been reduced to a series of technical questions. Fukuyama made the same fundamental mistake that Angell had made. He failed to see that the globalizing regime that he mistook for the permanent human condition was, in fact, the product of a particular power arrangement in which one imperial power dominated the globe. Threaten that empire, the truth was, and the global arrangements that went with it would quickly fall away.

Two specific shocks added to the pressures that were mounting on the British to end their isolation and seek allies. In the autumn of 1899, the South African War broke out. Confronted with two small Afrikaner republics, the mighty British Empire should have made short work of it. But the British army demonstrated that it had become a rusty instrument in an era in which it had faced few real tests. And the Afrikaners showed themselves to be first-class fighters. Their unorthodox guerilla methods made them hard to drive to the ground. The rest of Europe cheered on the Afrikaners, very much enjoying Britain's predicament. Because of the British navy's supremacy, no foreign power could even consider aiding the Boers, but foreigners could and did take note of how hard the war was for Britain. Ultimately, the British prevailed, but only after inventing a new system for detaining large numbers of foes that was to become notorious over the course of the twentieth century: the concentration camp.

Not long into the first decade of the twentieth century, the British found themselves in a grueling naval construction race with Germany. Both the Royal Navy and the German navy were launching a new generation of battleships, the dreadnoughts, heavily armored vessels that would be most useful in a great battle not far from European shores. Germany's insistence on building the monsters was a clear signal that the kaiser intended to threaten Britain's naval lifeline in the North Sea, in a direct fight that would cut the British Isles off from the food and raw materials and would open up Britain for invasion. The British fought back gamely, determined that the Royal Navy would not be out-built. As with all arms races, this one consigned older ships to obsolescence, thus making the threat facing the British even greater. In the end, the British did build more dreadnoughts than the Germans, who were also busy creating a huge army. The supreme test came in the Battle of Jutland in 1916; the Royal Navy, while suffering more casualties than the German navy, maintained its supremacy and kept the German fleet tied up in its home ports for the rest of the war.

The German threat pressured the British to take a new look at their cross-channel competitor and at their main rivals in the quest for overseas empire, the French. In 1905, the British forged an alliance of sorts with the French, the Entente Cordiale. The alliance was far from being a full-fledged military pact of the kind that existed between France and Russia, with spelled-out commitments for what each side would do in the event of conflict. But Britain had ended its isolation in Europe. Indeed, by the time the new arrangement was made with France, the British had already signed an alliance with Japan, the rising naval power of the Pacific.

A few years after the entente with France, the British arrived at a similar arrangement with the Russian Empire. This was a sign of how profoundly things were changing among the European powers. In the late nineteenth century, the war most commonly predicted by experts was the one that was never fought, a showdown between the British and the Russians. Their rivalry, which came to be known as the "great game," was a struggle for control over the rugged territory that divided southern Russia from the northern approaches to India. Whoever controlled this heartland, it was speculated, would have the upper hand in the struggle between the great land-based empire and its sea-based foe, the struggle that geostrategists thought was inevitable.

What drew the Russians and the British together was the same thing that drew the British and the French together—increasing concern about the rise of Germany. The Russians perceived a clash between Slavs and Germans as their great challenge. While the immediate German enemy was Austria-Hungary, the Russians perceived Germany as the real power that stood behind Austria. It took William II just over a decade and a half at the helm to preside over the division of Europe into the Triple Alliance—Germany, Austria-Hungary, and Italy—against the Triple Entente—France, Russia, and Britain.

The two sets of alliances pushed the military planners of the day, working with the technology and manpower of their time, to spell out how the great war would be fought when it came. And the planners, Norman Angell notwithstanding, were sure that the day would come. Theirs was an age of romantic militarism rooted in social Darwinist notions that war would prove the true worth of peoples. In the age of imperial rivalries prior to the First World War, a popular strain of thought was found in the application of the theory of evolution to the struggles among great powers. It was not difficult to transpose the idea of a struggle to the death among species for survival to the notion that among nations only the fittest would survive, or even ought to survive. It was easy for fevered minds to come up with the idea that beneath the surface of peaceful, bourgeois Europe there raged a struggle for dominance that was bound to erupt. In the end, the struggle would be a purifying affair, the fit would triumph, and the unfit would become extinct. Thus, the world would move forward to a higher level of civilization. These ideas were much in circulation in Europe during the period. Among other things, they reflected a perception that a new test of strength among the powers was coming, that the long peace of British dominance could not be sustained.

As the Germans witnessed the entente powers drawing together, quite naturally they saw themselves facing encirclement. Their military planning was, therefore, based on dealing with the conundrum of the two-front war that they were sure would befall them. Count Alfred von Schlieffen, chief of the German General Staff from 1891 to 1906, was the architect of Germany's plan for the great European war. The plan was premised on the assumption that a war with either France or Russia meant a war with the other as well. There was no point, in German thinking, trying politically to isolate one of these powers when an actual crisis arose. Inflexibly, the Germans simply planned for war against both, seeing the problem more in technical terms than in political or human terms.

All European planners of the day were fixated on the idea that the side that would win the war, which was expected to be of short duration, would be the side that most effectively mobilized its manpower and shipped its regiments by rail to the most advantageous places for the start of the conflict. Military plans, therefore, were drawn up in terms of the exact number of days from initial mobilization to the outbreak of hostilities to the achievement of victory in a decisive battle. Mass infantry was the critical weapon, and getting it into the field was the key to victory. Because the planners on both sides were locked into this logic, it followed that in the event of a serious political crisis, the military general staffs would insist on trying to mobilize as early as possible to get a head start against their foes. Even an advantage of one day could be decisive, they believed. Therefore, the way the system was set up, diplomacy was not to be allowed to work until the very last hour. At a certain point, mobilization had to be started, and once mobilization was underway the machine could not be stopped. War was inevitable from the day the troops were called up.

The Schlieffen Plan was based on these premises. General Schlieffen decided that since Germany faced a two-front war, it had to knock out one or the other of its foes early on so that it could then turn its attention to the other. He decided that for reasons of geography and speed of mobilization, France should be the first target. The problem with Russia was that it had so much territory that it could absorb an initial German onslaught, drawing the Germans further from their supply depots, where a counter-attack could be mounted. Meanwhile, the more efficient French, who could mobilize more quickly, would launch an assault on Germany. To avoid this disaster, Schlieffen concluded that the Germans had to attack France with overwhelming force at the beginning of the conflict, holding a small German force in place to counter the Russian steamroller when it finally got mobilized. Since the initial assault would be undertaken with an army of well over a million men, it would need favorable terrain from which to undertake a descent on Paris, whose capture would deliver a knock-out blow to France. Considering the difficult terrain and the extensive fortifications along the Franco-German border, Schlieffen decided that the only available option was to march the German army through Belgium and then turn south in a great arc across the flat lands of Flanders to capture Paris.

Ultimately, it was the implacable decision of the Germans to violate the neutrality of Belgium in August 1914 that drew Britain into full participation in the First World War at the side of France and Russia. While the violation of little Belgium was the event that galvanized British public opinion and the British government, underlying the British decision to go to war was the determination to prevent the domination of the continent by a single power. Britain went to war to preserve the world order over which it had presided for the previous century. With the exception of a few far-sighted individuals, including Britain's Lord Kitchener, almost all the military expected the conflict to be over quickly. Instead, as Kitchener had foreseen, the war became an affair of millions, an industrial horror in which the flower of the young manhood of the warring nations went to their deaths. Given the scale and duration of the war, beyond anything Britain had ever before endured, British global hegemony became a casualty. While the British Empire survived, its system of global finance, headquartered in London, gave way to a new system centered in New York. Not entering the war until the spring of 1917, the United States tipped the scales of the conflict in favor of the Allies and ensured the defeat of Germany and Austria-Hungary. And the United States did so without suffering casualties on anything like the scale of those that afflicted Britain and France. Destroying each other on the battlefields of Europe, the European great powers had opened the door to the rise of a new global hegemon.

PART 3
THE CRISIS
OF THE
AMERICAN EMPIRE

Imperial Overstretch

Presidents, emperors, and pharaohs travel in imperial finery to transmit the message to those they rule that their power is untouchable and permanent. They surround themselves with cliques of advisers who tell them what they want to hear because they are not so sure that they really are as all-powerful as the image they portray. Whether ancient or contemporary, empires are subject to one common problem—that of overstretch.

In the next twenty years or so, the United States' share of global economic output is likely to fall to about 15 percent. This is still a very significant proportion, but it is a far cry from the U.S. peak in 1945 (50 percent) and is much lower than the figure at the beginning of the twenty-first century (20 percent). This matters because empires continually need to spend blood and treasure to extend and sustain themselves. Imperial leaders must tread a fine line between making expenditures that reap profits or strategic benefits and risking imperial overstretch, in which they make expenditures in excess of what they can reasonably sustain. The empires of Rome, Spain, Britain, France, the Third Reich, and the Soviet Union eventually all suffered from imperial overstretch.

The United States is now being pulled in many directions simultaneously, as economic pressures, mounting debts, wars, and increased military spending weigh on decision makers. Those at the helm could do worse than to consider the fate of their imperial predecessors as they faced similar challenges.

The Roman Empire avoided imperial overstretch for centuries. During its rise, the Romans acquired territory and slave labor at a rate rapid enough that the profits that flowed back, and the strategic value of the territory acquired, more than offset the cost of patrolling and defending the empire from external attack or internal upheaval. Once the empire stopped expanding, however, the long-term balance began to shift against Rome. With conquests at an end, far fewer new cohorts of slaves fell into Roman hands. Beginning in the third century A.D., Rome suffered as a consequence of the unwillingness of its upper class to countenance the level of taxation needed to maintain the legions and the defense of the frontiers. As a result, pressure on the frontiers by Germanic and other invaders, which could have been halted in an earlier period, posed an increasing threat to the viability of the empire. The problem of imperial overstretch became insoluble as a consequence of both the absence of new benefits from empire and the inability of the state to marshal the resources to counter external threats.

For the Spaniards, their stupendous good fortune in falling upon a treasure house of bullion in America underwrote the rise of an empire in a country that otherwise lacked the resources to mount one. The flow of gold, and especially silver, into the Spanish treasury—the Spanish crown claimed one-fifth of the bullion, the quinto, as its royalty—gave the Spanish state the capacity to hire large numbers of foreign soldiers. A heavily armed Spain was in a position to fight wars to uphold the dynastic alliances forged by the Spanish monarchy. For a time, as a consequence of the bullion of the Americas, Spain became a world trading center, with sugar and silver from the Americas and silk from China, and much of this commerce was financed by bankers across Europe. Over the course of centuries, however, the initially favorable effects of empire turned negative and Spain suffered the consequences of imperial overstretch. Since Spain's expansion was mostly undertaken by financiers based in Genoa, Florence, England, Germany, and Switzerland, the profits of empire, for the most part, did not remain in Spain. Indeed, Spain suffered the effects of a higher-cost economy in key sectors as a consequence of its imperial rise, which hurt it over the long term. And while empire made it possible for the Spaniards to finance their wars, those wars proved highly damaging. In particular, there was the economically draining eighty-year struggle of the Netherlands to free itself from control by the Spanish crown and the occupation of Spanish armies. The Spanish Empire, very much a multinational affair, based on the energies and talents of many peoples, was ultimately challenged by rising powers against whom it could not compete. The Netherlands, England (whose naval victory over the Spanish Armada in 1588 at the height of Spain's greatness was a warning for the future), and France all learned to play Spain's imperial game more effectively than had the Spaniards. By the eighteenth century, the Spanish Empire was in decline and the struggle for dominance among the European powers had passed to other contenders.

The British Empire began its rise in a most unpromising way—as a scavenger feeding off plunder from the Spaniards during their days of imperial greatness. Henry Morgan and Francis Drake were among the storied pirates who demonstrated to the English that they, too, could win fabulous riches from the New World and from Asia. The English crown even licensed those pirates, who under the name "privateers" were financed by investors to roam the seas in search of booty, much of it from Spanish galleons. The First British Empire was carved out in the final age of mercantilism: the British had hoped to find gold and silver in North America but realized that furs, fish, and timber could form an alternative basis for the accumulation of wealth. In addition, Britain's North American realm was to be the site for the establishment of settler colonies that were ultimately to grow into a new metropolis. In the West Indies, the sugar trade was the source of enormous riches for British investors. And in the Indian subcontinent in the mid-eighteenth century, the British began their two centuries of control over India. Britain's Indian holdings became the crown jewel of the British Empire, the source of vast profits for the East India Company, a royally sanctioned monopoly that gained its wealth by tilting the terms of trade in its favor. The company combined the roles of a merchant operation underwritten by British investors and a military ruler of large parts of India. From the vantage point of trade monopoly and brute force, quite similar to the operations of the conquistadores in America, the British constructed their early empire in the subcontinent.

During most of the eighteenth century, the British Empire was locked in a deadly struggle with its French rival. While much of the British administration in the early eighteenth century was modeled after that of Louis XIV, the British were successful, despite serious internal corruption, in raising the public funds they needed to finance their military. During this perilous period, taxation was high in Britain, and the financing of the national debt played a crucial role in launching the financial sector in London. Despite catastrophes, including the British loss of the Thirteen Colonies, a defeat that had consequences in Europe as well as America, the British kept their state and much of their empire afloat. Britain survived the Napoleonic threat as well, and the reward for victory at the Battle of Waterloo was a dramatic decline in taxes and a century of cheap government during the Pax Britannica. Victory in the global struggle against the French allowed the British to dominate the world by maintaining the Royal Navy as master of the seas, according to the "two-fleet standard," by which Britain set out to ensure that its navy was the equivalent of the fleets of the next two powers combined.

It was not until the First World War that the problem of imperial overstretch caught up with the British Empire. The race against Germany to build new dreadnoughts for the navy pointed the way to the catastrophe to come. The war itself ended Britain's reign as the creditor of the world. New York replaced London as the globe's financial capital. The era 1914 to 1945 was the "Thirty Years' War" of the twentieth century. It was the age when British imperialism was no longer capable of dominating the world as it had for the preceding century. By the end of the Second World War, Britain's days as a major global power were ending. While it was the Axis powers that suffered military defeat, the war effectively eliminated the British Empire and opened the door to the era of the bipolar world, when the globe was dominated by two superpowers, the United States and the Soviet Union. While Winston Churchill gamely vowed that he had no intention of presiding over the dissolution of the British Empire, that is, in fact, exactly what he and his successors did. In 1947, the empire's crown jewel was lost with the independence of India and Pakistan. By the time Churchill died in 1965, almost every territory in the empire had achieved independence. It was the American Empire, not Britain's foes, that inherited Britain's mantle. At the Bretton Woods Conference in 1944, the Americans laid down the rules for how the postwar global economy was to be organized, even before the fall of Germany and Japan, and despite the objections of the British. The old empire was pushed aside by the new one.

The French Empire—at its zenith at the beginning of the eighteenth century, in the era of the Sun King, Louis XIV—suffered the consequences of imperial overstretch much sooner than did the British. The French appeared to be the logical successor to Spain and the Netherlands and seemed headed for a long reign as the world's leading imperial power. France was the most populous state in western Europe, boasting a well-organized state and bureaucracy and outfitted with a formidable military. Moreover, France had emerged in the era as the cultural capital of the continent, with French replacing Italian and Latin as the international language of diplomacy. In the century of the Enlightenment, French authors set the course that thinkers in the rest of Europe, and indeed in America, followed. French customs and style were copied everywhere. The Versailles of Louis XIV was the imperial capital of the day.

The problem was that, while the French pursued a course in its imperial affairs that was similar to that pursued by the British, France's strategic compulsions were fatally divided between the pressures of Europe and the opportunities of empire. At the beginning of the eighteenth century, the French Empire in America was vastly larger in area than that of its British foe, which was locked into the narrow confines of the Thirteen Colonies. The British, however, enjoyed the advantage of large settler colonies that were quickly expanding in population, while spacious New France had only about one French colonist for every twenty British colonists. Just as serious was the fact that France was distracted from its overseas empire by its designs in Europe. In the titanic struggles of the War of the Spanish Succession, the War of the Austrian Succession, the Seven Years' War, and, later, in the wars during the French Revolution and the age of Napoleon, the French were tied down in great European battles. The British, on the other hand, managed to keep their hand in Europe while never failing to devote the resources and manpower needed to fight imperial battles, the one crucial exception being the American Revolutionary War.

Unlike the British, the French failed to keep their fiscal house in order. During the draining struggles of the eighteenth century, France's dysfunctional social order proved fatal for the regime. Great landowners, the aristocrats who maintained the privileges that they had inherited from feudalism, refused to countenance serious tax increases. Unwilling to pay their share to keep the state afloat, they provoked the crisis that forced the royal government to call into session the meeting of the Estates General in 1789. The consequence was the unleashing of the French Revolution and, in August 1789, the abolition of aristocratic privilege and the transfer of the land to the nation's peasant farmers. This great achievement of the revolution was never reversed.

One effect of the revolution, entirely unexpected by all the other European regimes, was that France's military power became more, not less, potent. For the first time in history, France became "a nation in arms," with the manpower of the country mobilized. A fearsome new power, which the world would come to know over the next two centuries and more, had been unleashed. Ultimately, Napoleon became the heir to that power as the forces of revolution and counter-revolution combined to project his imperial regime onto the stage. Effectively hemmed in by the British navy, Napoleon strove for hegemony in Europe and came within an inch of achieving it. Overstretch came for his empire with the invasion of Russia in 1812, an invasion that was beyond the capacity of the Grande Armée. Like Hitler 130 years later, he took a step too far, beyond the capacity of the French state—an act of hubris that led inexorably to Waterloo.

Adolf Hitler, the next dictator to try to rule Europe, courted imperial overstretch with reckless abandon. The lessons he learned during his first years in power launched him on the course that led him to the invasion of the Soviet Union on June 22, 1941, his point of no return. What misled Hitler into thinking he could do anything he liked was the temporary weakness and shortsightedness of his potential foes during the 1930s. The Third Reich set out on its course to establish absolute power for itself within Germany as the foundation to achieve hegemony in Europe the day Hitler came to power, January 30, 1933. The Nazis' rise was precipitated by a combination of three factors: the unwillingness of a militarist right that could not accept the defeat of 1918 to live within the confines of the Weimar Republic; the fear of Bolshevism that infected so much of the German middle and upper classes; and the misery inflicted on the whole society by the Great Depression. Hitler came to power during the period of the interregnum between the end of British global hegemony and the emergence of the United States as the power that would replace Britain. With the Soviet Union, the self-proclaimed center for the promulgation of global socialist revolution, estranged from capitalist Europe, with Britain and France divided between appeasement and resistance to Hitler, and with the United States staunchly isolationist where Europe was concerned, Hitler had his chance. His first victories were achieved as a consequence of his brilliant knack for playing his foes off against each other and banking on Europeans' horror at the prospect of another war. The rearmament of the Rhineland, the Anschluss with Austria, and the occupation of the Sudetenland and then the rest of the Czech lands were all achieved without war. Then came his miraculous and, in retrospect, seemingly easy conquests of Poland, Norway, Denmark, the Netherlands, Belgium, and France.

Having achieved a truce with the Soviet Union as a consequence of the Nazi–Soviet Pact of August 1939, which provided for the division of eastern Europe between the two powers, Hitler was left in a highly advantageous position for his showdown with his only remaining foe, Great Britain. The nightmare of the German High Command during the First World War had been the two-front war. Hitler's pact with Stalin appeared to have solved this problem. With Britain driven off the continent, but still in the war, Hitler took the step that demonstrated his inability to calculate the strength of his foes. With Operation Barbarossa, his invasion of the Soviet Union, Hitler showed that he had not taken account of the vast resources, manpower, and industrial output of the Soviet Union. In 1941, the Soviet Union enjoyed significantly greater industrial capacity than Germany did. Hitler, of course, was counting on a knockout blow that would defeat the Soviet Union before it could bring its long-term advantages into play. But he failed to recognize the perils of overstretch: with the German army stymied at Moscow, Hitler declared war on the United States four days after the Japanese attack on Pearl Harbor. Already facing much stiffer resistance than he had contemplated in Russia, he blithely went to war with the world's greatest industrial power, thereby saving U.S. president Franklin D. Roosevelt from having to take the politically difficult step of choosing war with Germany when he was already embroiled with Japan. Although the Germans showed great resourcefulness in carrying on the war, developing new weapons, making do with substitutes for key strategic resources, the events of December 1941 sealed the fate of Hitler's empire.

The Soviet Empire took much longer than the Third Reich to display the fundamental weaknesses that brought it down in a remarkably short period of time. Indeed, only a few years before the peaceful revolutions that swept through Eastern Europe in 1989 and then brought down the Soviet Union two years later, very few analysts in the West had any idea that the whole Soviet system was in grave peril. As late as

1980, neo-conservative analysts in the United States were making the case that the Soviet Union had surpassed the United States in military might and that America would have to vastly increase defense spending just to keep up with the Soviets.

What undermined the Soviet Union and its empire during the postwar decades was the weight of its socioeconomic arrangements and the size of its military budget. Within the Soviet Empire certain basic costs—food, health care, education, and housing—were heavily subsidized. Since industry within the empire was notoriously inefficient, this was a heavy burden indeed. The system operated according to the commonly told joke by an Eastern European worker that "they pretended to pay us and we pretended to work." Two additional factors made this inefficient economy even more prone to breakdown. First, a comparatively large new governing class was put in place at the top of each country within the empire, first in the Soviet Union and then in the satellite countries after the war. This so-called *nomenklatura*, made up of the top members of the Communist Party, enjoyed luxurious living and costly perquisites. Second, the Soviet Union and the other members of the Warsaw Pact spent an enormous proportion of their GDP on defense. While the United States, during the 1970s and 1980s, spent about 6 percent of its GDP on defense, the Warsaw Pact countries spent at least 15 percent of their GDP on their military establishment. Taken together, the weight of the subsidies for ordinary citizens, plus the cost of keeping top Communists well outfitted as well as paying for a vast military, were too much for the inefficient economy to bear.

Moreover, as time passed, the availability of cheap resources, an input which had helped keep the system going, began to disappear. Higher resource costs for the inputs needed by the already unproductive industrial facilities proved to be a near fatal blow to the Soviets and their satellites. Signs that the system was being severely strained showed up in several Eastern European countries, notably Poland and Hungary, well before the end came in 1989. To prevent social upheaval, the Communist regimes in these countries began borrowing heavily from the West as a way to shore up the various elements of the system. Once this happened, it was clear that Communism in those parts of the empire was living on borrowed time. "Goulash Communism," as it was called in Hungary, was a stopgap measure to keep a dying system on life support.

An additional and severe blow to the ailing system came with the Soviet invasion of Afghanistan in 1979. The war on the empire's southern boundary landed the Soviets in a quagmire from which the military could not easily withdraw. Not only did the fearsome reputation of the Red Army suffer from its inability to see the war to a successful conclusion, the Soviets were forced to spend vast sums on a conflict that they could ill afford, in which fifteen thousand Soviet soldiers died.

By the time Mikhail Gorbachev became General Secretary of the Soviet Communist Party in 1985, an air of crisis had settled over the Soviet Empire. Gorbachev, the bold reformer, came to office determined to acknowledge the problems (*glasnost*) and confront them head on (*perestroika*). Gorbachev admitted publicly that, far from being on the road to a socialism that "would bury" capitalism, as former Soviet premier Nikita Khrushchev had boasted, the Soviet Union was economically unproductive and had fallen far behind the West in the technological revolution. As he attempted to reform the system, however, he soon discovered that every change he made simply contributed to the unraveling process that was underway. Beneath its solid-looking exterior, the Soviet Empire was in such dire condition that any effort to transform it merely propelled it toward collapse. Once it became evident that the Gorbachev regime was no longer willing to use overwhelming force in the satellite countries, as had been used in the invasion of Hungary in 1956 and in Czechoslovakia in 1968, the regimes in those countries quickly collapsed in the face of rising public protest. One by one, in Poland, Hungary, East Germany, Czechoslovakia, and then in Romania, the pro-Moscow regimes toppled in 1989.

It soon became clear that the rot was not confined to the satellites alone. The discontent that swept Eastern Europe infected the Soviet Union itself, in the Russian heartland, as well as in virtually all of the other republics of the USSR. The only attempt to halt the collapse was a poorly organized, botched coup attempt by Communist hard-liners who managed to seize Gorbachev but then flinched in the face of the popular tide in Moscow led by Boris Yeltsin. Like the *Titanic*, the USSR and its empire sank beneath the waves. What Russian president Vladimir Putin was to describe in 2005 as the "greatest geo-political catastrophe of the twentieth century," the failure of the Soviet system provided a spectacular demonstration that great empires can collapse suddenly, and not simply as a consequence of overwhelming military defeat. In the case of the Soviet Union, the concept of imperial overstretch can be seen plainly at work in terms of the stresses that were brought to bear on the system. In this case, however, the concept of overstretch extends to include an additional notion: that a dictatorial system whose legitimacy is tied to a highly rigid ideology is exceptionally difficult to reform. Throughout Eastern Europe and the Soviet Union, the Communist system relied on a publicly proclaimed ideology that declared that Communism had history on its side. The public calendar in the empire was tied to celebrations of the glorious events in the history of the social struggle. While cynicism about the achievements of socialism was practically universal in Russia and its satellites, as long as the skin of legitimacy was not ruptured, the system remained intact. Gorbachev tore at that skin, and the skeleton beneath disintegrated.

The recorded cases of imperial overstretch in the past are certainly no predictor of what will happen in the future. History does, however, alert us to the types of risks to which they are prone. In what ways does the American Empire face the problem of imperial overstretch? How viable is the American Empire for the mid- to long-term future? The challenges that confront the American Empire include economic competitors, challenges to American approaches to the economy, resource shortages, environmental degradation, military threats, ideological and cultural challenges, and the rise of new superpowers.

The American Empire differs from its predecessors in the extent to which it relies on its influence over sovereign states rather than on the military occupation of such states. It allows mainstream American politicians to deny that an American Empire even exists. In his State of the Union address on January 20, 2004, President George W. Bush declared that "America is a nation with a mission and that mission comes from our most basic beliefs. We have no desire to dominate, no ambitions of empire." American ideology, since the time of the American Revolution, contains a powerful streak of anti-imperialist rhetoric. The Declaration of Independence asserted the right not only of Americans but of all peoples to govern themselves. Americans have always been conscious that their nation was born in an armed struggle against an imperial power. The irony of that anti-imperialist legacy is that it has effectively inoculated Americans against the very idea that they too have become an imperial power. Americans have always believed that their nation has a special calling to spread liberty to the world. For this reason, invasions of other countries and the deployment of the military have rarely been understood for what they are: the signposts of imperialism and militarism.

How has the American Empire grown so mighty with so little formal annexation of other territories? While empires have evolved in very different ways over the course of thousands of years, we can take as a constant the notion that the underlying purpose of empire is to extract labor from others. The imperial motto in all times and all places is that it is better to make someone work for you than it is to be forced to work for them. In the case of the earliest empires, the slave empires, territorial occupation, combined with the practice of turning the conquered into slaves, was the only way to extract the labor of other peoples. Previous empires, the British most notably, were also able to control other peoples and nations as an integral aspect of their broad imperial design without annexing them.

American anti-imperialist rhetoric aside, the United States has resorted to the military occupation of foreign states and territories whenever that has been necessary. Conquest has been central to the rise of America. The great conquest on which the American Empire was erected, of course, was that of the territory that became the United States. That conquest involved ceaseless war against native peoples, and periodic wars against others, such as the British and the Mexicans. By 1823, when the U.S. government proclaimed the Monroe Doctrine, the United States was already insisting on a special role for itself as protector and overlord of the western hemisphere. The Monroe Doctrine asserted that the United States would block any attempt by a European power to establish a new empire in the hemisphere. At the time the Doctrine was issued, there was an element of bravado in it. The true protector of the hemisphere from marauding European imperial powers was the British navy.

GEORGES CLEMENCEAU, the early twentieth-century French statesman, once remarked that the United States had gone from "barbarism to decadence without an intervening period of civilization." Another way of putting this sour remark is that the journey from calling in the cavalry to quell the natives to suffering from imperial overstretch has happened rather quickly. Today, the Americans face the classic problem of long-established empires: convincing their upper classes to submit to a level of taxation required to sustain the empire. Ruling classes never submit easily to the idea of paying their way, but some have relented more easily than others. The British ruling class, for instance, with its quasi-aristocratic background and its schooling in traditional Toryism, proved more capable than present-day Americans of taking the long view that society is better served by discipline. The American ruling class, by contrast, has lacked the ideological and class cohesion that served the British ruling class so well. Moreover, the American ruling class has been deeply attached to the liberal idea of the small state. This idea, whose practical outcome has meant low taxes for them, makes it extremely difficult for political leaders to convince the rich in America to pay enough to safeguard their position for the long term.

The segment of the American political elite that most fervently favors a higher military budget for the United States is also the wing of the American leadership that is most strongly opposed to high taxes. Since George W. Bush was sworn in as president in January 2001, that militarist wing of the U.S. leadership has held the reins of power, controlling not only the White House, but, until the Congressional elections of 2006, both houses of Congress as well. The Bush administration launched invasions of Afghanistan and Iraq in 2001 and 2003, while simultaneously pushing tax cuts through Congress, tax cuts that disproportionately benefited the wealthy. As a consequence of its militaristic policies during a period of reduced economic growth, the Bush administration saddled the United States with record high government deficits—close to half a trillion dollars in 2004. The deficit was halved by 2006, but the administration's policies meant that eliminating them was a forlorn hope. The deficits came just a few years after the Clinton administration achieved the first balanced budget and surplus in many years. The result is that the U.S. federal government is mired in debt, a debt on which interest must be paid. A high proportion of the treasury bills sold to finance the U.S. debt are held by foreign countries, approximately $2 trillion of this by the central banks of Japan and China.

It is not the first time that American involvement in foreign wars has imperiled its economy. In Vietnam, the United States had to cut its losses and concede defeat, not only because of American casualties in a war with no end in sight, but also because of the ways the war impeded American global competitiveness. By 1970, foreign central bankers held $60 billion (a paltry sum today) and the United States was running an ever-higher current account deficit. The red flag that signaled how the years of the war had changed America vis-à-vis its competitors, however, was the fact that for the first time since the end of the nineteenth century, the United States actually ran a manufacturing trade deficit. In our era, the United States runs a manufacturing trade deficit every year in addition to a rising and enormous current account deficit ($880 billion in 2006).

In 1970, however, that first deficit was a signal that America had lost its competitive edge in manufacturing against West Germany and Japan. On August 15, 1971, in a television address to the American people, President Richard Nixon responded to the new economic realities by announcing that the United States was changing the rules of the game. Nixon unilaterally cut the link between the U.S. dollar and gold, a pillar of the Bretton Woods system established in 1944 to manage the postwar global economy. No longer could foreign central banks request gold, at $35 an ounce, to replace the U.S. dollars they held. In addition, Nixon slapped a 10 percent tariff surcharge on all imports into the United States. In the weeks to come, his administration established a tax scheme to encourage U.S. corporations to export more and keep jobs at home rather than create jobs in their subsidiaries abroad. And the government put pressure on other leading countries to accept a downward revaluation of the U.S. dollar against their currency to help make American exports more competitive. As these currency revaluations were made, the fixed exchange rate system established at Bretton Woods disintegrated, to be succeeded by the floating exchange rate system that still prevails today.

The American economy continued to decline against foreign competitors through the 1970s and 1980s. A series of crucial developments at least partially reversed that trend during the 1990s. The collapse of the Soviet Union and its empire not only removed a major geostrategic competitor, it opened the door to reduced defense spending in the United States, the so-called peace dividend. Japan, America's great economic challenger in the previous two decades, experienced economic turbulence at the end of the 1980s, triggered by the implosion of property values. The bursting of the real estate speculative bubble placed immense pressures on Japan's leading banks, whose assets were closely tied to inflated property values. As Japan struggled to deal with the restructuring of its financial sector, the country's economy was further threatened by a series of scandals that exposed the corrupt links between leading politicians and the private sector. The whole system of public–private planning on which Japan had thrived for decades was thrown into doubt and disrepute. Soviet disintegration and Japan's woes coincided with a great technology-related boom in the American economy. As these challengers fell by the wayside, the American economy, particularly its financial markets, soared alongside the rise of the tech sector.

By the year 2000, America's strong performance against competitors was running out of steam. In April 2000, the American tech boom reached its high point when the NASDAQ passed the 5000 level. Then the bubble burst and the sector on which the American miracle of the 1990s had been based was thrown into a long period of retrenchment and restructuring. By the time George W. Bush became president in January 2001, the boom years were over, and America was sliding into recession.

The government deficits that followed, the consequence of slower growth, tax cuts, and higher military spending, forced a consideration of how the Americans were going to manage their empire. Could they finance the military costs of controlling the Persian Gulf region, a region that had been designated as crucial to the American national interest by every president since the mid-1940s? Furthermore, could they sustain their position in the region without building a wide coalition with their allies, who could be convinced to pay a part of the bill there, either by sending troops to assist the Americans or by contributing to American efforts to rebuild Iraq?

Though they were certainly not analyzed this way by the American media at the time, those were the central issues on which the major candidates, George W. Bush and John Kerry, conducted their debate during the 2004 presidential election campaign. President Bush argued that the best way to advance the global interests of America was to wage war in Iraq on its own terms supported by the countries that chose to come aboard. John Kerry retorted that the war in Iraq had been a diversion from what should have been the top priority, combating Al Qaeda and its leaders, principally Osama bin Laden. Kerry did not propose to withdraw from Iraq, however. He agreed with Bush that victory there must be secured. The difference was that he proposed to achieve this by enlisting the support of a wider international coalition. Kerry stated that the American Empire required military manpower and capital from its allies. This was a debate not about the fundamental goals of the empire but about how best to cajole other countries into supporting those goals.

The victory of George W. Bush in the November 2004 presidential election confirmed that the radical, unilateralist wing of the American leadership would remain in charge of the executive branch of government in the United States. In the same election, the Republicans also retained control of both houses of Congress. It was a matter of great consequence that the unilateralists represented the regions of America and the segments of American society that were the least secular and that were most out of touch with the world beyond the United States. That situation constituted a historic reversal within the United States that had major implications for the American Empire and the rest of the world. In the lead-up to the Second World War, it was the Americans in the northeast and on the west coast who were most inclined to support American involvement in war against the Axis powers. Isolationism, on the other hand, was most strongly present in the great heartland of the country. In one sense, this has not changed, while in another it has changed completely. It remains true that it is Americans in the northeast and on the west coast who favor multilateral engagement with the rest of the world. What has changed is that isolationism in the heartland has metastasized into isolationism-unilateralism. While those regions that were most disposed to keep their distance from the wider world are still inclined in that direction, the enormous expansion of American military power and the collapse of distances in the age of missiles and terrorism have turned many isolationists into unilateralists.

The political constituency that was least responsive to the concerns of foreigners was the one that provided the decisive backing for a foreign and military policy that featured unilateralism and the resort to pre-emption.

This was highly advantageous to the Bush White House because it meant that the American leadership could take initiatives while remaining substantially insulated from public opinion.

The days of unfettered neo-conservative control of the American Empire were numbered, however. With U.S. combat deaths in Iraq approaching 3,000 and dead and wounded exceeding 25,000, and with Iraq sinking into civil war, American voters handed both houses of Congress to the Democrats in the midterm elections in November 2006. The day after the election, Defense Secretary Donald Rumsfeld resigned. His designated replacement, Robert Gates, in a congressional confirmation hearing, frankly acknowledged that the United States was not winning in Iraq.

Moreover, popular discontent was mirrored by a serious division of opinion within the American political establishment. On December 6, 2006, the Iraq Study Group, headed by Republican James Baker and Democrat Lee Hamilton, reported its recommendations to the Bush administration. Established to find a way to get the United States out of the Iraq quagmire, the Study Group's recommendations amounted to a flat repudiation of the foreign and military policies of the administration. The report recommended the withdrawal of large numbers of U.S. forces from Iraq by the beginning of 2008 and advised that overtures be made to seek the collaboration of Syria and Iran in finding a settlement to the conflict in Iraq.

While releasing his report, James Baker, a patrician elder statesman from the Bush Sr. administration, reminded the media that it had been American policy to talk to foes during the more than four decades of the Cold War and, by implication, that the Bush administration's highhanded avoidance of dialogue had to end.

The Baker-Hamilton report was a clear signal that an important rift had opened up within the American political establishment, not only about the Iraq War, but about the United States' approach to global issues.

As was the case in earlier empires, the onset of imperial overstretch in the United States has generated a heated debate in elite circles. The twin problems of legitimacy and sustainability that bedevil every empire threaten the American Empire in very particular ways, as we will see in coming chapters.

Islam and Oil

During the past century, the American Empire emerged triumphant in three global conflicts: the two world wars and the Cold War. The First World War vastly heightened the power of the financial oligarchy in the United States. Before 1914, the United States operated within the broad confines of a British-centered global system of military and financial power. The British navy ensured that the rules under which the Pax Britannica functioned would not be violated, and the Bank of England managed interest rates and oversaw the global flow of capital. During the Pax Britannica, American economic development was vastly affected by the ebbs and flows within that British-centered system. The United States was a net debtor nation, with British lenders collecting interest on funds borrowed by Americans. As a consequence of the First World War, the United States broke out of the British global system.

During the 1920s, American finance capital was in the driver's seat. It was an era of political reaction, with its "red scare" and its vicious assaults against the working class and progressive politics. The gains of the progressives and the muckrakers in the decade before the First World War were trampled underfoot. A decade after the end of the war, with the onset of the Great Depression, however, a new global conflict was already in sight, and with it opened a vast new role for the United States in the world and a transformation of the social coalition that held power in America. If the First World War brought American finance capital to power, a much broader alliance of social classes was needed to win the Second World War. That alliance first appeared in the form of Franklin D. Roosevelt's New Deal in 1933. To the power of finance capital, which had been cast under a cloud by the Depression, was added a coalition of interests that included not only finance capital, but also manufacturers and, to a degree, organized labor and organized farmers. This was the social coalition, despite its many internal crises, that prevailed against fascism and Nazism during the Second World War.

Victory in the third global conflict of the twentieth century, the Cold War with the Soviet Empire, played a major part, along with technological change and economic deregulation, in causing a further shift in the nature of capitalism. The social coalition that prevailed at the end of the Second World War had promoted high social spending, a growth in workers' incomes, increased consumption within the advanced countries, and a concentration of trade and investment in the developed world. It was an age in which the old colonial empires were disintegrating. The nation-state was accumulating new roles as a welfare state in the advanced countries. American power was much enhanced but it was mediated by the increased power of the state in delivering social programs and education.

Economic deregulation, new technology, and the demise of socialist alternatives reconfigured capitalism. Investment in productive operations shifted away from the advanced world to the Third World, with an enormous emphasis on China and India. The Keynesian interlude was over and capitalism was reverting in important ways to the character it had had during the age of imperialism that began in 1870. For capitalism to avoid collapse, it needed the new outlets it had been able to find during the age of imperialism. During the period after the Second World War it had appeared for several decades that capitalism, through higher social spending and rising workers' incomes, had solved the problem that had previously driven capitalism to imperialism.

By the 1970s, the curtain came down on the golden age of the great social compromise, the era in which the majority of people in the advanced countries, for the first time in history, enjoyed a modicum of prosperity. Battered by the inflation generated by the Vietnam War and the oil price shocks, the postwar system gave way to a tougher, meaner capitalism. Monetarism replaced Keynesianism. Neo-conservatism launched its assault on the welfare state. The war on inflation launched by British prime minister Margaret Thatcher and U.S. president Ronald Reagan succeeded in reining in the power of organized labor by generating higher unemployment, which always undermines workers' bargaining power.

Empire was once more in the air, and after the fall of Soviet Communism, the celebration of inequality that was the hallmark of classical capitalism was again the order of the day. In the writings of Milton Friedman and others, the emphasis was on merit, competition, and the energizing benefits of inequality. The same authors denigrated the concept of social solidarity as stultifying. With the vast labor pools of China and India coming fully into the global system, capitalists could reckon on the massive profits that only result from what economists call "green" labor—the addition of a new cohort of workers who will work hard for very little. But for this glorious opportunity to be realized, very difficult problems needed to be surmounted. And the only vehicle that could achieve this was the power of an imperial state.

The road to a truly global system required stubborn obstacles to be overcome. In many places in the world, nationalists, religious sects, drug dealers, and other criminal elements barred the way to the creation of functioning states and orderly markets. As a consequence, access to resources and labor and the ability to market products were imperiled. In the minds of some thinkers, this set of interconnected tasks could only be undertaken by an empire.

"I believe the world needs an effective liberal empire," Niall Ferguson has argued, "and that the United States is the best candidate for the job. . . . There are parts of the world where legal and political institutions are in a condition of such collapse or corruption that their inhabitants are effectively cut off from any hope of prosperity. And there are states that, through either weakness or malice, encourage terrorist organizations committed to wrecking a liberal world order. For that reason, economic globalization needs to be underwritten politically, as it was a century ago."[1]

On a more or less piecemeal basis, the American Empire has been doing the job. Its success over the mid- to long-term future depends on how it copes with four strategic challenges: the relationship between the United States and the Islamic world; the looming showdown with China; the emerging crisis in Latin America; and the conundrum of how to ensure access to sufficient supplies of petroleum while coping with the emerging global environmental crisis.

The United States has been drawn into its struggle in the Islamic world as a consequence of its long-term pro-Israeli stance in the Middle East. But what has radically reshaped and vastly raised the stakes in the conflict have been the U.S.-led invasions of Afghanistan in 2001 and Iraq in 2003. The invasions were supported by the new neo-conservatives, such as Michael Ignatieff and Niall Ferguson, as crusades that could transform these nations into liberal democracies. Further, it is argued, success at reforming these countries could provide a model for other countries in this crucial region of the world. This "missionary" outlook does not shed much light on the huge geostrategic stakes that are involved in its outcome. If the United States and its partners were to fail in these "beachheads" in the heart of the Islamic world, it would constitute a major blow to the American Empire.

When George W. Bush was sworn in as president on January 20, 2001, the common assumption among analysts of global power was that a showdown between the Americans and the Chinese could pose the most dangerous threat to global peace. The Republicans displayed a more muscular stance toward China during Bush's campaign for the White House than the Democrats. Mainstream Republicans saw China as a competitor at best, while a powerful section of the party saw the Beijing regime as the greatest threat to U.S. global power, a successor to Moscow in the days of the Cold War. The terror attacks on New York City and Washington, DC, on September 11, 2001, changed Washington's attitude to China, at least on the surface. Engaged first in Afghanistan and then in Iraq, the Bush White House wanted to keep things calm in East Asia, if possible. It was even hoped that Sino-American cooperation against the threat of terrorism generated by Islamic fundamentalists could establish a new era of trust between the two countries.

In the Middle East, the Americans have faced the harrowing effects of imperial overstretch. The American military has been severely challenged in Iraq, with National Guard units forced to do extended tours of duty. The claim that the U.S. military is able to fight at least one other major conflict at the same time as the Iraq operation is regarded as doubtful by military experts. Like Britain during the Boer War, America during the Iraq conflict has been seen by competitors as exposed and, therefore, open to challenge.

It has always been a rule of empire that when an imperial power invests an inordinate amount of energy in one corner of its realm, cracks and fissures appear elsewhere. That, in turn, encourages challengers, even those who are determined not to take inordinate risks. Empires take great care to punish those who violate the rules, not only to deal with the immediate violator, but also to warn all other potential violators of the consequences of misbehaving. The Americans have always been highly aware of the "demonstration effect" of prevailing over foes. During the Vietnam War, for instance, when criticism developed in the United States about the utility of the conflict, the counter-argument was constantly made that whether or not the war had been a good idea in the first place, once engaged, it had to be won. The consequences of defeat, the argument went, were too great to allow this to happen. U.S. failure would lead not only to a domino effect in Southeast Asia that would encourage other countries in the region to undertake nationalist-Communist revolutions, but also to a general tendency for nations around the world not to believe the solemn word of the United States. Or, to put it another way, once fear of the imperium subsides, people begin to test its limits.

In the case of Iraq, the same set of arguments and calculations are evident. An American victory in pacifying Iraq and installing a pro-American regime in Baghdad would be a stern warning to others. Those in the immediate area, principally the Syrians, Iranians, and Saudis, would learn that they could not effectively challenge America's will. It would also serve as a warning to the Palestinians that any hope of reaching a deal with Israel that was not to the liking of Washington was out of the question. And the warning would be heard at a much greater remove in Europe, Asia, and Latin America. In the weeks following the elections in Iraq on January 30, 2005, pro-American voices were heard in Europe telling Europeans that, notwithstanding their opposition to the war, George W. Bush had been shown to be right in the end. Or, a version of the message went, even if the Americans were not right about going to war initially, they had prevailed and this was the time to get back onside with them and to abandon the idea of Europe emerging as a counter-force to America in global affairs. Similarly, American victory in Iraq would send a message not only to North Korea that it must make a deal with Washington, but also to Beijing that too rapid an effort to expand Chinese influence in East Asia, in Taiwan in particular, would meet with a sure-footed U.S. response. And in Latin America, U.S. victory would remind that region that the Yankee remained powerful and that siding with rebellious leaders like Hugo Chavez was fraught with peril.

Naturally, an American defeat in Iraq, or the perception that the United States has sunk into a quagmire, would be a signal that the empire was in trouble and that it would be safe to disobey Washington's edicts. The stakes, therefore, in George W. Bush's Iraq adventure are immensely high. Magnifying the problems that flow from this severe regional crisis is the structure of the American Empire, which strongly resembles a vast holding company. American power is exercised over self-governing states rather than through annexation and military occupation, as was the case with most previous empires. Those at the apex need not concern themselves with everyday decisions at lower levels that do not much affect the overall operation.

This structure is simultaneously the great strength and the great weakness of the American Empire. The strength arises from the fact that routine administration is handled by the sovereign states within the American global sphere. But this can generate weakness as well. When the empire experiences crises, national governments can choose the occasion to reclaim more power for themselves.

The American Empire differs from the great European empires of the nineteenth century and its predecessors that relied on slave labor and on plunder in that the goal of the imperium is to enforce the rules for the free flow of capital in every part of the world. That is what allows a wider separation between direct imperial rule and effective imperial control than has existed with any previous empire. In that sense, the American Empire is more fully a capitalist empire, in the most essential meaning of that term, as compared even with the British Empire.

In the case of the British Empire, imperial territories were subjected to force and to regulations whose purpose was to create a profitable environment for British industry and British financiers. In India, for instance, the British put in place regulations whose purpose was to drastically weaken the local textile industry so that Lancashire textile producers could rule the world, including the Indian market. When British industry lost out to American, Japanese, and German industry, the British Empire, with the exception of the self-governing dominions, was turned into a protected market. The only beneficiaries of this arrangement were British industrialists, certainly not the consumers, who were forced to buy more expensive and, in some cases, second-rate products, rather than being able to buy cheaper imports.

One must not overstate this distinction between the American Empire and the British Empire, however. While the Americans are much less involved in administering the territories of their empire than were the British, there are special cases in which American financiers and industrialists are granted stupendous opportunities to reap profits as a consequence of U.S. military occupation. The U.S. invasion of Iraq in 2003 provides an outstanding example of this phenomenon. While American taxpayers have been hit with the bill for the invasion and occupation of Iraq, U.S. companies such as Bechtel, the world's largest engineering firm, have made billions in profits, shoring up infrastructure, installing security systems, upgrading petroleum pipelines, and outfitting U.S. military bases. And just as the long-running debate about whether European empires in the nineteenth century were profitable for the imperial powers themselves made sense only if one took account of the special interests for whom they were highly profitable, the same has been true of American operations in occupied countries such as Iraq. While Americans as a whole have certainly not profited from such occupations, very powerful U.S. corporations, with close ties to Washington, have found the occupations exceptionally profitable.

In the occupation of Iraq, the United States has departed from the customary behavior of its empire to revert to a more primitive imperialism in which rules are established that are specifically designed to benefit a handful of corporations with close ties to the administration. In the Iraq case, the practice of the United States strongly resembles that of the practice of states in the age of mercantilism, when government-licensed monopolies were granted special opportunities to make profits. This is a reminder that where empires are concerned there are no pure types, that under certain circumstances, an empire can turn to methods that characterized imperial practice in earlier periods. Where necessary the United States is prepared to occupy a country and to oversee its formal government, and in those conditions, it is willing to hand over extravagant benefits to major American corporations.

The first basic requirement of empire is that an imperial center must be sustained by a sufficiently large volume of economic output to serve as a platform on which to erect its expansion, crucially including the creation of a military to take on competitors and challengers. The size of the economy, therefore, matters enormously. Britain reached its zenith in terms of the proportion of global economic output for which it accounted in the mid-nineteenth century, when it produced about 35 percent of the global economic total. At the end of the Second World War, the United States reached its incredible peak when it produced 50 percent of the world's goods and services. At the beginning of the twenty-first century, the United States accounted for just over 20 percent of global economic production, a little below the European Union and about double the production of Japan. What is immediately apparent is that while the American economy is far larger and more productive than it was in 1945, it has undergone a steep decline relative to its competitors over the past six decades. The word "relative" must be emphasized here. We are not speaking of absolute decline. But relative decline is crucial because the United States' competitors have grown economically much more rapidly than has the United States since the end of the war. This growth has occurred in the First World in relation to Europe and Japan, although over the past fifteen years or so, these regions have not grown relative to the United States. Over this recent period, the extraordinary change has come as a consequence of the rise of China and India, primarily, but also other countries such as Brazil and Nigeria. Over the next couple of decades, first China and, not long after, India, are virtually certain to reach and surpass the overall economic output of the United States. This does not mean that these countries will reach the level of productivity and technological sophistication of the United States in anything like so short a time. But the mere fact that the volume of output of these economies will surpass that of the United States will change the geopolitical shape of the world.

The rise of the great Asian powers inexorably highlights the question of the global scramble for petroleum and other strategic resources, and the flip side of that question, the emerging global environmental crisis.

The career of the United States as a world power has been inexorably linked to the availability of strategic resources, especially petroleum. It was on the eve of the American Civil War in 1859 that explorers struck oil in Titusville, Pennsylvania. What followed was the rapid emergence of the petroleum industry and the technological transformations that accompanied it, with the United States as the global leader in these developments right from the beginning. During the first century of this revolutionary industry, the United States was the world's largest petroleum producer. The first oil fields in Pennsylvania were soon dwarfed in importance by the discovery of vast oil reserves in Texas. John D. Rockefeller, the world's first billionaire, established the Standard Oil trust, which later spawned many other mighty companies, among them Exxon Corporation.

In combination with the automobile industry, petroleum transformed life in America, reshaping the cities with the emergence of suburbs, and gave Americans a freedom of movement and personal choice never before enjoyed by any other society. The petroleum industry was crucial to the transformation of the United States into the world's largest national economy, an integrated transcontinental giant that soon relegated the great powers of Europe to the second tier. No less important was the role of petroleum in the rise of the United States as the world's greatest military power. By the end of the Second World War, the U.S. military had achieved vastly greater mobility on land, at sea, and in the air than any other power. If the atomic bomb was the symbol of America's unique military might at the conclusion of that conflict, it was oil that had driven the American forces to victory. Indeed, oil had been one of the causes of America's war with Japan. The Roosevelt administration's decision to limit the export of oil and other strategic resources to Japan to restrain Japanese military expansionism was one of the main reasons Tokyo decided it had to launch a war against the United States with its aerial attack on Pearl Harbor on December 7, 1941. Similarly, during the last two years of the conflict, despite its development of revolutionary new weapons, Hitler's Third Reich was severely hobbled by its growing shortage of petroleum.

Over the past six decades, America's economy and military have continued to run on oil. What was once a great strength for the United States in its rivalry with other powers has now become an alarming area of vulnerability for the American Empire. While in the early decades of oil production, the United States was able to supply all of its domestic needs and to export petroleum as well, by the early 1960s, the United States was dependent on imports to meet 20 percent of its oil demand. By 1977, 45 percent of the oil consumed in the United States was imported. In 1998, over half the oil used by Americans was imported.[2] Over the next two decades, U.S. dependence on imports is forecast to increase. By 2025, according to the long-range projection of the U.S. Department of Energy, the United States will need to import 69.6 percent of the oil Americans consume.[3]

As the known international reserves of conventional oil reach their peak of production—likely sometime in the next couple of decades, according to experts—the world will become ever more dependent on the petroleum reserves located around the Persian Gulf. Six Persian Gulf countries—Saudi Arabia, Iraq, the United Arab Emirates (UAE), Kuwait, Iran, and Qatar—sit on 64 percent of the world's known conventional reserves.[4] With falling domestic oil production and rising dependence for imports on the highly volatile Persian Gulf region, the U.S. government has identified access to the oil reserves of the region as crucial for its national security.

In July 2006, at 1.6 million barrels a day, Canada was the largest single exporter of crude oil to the United States. Rounding out the top five exporters to the United States were Mexico with just over 1.5 million barrels daily, Saudi Arabia at over 1.2 million barrels, Venezuela with nearly 1.2 million barrels, and Nigeria with just over 1.0 million barrels. These five countries made up 66 percent of American oil imports. What these totals make clear is the high dependence of the United States on oil from Canada and other western hemisphere sources and its relatively low reliance on Middle Eastern sources compared with Western Europe and Japan, which are much more dependent on the Middle East.

America's direct interest in the oil of the Persian Gulf dates back to 1933, when the Standard Oil Company of California (SOCAL) was the recipient of a sixty-year concession to explore for and develop the oil reserves in a large area along the Persian Gulf coast of Saudi Arabia. Within a few years, exploration of the region revealed that the territory was fabulously rich in petroleum, which led the U.S. government to take an increasing interest in it. Following his meetings with Joseph Stalin and Winston Churchill at Yalta, President Franklin Roosevelt flew to Egypt, where he held a meeting with King Ibn Saud of Saudi Arabia on February 14, 1945.

Historians believe that during their five-and-a-half-hour conversation, of which no record was kept, the two leaders reached an understanding. Saudi Arabia would allow American oil interests to dominate the kingdom's oil fields, and in return the United States would undertake to protect the sovereignty of the kingdom from external threats. As part of the understanding, the United States would be permitted to construct an air force base on Saudi soil at Dhahran.

A 1945 U.S. State Department memo bluntly outlined the American attitude to the kingdom: "The oil resources of Saudi Arabia [are] among the greatest in the world" and they "must remain under American control for the dual purpose of supplementing and replacing our dwindling reserves, and of preventing this power potential from falling into unfriendly hands."[5]

In the past, a plentiful supply of oil helped the United States rise to a position of global power. Today, with its own oil reserves inadequate to meet its needs, the United States spends blood and treasure to keep open its vital access to Persian Gulf oil. Domestic oil once helped make the U.S. military invincible; now the U.S. military consumes vast quantities of oil to ensure that the spigot of oil from foreign sources stays open. As the world demand for oil swells, and while supplies of this depleting resource can only dwindle, the great economic and military powers—the United States, Europe, Japan, China, and India—are locked in a struggle to secure enough oil to meet their needs. Among the major powers, only Russia has enough oil both to supply its own domestic market and to export to others.

For decades, a central aspect of American oil policy has been to foster a close alliance with Saudi Arabia, sustained by the sale of advanced U.S. warplanes and other weapons systems to the kingdom. The United States has also supplied weapons to the Saudi internal security forces, whose purpose has been to shield the regime against internal challenges. The American support for Israel in the 1973 Arab–Israeli War led to the embargo by Arab countries of the sale of oil to the United States and other Western countries. During this period of turbulence, the government of Saudi Arabia nationalized the concession held by Aramco, although U.S. petroleum companies were still allowed to market Saudi oil internationally.

The oil embargo was followed by the quadrupling of world oil prices from approximately $3 a barrel to $12 a barrel between December 1973 and the spring of 1974. This oil price revolution had mixed effects on the United States. On the one hand, it slowed the rate of economic growth in the United States and in other industrialized countries, but on the other hand it prompted exploration and development of U.S. domestic petroleum reserves that would have been uneconomic at lower prices.

On the eastern side of the Persian Gulf, and of great importance in the petroleum equation, is Iran, not only because it has enormous oil reserves, but because it poses a potential threat to American interests in the rest of the region.

Historically Iran was a theater of struggle for power between the British and the Russians. In 1953, in response to the nationalism of the Mossadegh government in Iran, the United States engineered a coup d'état that brought the pro-Washington regime of the Shah to power. In 1979, the Shah, in turn, was toppled by a broadly popular revolution whose leader was the Paris-based Ayatollah Khomeini. In place of the Shah, an Islamic fundamentalist order that was deeply hostile to the United States came to power. The Iranian revolution effectively removed the country's oil from the global supply, provoking a temporary doubling of world oil prices—of major importance in triggering a sharp global recession at the beginning of the 1980s.

A victim of the Iranian crisis, which sharply worsened with the taking of hostages at the U.S. embassy in Tehran, was President Jimmy Carter, who was defeated by Ronald Reagan in the election of November 1980. The supreme prize to be guarded, as always, was the oil wealth of Saudi Arabia. If possible, according to American strategists, the contagion of Iranian fundamentalism must be kept away from the kingdom. For its part, the Saudi monarchy hoped that autocracy, repression, and a conservative version of Islam would be sufficient to inoculate Saudi society against fundamentalism.

During the Iran–Iraq War of the 1980s, the United States "tilted" in favor of Iraq, opening the way for the sale of weapons to supply Saddam Hussein's hard-pressed forces. Washington had feared that an Iranian victory would put the hostile Tehran regime within striking distance of the crucial Saudi oil fields. During this period, as well, the United States pumped funds to Islamic opponents of the Soviet occupation of Afghanistan. One of the recipients was a Saudi entrepreneur by the name of Osama bin Laden. In this way, the United States helped underwrite the creation of both Al Qaeda and the Taliban.

In the summer of 1990, Saddam Hussein gambled, in a vast miscalculation, that the United States would stand aside and allow Iraq to occupy Kuwait, giving Baghdad control of that country's petroleum reserves and putting the Iraqis within easy reach of the oil fields of Saudi Arabia. In response, the administration of George H.W. Bush assembled a large coalition of states to expel the Iraqis from Kuwait. In the winter of 1991, the United States and its allies unleashed Desert Storm and swiftly drove Hussein's forces out of the emirate, while stopping short of marching on to Baghdad and toppling the Iraqi dictator's regime.

For the next decade, the Americans were successful in keeping Saddam "in his box" as they referred to it, by mounting flights from the U.S. base in Saudi Arabia to patrol the no-fly zone the United States proclaimed in southern Iraq. A severe downside of this strategy was that the continuing presence of the U.S. military in Saudi Arabia provoked the extreme wrath of Osama bin Laden and his brand of Islamic fundamentalists. Al Qaeda proclaimed the twin goals of overthrowing the Saudi regime and pushing the Americans out of this land where the holiest Islamic sites were situated. Al Qaeda's attacks on the United States climaxed with the September 11, 2001, assaults on New York City and Washington, DC.

The subsequent U.S. invasions of Afghanistan and Iraq had the twin objectives of countering the growth of hostile forces in the region—both the Taliban and Saddam's regime—and safeguarding U.S. access to the oil of the Gulf.

The first Gulf War led to a strategic upheaval in the region. The use of Saudi Arabia as the major staging area for the attack on Iraq contributed to the destabilization of Saudi society and the rise within the kingdom of a variety of militant Islamic fundamentalism that was virulently anti-American and anti-Western. The formerly prized (from the American point of view) balance of power between Iraq and Iran in the Gulf was shattered in favor of Iran. The balance of forces within Iraq, a country shackled together by Saddam's brutal regime, was blown apart so that Sunni control over the Kurdish north and the Shiite south were seriously undermined. (Sunnis and Shiites are two Islamic sects with a long history of antagonism toward each other. The Kurds are an ethnic minority who live on both sides of the Iraqi-Turkish frontier.)

In the years following the first Gulf War, the American policy of "keeping Saddam in his box" remained in place until the terror attacks on New York and Washington. By then George W. Bush was in office, and the key figures in his administration had a quite different strategic outlook on how to maintain American hegemony in the Persian Gulf from that of their predecessors. Previously, the U.S. policy had been to anchor its position in the Gulf to its alliance with and presence in Saudi Arabia. George Bush, the elder, had held to this posture and had made the decision not to march on to Baghdad during the first Gulf War. After September 11, 2001, however, the White House had become convinced that the U.S. position in Saudi Arabia was shaky and needed to be buttressed. The radical idea that quickly gained ground among top decision makers was that the American position in the Persian Gulf would be greatly strengthened through an invasion and occupation of Iraq. Paul Wolfowitz, deputy secretary of state, played a key role in convincing the top decision makers in the administration that an occupied Iraq could be molded along American lines to become a model democracy in which Islamic fundamentalism would be countered by a secular Islamic society. The Bush administration talked itself into the notion that the invading American troops would be met as liberators by a grateful population, not only in the Shiite south and Kurdish north, but in the Sunni center as well. Iraq was to be America's tabula rasa in the Middle East, a blank slate on which a new beginning could be written. Once Iraq was liberated from Saddam's grip, the Americanized regime could quite easily be made to see the utility of maintaining permanent U.S. military bases in the country.

The invasions of Afghanistan and Iraq were radical departures whose outcomes not only would determine the fate of the American Empire in the Middle East, but would have an enormous effect on the durability of the empire worldwide.

By the spring of 2006, for the first time since the terror attacks of 2001, mainstream voices in the United States spoke out in opposition to the Bush administration's strategy in the Middle East, as well as on issues concerning petroleum and the environment. Around the personality of Al Gore, the former vice-president who had lost the election of 2000 to Bush, an alternative approach to these interrelated questions was being advanced. With the release of his film, *An Inconvenient Truth*, in January 2006, Gore found a vehicle for placing the issue of global warming and catastrophic climate change on the front burner of American politics. The burden of Gore's argument, noteworthy not as science but because it came from a leading political figure, was that climate change was the most important issue facing the world and that failing to address it would lead to catastrophic consequences. Gore's initiative revealed, in a serious way, how the United States was unprepared to face the fact that the era of cheap and plentiful petroleum had come to an end. If the United States was to make a concerted effort to reduce greenhouse emissions and to increase energy efficiency and reduce its dependence on hydrocarbons, the effect would be to diminish the strategic importance of the Persian Gulf to the American Empire. That some people were taking him seriously was reflected in the fact that Al Gore's fee for a lecture shot up from $25,000 to $100,000 in the early months of 2006.

Latin America: Taken for Granted

While U.S. policymakers have shifted their calculations about the threats posed by the Middle East and China over the middle term, a region much closer to home has been showing disquieting signs of moving out of Washington's orbit. Latin America is the often-forgotten and underestimated backyard of the American Empire. In many geostrategic studies of the American global position and its future prospects, Latin America is given short shrift or is completely ignored. For instance, in his strategic study, *The Grand Chessboard*, Zbigniew Brzezinski believed the fate of American global power would be decided in Eurasia, but he did not bother to discuss the western hemisphere at all. During his days in power, Henry Kissinger famously believed that nothing that happened in the global south mattered much in the exercise of power worldwide.

In truth, however, while the Bush administration's efforts have been focused on the great test in the Middle East, Latin America has been making a concerted turn toward the political left and away from Washington. Today in Latin America, the largest democracies, Chile, Argentina, Venezuela, and Brazil, have socialist or left-leaning regimes, leaving only Mexico with a right-of-center government.

In the past, challenges to America's chosen course for the western hemisphere have been met with brutal repression, through direct or indirect U.S. intervention. There is no need to list the dozens of American missions and interventions in Latin America; a few key cases make the point. In 1954, a populist-democratic regime in Guatemala that threatened the interests of the United Fruit Company was overturned by a CIA-sponsored coup. In 1973, the Salvador Allende regime in Chile, in office as a consequence of a fair and competitive election, was overturned in a bloody coup, in part engineered in Washington, and was followed by the brutal dictatorship of Augusto Pinochet. The Americans have shown that they are perfectly willing to overthrow democratic regimes in Latin America that stand in their way.

Recently the focus of America's concerns in Latin America has been the populist left-wing regime of President Hugo Chavez of Venezuela.

Because of Venezuela's bountiful petroleum reserves, and the clout this gives him, Chavez has replaced Fidel Castro as the leading leftist bogeyman in Latin America in the eyes of American strategists.

In April 2002, a coup hatched by Venezuelan business leaders and military officers forced Chavez out of power for two days, before he was reinstalled by a popular movement that compelled those who had seized power to stand down. The precise role of Washington in the failed coup is not yet known. However, U.S. intelligence was well informed about the nature of the impending coup. Given the long history of American involvement in overturning regimes in Central and South America, no one would be shocked a few years from now to learn that the Bush administration had been actively involved in planning the operation in Venezuela. The difference, of course, was that this attempt to eliminate Chavez failed, as did a subsequent effort to remove him in a referendum.

What made Chavez's success particularly worrying from the Bush administration's standpoint was that Venezuela is the fourth-largest foreign supplier of oil to the United States. In 2005, Chavez forged a major energy deal with China. Everywhere the Americans look these days they encounter the Chinese, who are avidly competing for available oil on the international market. The United States can no longer assume that Venezuelan oil is a special American preserve that can be drawn on at will. Chavez has gained appreciable power by being able to sell oil to China and others, to earn the means to fund popular programs that benefit his power base among Venezuela's lower classes, as well as to purchase armaments. Chavez has not only thrown American military advisers out of Venezuela, he has warned Washington that American efforts to destabilize his regime will be met with an oil embargo. In March 2005, when Chavez purchased weapons from Russia, U.S. Defense Secretary Donald Rumsfeld questioned his motives: "I can't imagine why Venezuela needs 100,000 AK-47's."[1] Attempts by Rumsfeld and by Secretary of State Condoleezza Rice to win over Latin American governments to membership in an anti-Chavez common front have fallen flat. Instead, Chavez and other Latin American leaders have been thinking through alternatives for the region to counter Washington's aim of extending the North American Free Trade Agreement (NAFTA) south through a Free Trade Area of the Americas (FTAA).

What has imperiled the U.S. position in Latin America has been the latest in a succession of political transformations in the region over the past quarter-century. The statism of many regimes, accompanied by high inflation and slow growth, was succeeded by a wave of neo-liberalism in much of Latin America in the 1990s. Neo-liberalism, the economic recipe favored by the Americans, as well as by the International Monetary Fund (IMF) and the World Bank, was ideally suited to fitting Latin America into the scheme of globalization. For a brief time it appeared that Latin Americans were adopting the orthodoxy of the Washington consensus and erecting market states that could be ripe for the extension of NAFTA all the way south to Tierra del Fuego.

While neo-liberalism enriched a few and made Latin America safer for foreign financiers, it worsened the condition of the region's vast marginalized population, robbing the people of the few social benefits they enjoyed. For instance, in the shanty towns surrounding Caracas, where most people lived without running water and other amenities before Chavez came to power, neo-liberal control of Venezuela directed oil wealth to a minority, leaving the majority impoverished. By the time George W. Bush and the other heads of government of the hemisphere, with the exception of Fidel Castro, visited Quebec City in the spring of 2001 to plan for the launch of the FTAA, the third wave of change in Latin America—this time to the left—was already underway.

The new left wave was populist and strongly anti-American. It featured a range of leaders with different constituencies and distinct ideological outlooks. Brazil's Lula da Silva leaned toward the traditional social democratic end of the spectrum. Hugo Chavez, the fiery Venezuelan president, was the exemplar of the new revolutionary anti-imperialism.

At the core of Chavez's political constituency were the impoverished people who dwelt in marginal, impoverished communities on the edge of Caracas. Formidable in large measure because of the vast revenues from Venezuelan oil, Chavez has become the prophet of an alternative economic and social policy throughout Latin America. Authoritarian, pro-Castro, but still reconciled to constitutional democracy, Chavez saw himself carrying forward the liberating work of Simón Bolívar, the great revolutionary leader who led the fight for Latin American independence from Spain in the early nineteenth century.

Unlike Castro, Chavez has not opted for a publicly owned, command economy. While there is plenty of private enterprise in Venezuela, and it is not hard to find virulent opponents of Chavez in the middle-class quarters of Caracas, the president sees himself as leading a concerted struggle against the American Empire. He has surrounded himself with socialist intellectual exiles from Britain, the United States, and other parts of the world. Not only has Chavez forged strong ties with other Latin American leaders, using the provision of cheap oil and capital as his tools, he has reached out to the anti-American regime of Iran and to the Chinese government in his efforts to offset the power of Washington.

Chavez's political appeal extended north into Mexico into the heart of NAFTA. In a famous spat with Vicente Fox, in which Chavez accused the Mexican president of being a toady to George Bush, a slight which initially annoyed most Mexicans, his point was not without effect. Although he often presented himself as something of a buffoon, Chavez found Fox's area of vulnerability with stiletto-like precision.

Fox's grand design—to achieve a historic new deal with the United States—was foundering as he neared the end of his seven-year term. Fox came to the presidency hoping to find a way to normalize the position of the millions of Mexicans who work illegally in the United States. Shortly after he entered the White House in January 2001, George W. Bush's first meeting with a foreign leader was with Fox. Bush described Mexico as America's closest partner, a pointed insult to Canada that was intended to curry favor with America's southern neighbor. As the former governor of a state bordering on Mexico, Bush had his own reasons for wanting good relations with Fox. He badly wanted to win Latino voters to his banner to assure his victory in the 2004 presidential election.

What dashed the hopes of the two presidents were the terror attacks of September 11, 2001. With national security suddenly at the top of the American political agenda, the idea of a sweeping deal to ease the way for Mexican workers in the United States had to be put on the back burner. Even though American employers, especially those in border states such as California, had come to depend on cheap, illegal Mexican labor—to the point where Federal Reserve Board President Alan Greenspan acknowledged its importance in keeping U.S. inflation low—there was always the potential for an anti-immigrant backlash to develop among Americans,

THE PERILS OF EMPIRE

particularly among those on the political right, who form the core of Bush's constituency. September 11 vastly heightened the danger of a sharp revival of nativist sentiment among Americans. While paranoia was directed mostly toward Muslims, the rapid increase of the Latino population in California and other states in the southwest fueled the anxiety of many white conservatives. What worried them was the palpable sense that America was no longer recognizable, that the presence of Mexicans in large numbers on their streets was changing their homeland. Fear of change and anxiety for the future have incited the waves of nativism that have roiled America periodically for more than two hundred years. In the period following September 11, Bush was in no position to advance a policy to secure the rights of illegal Mexican immigrants in the United States.

The American invasion of Iraq in March 2003 further complicated relations between Washington and Mexico City. In the lead-up to the war, Mexico did not support the United States in its efforts to win United Nations support for the invasion. The Iraq issue again pushed any thought of a sweeping deal to the side. In the early months of 2006, the immigration issue exploded in the United States in an angry confrontation between illegal immigrants and those on the political right who wanted to block an amnesty for illegal aliens from Mexico. The issue made its way to the top of the American political agenda at a time when George W. Bush's approval ratings hovered around 36 percent in U.S. public opinion polls. Hard-edged, right-wing politicians, who were quite prepared to ignore the unpopular president, built political followings by calling for the application of the letter of the law where illegal aliens were concerned. Impractical, disruptive, and unworkable as the expulsion of more than ten million people from the United States would be, those supporting such an extreme approach drew massive support to their cause. On the other side of the gulf were the illegal immigrants who took to the streets in enormous demonstrations, with hundreds of thousands of people protesting in Washington, DC, New York, Los Angeles, and other American cities. In the past, illegal immigrants had maintained a low profile, hoping that their utility to employers—for whom they worked as farm laborers, in factories, cleaning streets, and gardening and serving as nannies for the affluent—would cause the authorities to leave them alone. But vigilantes, who began to launch their own private efforts to monitor the border, and the protests of taxpayers against funding the education of the children of aliens and picking up the tab for their health care, forced the immigrants to draw open attention to themselves.

Well aware of their huge numbers and of the wide support for them among millions of American citizens of Hispanic origin and generally among liberal Americans, the illegals were emboldened to demand rights for themselves and their families. In their demonstrations, they wrapped themselves in the American flag and announced that all they wanted was to become Americans. They made the case that they were hard-working people who only wanted the chance to do jobs that Americans were largely unwilling to do, that their contribution to the country was much greater than the tax revenue that was spent servicing them.

Bush tried to work with Congress to find a middle ground that would open the way to citizenship for illegal immigrants who had lived in the United States for five years or more and that would set up a system to create a status for non-citizens to work in the United States as transient laborers. With Congressional elections approaching in the autumn of 2006 and with the occupant of the White House unable to exercise much political clout, the angry fissure widened with no solution in sight.

Bush's misfortune was also Fox's. The Mexican president's strategy of seeking closer ties with the United States appeared to be a grand failure. Not only was the United States unwilling to legitimize the position of illegal Mexican immigrants, but the Mexican gamble in favor of NAFTA had been beneficial only to a small segment of the country's population while doing little or nothing for the large majority.

While American policymakers were well aware of the problems posed by the immigration issue and by the turn of Latin America to the left, these questions were rarely perceived in strategic terms. The well-funded and sophisticated Chavez threat, for instance, was seriously underestimated in Washington. Latin America, as American strategists saw it, continued to be a source of irritation, but there was little understanding of the implications for the American Empire if Latin American countries truly found a path that could lead them out from under the American shadow. Much more attention was devoted to thinking through the challenges in the Middle East, even though over the long term what was happening in the western hemisphere could be as important as any other cause in the ultimate undoing of America's global enterprise.

The immigration issue illustrated that the Latin American question was an internal, as well as an external, question for the United States. Official American census projections forecast that by the middle of the twenty-first century, 25 percent of the U.S. population would be of Hispanic origin. By that point, not only California, but Arizona, New Mexico, and Texas were forecast to have Hispanic majorities. Notwithstanding the immense power of the American dream to draw newcomers into its cultural and social matrices, the consolidation of such an enormous Latino population in the arc of states the United States seized from Mexico in the movement for Texan independence and the Mexican–American War of 1846–48 was bound to pose an unprecedented challenge to the English-speaking, white establishment of the United States.

American political culture is ill equipped to cope with the cultural, linguistic, educational, and social demands that are bound to flow from the rise of the Hispanic fact within the borders of the United States. While Latino Americans from Cuba, Puerto Rico, Central America, and Mexico have been far from homogeneous, they have much in common, linguistically and culturally. The demand for official status for the Spanish language in cities and states, and for the right to public education in the Spanish language, is bound to come at some point in the future. Hostility to bilingualism in the United States has long existed. Attempting to force the American Republic to change its basic nature and to acknowledge a bicultural reality in its midst promises to generate severe political conflict. Governors of Hispanic origin will soon be elected in key American states. While they may initially act as a bridge between fellow Latinos and other Americans, as Hispanic numbers grow and their power is felt, leaders may emerge with a political agenda that demands fundamental changes to the American political order.

The rise of the Latin fact inside the United States is bound to condition the ways the United States seeks to continue to keep Latin America under control as the backyard of its empire.

The Coming Sino-American Collision

Over the next two decades, the rise of China is bound to have an appreciable effect on the global space accorded to the American Empire. With vast resources and territory, a population of 1.2 billion people, and an economy that has exploded over the past quarter-century, China has already transformed the geopolitical situation in East Asia. Not only has China established major trading relationships with a long list of Asian countries, but its demand for resources, particularly petroleum, its vast exports of manufactured products, and its attraction as a location for direct foreign investment have been felt across the globe. Although large parts of China and most of the country's population remain poor, its economic takeoff has enriched a significant portion of the country, making it a crucial new market for a long list of commodities, from automobiles to appliances, electronics, luxury hotels, and construction materials. China has accumulated huge pools of capital. Between them, the Chinese and the Japanese hold 50 percent of U.S. short-term treasury bills. With the United States saddled with an enormous federal government debt—$8.9 trillion by the end of 2006, on which interest payments of $406 billion had to be paid in 2006—China and Japan now play an indispensable role in financing Washington's deficit and debt.

China's policy of acquiring such a huge sum of U.S. treasury bills bears a resemblance to the postwar U.S. Marshall Plan in Western Europe. The Marshall Plan pumped capital into Europe, creating a large market for American products. The irony, of course, is that in this case it is a developing country that has been helping meet the capital needs of a global empire. By helping finance the U.S. government debt, even though it loses out on low rates of interest on a falling U.S. dollar, China helps ensure the continued buoyancy of the U.S. consumer demand for Chinese exports. China's contribution to sustaining brisk U.S. consumer spending has been a key element in the Chinese strategy to industrialize its country.

It is not, however, a strategy that is likely to persist over the long term. As China matures as an industrial power and reshapes the markets in neighboring Asian countries, countries that make up half the population of the world, Chinese aid to support the strength of the American consumer market will surely decline.

China is much more than an economic giant. Unlike Europe, which remains substantially divided into nation-states with long histories and distinct cultures, China is a nation with a powerful identity and sense of itself as having a rightful place at the center of things. For centuries, the Chinese saw themselves as the "middle kingdom," the empire at the center of the earth's affairs, surrounded by other and lesser peoples. Looked at over the long sweep of Chinese history, the era of China's domination by European powers and Japan, which ended decisively in 1949 with the victory of the Communists in the nation's civil war, can be seen as an exceptional period of Chinese weakness. Today as their nation rebounds, the Chinese display a potent nationalism that proclaims the idea that their nation is resuming its rightful position in the world. Over the middle- and long-term future, this aggressive outlook is not only highly likely to engender a crisis over Taiwan, it is also likely to provoke tensions with Asia's other giants, Japan and India. How the United States chooses to manage these predictable crises will be crucial in determining the future of the American Empire.

Taiwan is a ticking time bomb. Most countries around the world, including the United States, adhere to a "One China" policy that recognizes that Taiwan is a province of China and that over the long term the issue between Beijing and Taipei will have to be resolved. The United States, however, insists that the solution to the Taiwan question must be peaceful and evolutionary. While steering clear of any challenge to Beijing's claim that Taiwan is a part of China, the United States has been Taiwan's defender. Not only have American arms manufacturers supplied the island state with the latest weapons, but the U.S. navy patrols the Straits of Taiwan, where it deploys its largest fleet of aircraft carriers. Ever since the Communist victory in the Chinese Civil War in 1949, the United States has been Taiwan's protector. For over two decades, while the United States refused to recognize the regime in Beijing, the pretense was maintained in the United Nations and elsewhere that the Republic of China, with its capital in Taipei, was the legitimate government of the whole of China. During these years, the Taiwan regime occupied China's seat in the UN as a permanent member of the Security Council. During these decades, military rumblings occurred on occasion, as in the late 1950s, when the Beijing government carried out artillery assaults on the offshore islands of Quemoy and Matsu, small islands controlled by Taipei that are only a few kilometers from the Chinese mainland. At times of such crisis, it seemed possible that the struggle over the offshore islands might even draw Washington into war with Beijing. The transformation of the 1970s led to U.S. recognition of Beijing and the replacement of Taipei by Beijing in the UN and on the Security Council, but it did not end the role of the United States as Taiwan's protector.

Taiwan could still be the trigger that sets off a more deep-seated, general struggle between the United States and China. While resembling other momentous collisions between empires in the past, the coming showdown between the United States and China has features that are entirely unique. First, it is truly a struggle for global power between the giant of the First World and a state that two decades ago was still counted as being in the Third World. The Soviet Union, by the time it entered the era of the Cold War in the years following the Second World War, had industrialized well beyond that status. The United States–China contest compresses the great issues in the contemporary world into one struggle, at the same time as it revisits crucial questions about the nature of empires and of inter-imperial struggles that have beset humankind for thousands of years.

Despite China's record of explosive economic growth, the large majority of the Chinese population remains poor, still locked out of the huge changes that have caught up perhaps three hundred million people in the upward mobility that has accompanied China's economic transformation. Were China to prevail in this struggle for power, it would not only overturn the Western domination of the globe that has existed for over five hundred years, but it would bring to the fore a power in which the majority of the population still lives in Third World conditions.

In considering the stakes in the contest between the United States and China, it is useful to recall previous momentous showdowns between empires. Although it was fought in the much smaller arena of the Mediterranean, the Rome–Carthage encounter involved incalculably high stakes for the future of the West. Had Carthage rather than Rome emerged triumphant, the history of the past two millennia would have been dramatically different. Similarly, a China–U.S. collision, should it end in a conflagration in which only one contender emerges as a global power, could prove to be a veritable fork in the road for humanity. Of course, it is to be hoped that the contest will not end in such dramatic fashion. In the late nineteenth century, the "great war" that many analysts anticipated was a struggle between Russia, the great land power, and Britain, the great sea power. Known as the "Great Game," and centered on control of the territory lying between northern India and the southern frontier of the Russian Empire, this war was never fought. And just as the Soviet–American Cold War did not end in a conflagration, not least because of the presence of nuclear weapons on both sides, a contest between China and the United States could endure for many decades with no dramatic and single conclusion.

As the United States and China begin to test each other's strength, each with different assets at its disposal, there remains considerable room for accommodation. To date, the two countries have enjoyed a substantial harmony of interests on economic matters. As China has opened itself to foreign capital, American investors have rushed head-long into the country, along with their peers elsewhere in the world, to take advantage of China's huge pool of inexpensive labor and its vast and expanding consumer market. Sino-American synergy is best captured in the case of the U.S. corporation Wal-Mart, the largest retailer in the world. In the United States Wal-Mart has become the conduit for the sale of an enormous quantity of goods manufactured in China. This achievement, unprecedented in its scale in the history of capitalism, has promoted Chinese industrialization at the same time as it has undermined manufacturing and industrial employment in the United States. While the impact of the Wal-Mart conduit has not gone without notice in the United States and the U.S. trade deficit with China has become a hot political issue, the arrangement still suits the interests of both countries. American and Chinese business interests and the Chinese state are content with the rise of industrial production in China from which immense profits are being made. American consumers flock in the millions to Wal-Mart outlets across the United States, even though some local businesses and concerned citizens have fought hard to keep the retailer out of their communities. And although U.S. industrial workers have steadily lost jobs in the face of imports from low-wage countries, with China at the head of the list, the most powerful American capitalists have been winners in the process. What is happening is analogous to the hollowing-out of agriculture in Italy as a consequence of imports from other provinces in the Roman Empire, in particular Egypt. At some point, the concern with the rising trade and current account deficits and the loss of industrial jobs at home may cause the calculus to shift, but that point has not yet been reached.

At this stage, American imperial interests have managed to subsume China within their broad realm in a way that has been profitable and that has contributed to reasonably good relations between the two countries. This, however, is a dynamic process and a potentially unstable one. The U.S. government is wary of the rise of China's economy, and the Chinese government is adamant that the acceleration of American investments in China must not threaten Beijing's political control.

As China's economy expands, its demand for resources and its commercial relations with other countries are already creating anxiety in Washington. China's demand for petroleum has forced Beijing to seek supplies in Russia, the Middle East, Africa, and South America. Not only does this put China into direct competition with the United States for petroleum, it interferes with the American ability to dominate oil-producing countries such as Venezuela and, even more explosively, in the Persian Gulf, where the Iranian leadership hopes oil sales to China will help their country in its confrontation with Washington. Around China's enormous perimeter countries are being drawn into ever more important commercial relationships with the rising giant that are often more important than their ties to the United States.

As a consequence, China's sphere of influence in Asia is rapidly expanding. Half the world's population lives in China and the countries that surround it. This is a very crowded neighborhood, and the power stakes couldn't be higher. A century ago, Europe was still the center of the world in geopolitical terms, and Asia was being carved up by Europeans, the Japanese, and to a lesser extent, the Americans. India was the jewel in the crown of the British Empire, and China, the greatest prize of all, was being forced to concede special zones of influence to the major powers.

Today, both China and India are rising economic powers, with strong states that wield nuclear weapons. And Japan, despite its economic woes over the past fifteen years, remains a highly advanced country, and the world's greatest creditor nation, with vast sums to invest around the world, including a huge and critical stake in the United States.

The Asian balance of power in the early years of the twenty-first century is as complex as was the European balance of power a century ago. One difference, of course, is that the greatest power of all, the United States, is a non-Asian power now attempting to manage the balance of power in Asia to its advantage. Having leaned toward Pakistan for decades, the United States has been seeking a stronger relationship with India. In the winter of 2006, President George W. Bush traveled to India, where he made a highly controversial deal with New Delhi that recognized India as a legitimate nuclear power, despite that country's violations of the Nuclear Non-Proliferation Treaty. Establishing strong ties with India and Japan is Washington's way of seeking to balance the rising might of China.

For its part, China has engaged in a war of words with Japan whose purpose is to lessen the influence of its long-term nemesis and rival. China has revisited the question of Japanese wartime atrocities against the Chinese people, an issue that resonates in other parts of Asia. As a consequence of the Japanese invasion of China in 1931, and in subsequent years, approximately twenty million Chinese lost their lives. Among the atrocities featured in the recent Chinese campaign have been the bombing and massacres in Nanking in 1937–38 and the subjugation of Chinese women as prostitutes for the Japanese armed forces.

Japanese obduracy about acknowledging the atrocities committed by its forces in the 1930s and 1940s has made it easier for China to press its case. Unlike the Germans, who have shouldered the burden of responsibility for the crimes of the Third Reich, Japan's apologies for the crimes of its militarist regime have been half-hearted and grudging. Moreover, the rise of a new right in Japan has brought to the fore political leaders who are more inclined to celebrate the militarism of the Japanese past than to deplore it. Japanese leaders have visited shrines that house the remains of men regarded as war criminals in China and other Asian countries, thus exacerbating the issue. So, too, has the alleged failure of Japanese school textbooks to chronicle Japanese war crimes. In truth, Japan has many textbooks, some of which are more forthright about the country's wartime atrocities than others. The Sino-Japanese tension has been punctuated by mass demonstrations in Chinese cities against Japan, some of them involving attacks on Japanese commercial establishments. One tactic employed by China in this political struggle has been to fund delegations of foreigners from many countries to visit China to learn first-hand the Chinese version of wartime events and to meet survivors of the Japanese atrocities. A clear goal of the campaign has been to undermine any attempt to elevate Japan to permanent membership in the United Nations Security Council.

China's campaign to push Japan to the sidelines as an Asian power is only part of its drive to achieve greater status for itself. Beijing will host the Summer Olympics in 2008, an opportunity to showcase China to the world.

Membership in the World Trade Organization has helped China in its effort to achieve superpower status. In the first decades of its existence, the People's Republic was shut out of world organizations; now, the new China presents itself as a pillar of order and stability. So far China has been careful not to push its weight around in power struggles with the United States at the United Nations. For instance, while China would not endorse Washington's invasion of Iraq in 2003, Beijing was not prepared to make the issue a test of power between the two states. And for its own reasons, China has been willing to go along with the United States in broadly opposing global terrorism, not least because it allows China to tighten its grip on dissident minorities at home, including the Tibetans.

At some point, this policy of accommodation could change. Beijing could decide that some American policy initiative—perhaps a decision to bomb Iran to neutralize the country's nuclear facilities—goes too far. China could decide that it is in a position to win world opinion and to isolate the United States. Such a step would be a signal that China is ready to take on the United States much more overtly than it has up until now. An event of this kind would constitute a direct challenge to American power and would gravely worsen relations between Beijing and Washington.

If the economic balance in the Sino-American equation can be said to be shifting in favor of China, the United States retains other substantial assets that will be difficult for China to challenge. Two of these are the diplomatic advantage and the cultural advantage.

What can be called the diplomatic advantage arises from the fact that the United States has been at the center of a web of relationships and institutions that dates back to the last days of the Second World War and that has been sustained and updated ever since then. In the summer of 1944, the United States and its allies met at Bretton Woods, New Hampshire, and under firm American direction planned the architecture of the postwar economy. In addition to making the U.S. dollar the reserve currency of the international system and establishing such organizations as the International Monetary Fund, the World Bank, and the General Agreement on Tariffs and Trade, the American-centered system was motivated by two seminal objectives: freer trade and freer rights for capital to flow from country to country without hindrance. While the details of the American-initiated system were to change, sometimes dramatically, the essentials of the American-centered global economy remain in place today.

This fundamental fact provides enormous advantages for the United States against its competitors in the global system. The fact that the U.S. dollar is the world's reserve currency, for instance, has allowed the United States to run a perennial current account deficit in a way no other country could. Other countries have parked trillions of dollars in U.S. securities, and this has underwritten the capacity of the United States to live beyond its means for decades. The arrangement operates as an informal tax on other countries for the security and governance provided for the global system by the United States. In some ways, it resembles the system of contributions made by the cities that made up the Delian Confederacy and the later Athenian Empire. Not only does the United States provide governance for the system as a part of this arrangement, it functions as the creditor of last resort in times of economic crisis, thereby helping avert international economic recessions or, even worse, economic meltdowns. In the cases of the Mexican economic crisis of the early 1990s and the more serious Asian economic crisis of the late 1990s, the U.S. Federal Reserve helped pump liquidity back into the system and thereby averted collapse of countries and financial institutions. These timely interventions by the U.S. central bank did what the United States failed to do in the months and years following the collapse of the U.S. stock market in October 1929. The failure of the most powerful creditor and economic nation to intervene in the early 1930s worsened the economic crisis and contributed to the political chaos that helped the Nazis and the Japanese militarists achieve power. In its role as overseer of the global system, the United States would not make that kind of mistake today.

In the web of relationships that exists in the global economy, the United States plays the role of puppetmaster, pulling the strings that need to be pulled, able to reward those who favor the United States and punish those who do not. It is very much the role that was played by Britain and the Bank of England during the Victorian age. It is the role played by an empire at the height of its powers, and the use of those powers makes that empire difficult to dislodge. Such powers do not make a great state unassailable, however, as the case of Britain illustrates.

If U.S. primacy in economic relationships gives the American Empire a great edge over China as a challenger, so, too, does its cultural advantage. In an age when instant communication plays a vast economic role, the United States is empowered by the primacy of English and the reach of American popular culture. While aspects of China's culture have been spread by the millions of Chinese migrants who have settled in many parts of the world, the culture of China remains highly unique in relation to that of other countries, even the countries that are its close Asian neighbors. The enormous achievement of the Chinese Empire—creating the world's largest nation out of its disparate parts—was only realized as a consequence of its relative isolation. And that, in turn, means that this nation of over one billion people has great difficulty reaching out to other nations to make common cause with them, except through the use of the lingua franca of the Americans and the American way of doing things. In the quest for superpower status in today's world, China has to play the game of spreading influence according to American rules and norms. While China has the advantage of being an immense power in the heart of what is becoming the world's economic center in the twenty-first century, the United States is the established cultural power that can reach out to nations on every continent, even to nations in which there is a high degree of anti-Americanism. Cultural power has never counted for as much as it does today in the inter-imperial struggle for power, and the advantage in this domain lies solidly with the United States.

The American strategy is to encircle China with countries that are closely aligned with Washington and to embed China as much as possible in the American global system. This is a stick and carrot approach, confronting China with alliances and military supremacy that appear unchallengeable while encouraging China's capitalist economic explosion. What makes the looming collision dangerous is that the calculus of power on both sides is far from perfectly understood and that the signals sent by each side are not necessarily going to be completely clear to the other. Moreover, the danger becomes much more evident when we focus on the fact that the crucial decisions will be taken by leaders in both countries who have their own narrow interests to worry about in addition to those of their countries.

Political leaders grapple with a whole series of challenges, both domestic and external, in their struggles to hold onto power in their own countries. In the United States, when the occupant of the White House for whatever reason falls to low levels of popularity with midterm or presidential elections approaching, desperate risks can be taken to bolster support. In the last year of Richard Nixon's embattled presidency in 1973–74, for instance, political analysts feared that a president facing impeachment could try to use a foreign policy adventure as a way to shore up support among Americans. Although Nixon did consider trumping up a crisis with the Soviet Union while his presidency was crumbling, his secretary of state, Henry Kissinger, had the political weight and wisdom to counsel against any such rash action.

It may be difficult for a president to make use of his massive powers to save his own skin in the American system of team or corporate government. As the American neo-conservative elites around George W. Bush have watched his presidency lose authority due to the catastrophes of Iraq and Hurricane Katrina, much more has been at stake than the mere fate of one individual. An entire inner elite and its ideology face the prospect of losing their command over the American Empire and all the privileges that go with it. Collective leaderships of this sort are capable of taking dramatic risks when the alternative is a fall from power.

In the relationship between the United States and China, such a moment of crisis in the American government could lead Washington to take risks in confronting Beijing.

It is virtually certain that when the immediate crisis faced by the United States in the Middle East is resolved one way or another, American strategic thinkers will once more focus on China as the principal threat to their country. A book edited by Robert Kagan and William Kristol, entitled *Present Dangers*, a publication that was seen as representing the views of highly influential neo-conservatives, presents an incendiary view of the threat from China: "China's goals in Asia," wrote Ross H. Munro in his chapter titled "China: The Challenge of a Rising Power," "voiced with increasing frankness during the 1990s, amount to a program for domination of the region. China has openly declared that it aims to occupy Taiwan and control the South China Sea, to end the U.S. military presence in Asia, to break all U.S. military alliances with Asian countries, and to force Japan into 'permanent strategic subservience' without the right to a full-fledged military. What China wants is an Asia where no country could oppose its will."[1]

And just as neo-conservatives in the United States are inclined to see China through a hostile lens, this argument also works the other way. While the Chinese system of government is less transparent than the American system, it is just as surely a system in which groups of leaders battle for supreme power. During a power struggle, one leader or group of leaders could well decide to play the card of expansionism or confrontation with Washington to increase its own internal standing.

In the winter of 2007, China launched an anti-missile missile into space that succeeded in hitting its target. The test alarmed the Pentagon and reminded the world that China and the United States are involved in a power struggle that could end in collision.

Resisting Empire

The rulers of all empires have one common nightmare—the threat of rebellion from below. While imperial strategists have to consider what boundaries their state can sustain without straining resources too severely, the threats from within are constant. Empires collide with one another in spectacular showdowns that change the course of history, but the fear of slaves, helots, serfs, peasants, and citizens of subject cities have been the stuff of daily governance. Because empires are based on the rule by one people of one or more other peoples, there is always a sharp line dividing the dominant from the dominated within an imperial system. The empires that endure for centuries, or even millennia, have found effective strategies for coping with the problem. Force is always one aspect of the solution. Empires are created through military victories, through the conquest of peoples. And force must always be present as an option for rulers to deploy. But force alone is seldom sufficient for an empire to survive for a lengthy period. The ruling people must be convinced of the legitimacy of its rule, and the subject people must be taught that it is futile or, in the best-case scenario, not in their interest to resist.

Even in the best-governed empires, revolts occur. In rare and spectacular cases, such as the American Revolution, they succeed. Most revolts against imperial control do not succeed, but the threat of such rebellions does impose enormous costs on imperial regimes.

The helot revolt against Sparta in the aftermath of the great earthquake in the fifth century B.C. showed the ability of the members of a desperate underclass, poorly armed and untrained as they were, to seize an opportunity and to resist the Spartan military for a number of years. The most famous slave revolt in history broke out in Italy in the first century B.C. and was led by the slave-gladiator Spartacus. Under his leadership, a formidable slave army was assembled and succeeded in taking control of most of mainland Italy against the armies of Rome. In the end, the Romans triumphed, and to underline both their fury and the futility of resistance to their authority, they crucified six thousand of Spartacus's warriors along the Appian Way.

The defeat of popular rebellions against established authority has often included ferocious reprisals. When royal forces regained control from Wat Tyler and his peasant followers in England in 1381, despite promises of clemency made by the king when he had been in the hands of the rebels, Tyler and his supporters were butchered. Similarly, when the forces of the French government crushed the revolutionary Paris Commune in 1871, tens of thousands of people were put to death in summary executions; the scale of bloodletting dwarfed the number executed during the much better-known Reign of Terror during the French Revolution in the 1790s. There is a corner of Père-Lachaise Cemetery in Paris where hundreds of Communards were stood up against the wall and massacred. The pock-marks where the bullets hit the stone wall can still be clearly seen today.

During the first weeks of the First World War in August 1914, as German armies swept across Belgium and northern France, there was occasional popular resistance to the invaders, in the form of so-called *francs-tireurs*, who shot at German troops with their hunting rifles. The German response to such incidents was to round up the men from nearby villages and execute them. Three decades later, the Nazi armies that occupied Poland, Yugoslavia, and the western regions of the Soviet Union responded to partisan resistance with huge reprisals, the general formula being the execution of fifty civilians for every one of their men killed. In some cases, in Belgium, Czechoslovakia, and the Soviet Union, whole villages—men, women, and children—were wiped out in response to a partisan attack on the Germans.

During the two and a half centuries when slavery existed in the Thirteen Colonies and the United States, slave revolts, although often neglected in standard histories of the United States, were much more common than popularly thought. What was probably the largest slave revolt in American history occurred near New Orleans in 1811. Between four and five hundred slaves assembled after a struggle at a plantation. Armed with primitive weapons, they marched from plantation to plantation gathering recruits. When they were met by U.S. army and militia units, sixty-six of the rebels were killed at once. Sixteen more were tried and executed. In 1822, an audacious conspiracy led by Denmark Vesey, a free black, planned the burning of Charleston, South Carolina, to be followed by a general slave uprising throughout the region. The conspiracy was thwarted and thirty-five blacks, including Vesey, were executed.

Campaigns to achieve independence for nations within the British Empire often involved armed struggle and vicious repression. The first of those struggles, and the one that involved the lengthiest and most bitter war, was, of course, the American Revolution. In the Thirteen Colonies, war broke out in 1775, a year before the Declaration of Independence, and continued until 1783, when the Treaty of Paris was signed to recognize the sovereignty of the United States of America. Later campaigns for self-government did not result in lengthy wars, but they did feature armed rebellions. In British North America, armed rebellions were launched by Reformers in English-speaking Upper Canada and by Patriotes in French-speaking Lower Canada in 1837–38. In both cases, the British army was able to defeat the rebels, but not without considerable loss of life in Lower Canada. In the aftermath of the struggle, some rebels were hanged and others were exiled to Australia.

One successful slave revolt against a major European empire involved the struggle of Haitians to free themselves from French rule. Ninety percent of the people of Haiti, formerly called Saint-Domingue, were black slaves who worked on the sugar cane plantations of the island, which made it France's most profitable colony during the eighteenth century. The slave rebellion began in August 1791 and continued until Haiti won independence in 1804. The most prominent leader to emerge from the struggle was Toussaint L'Ouverture, a former slave, who organized and led armies that defeated Spanish and British forces. In 1801, Napoleon Bonaparte sent a French army numbering thousands of men to suppress the Haitian revolution. Toussaint was tricked by the French, captured, and sent to France, where he died in prison in 1803. Jean-Jacques Dessalines, also a former slave and one of Toussaint's generals, assembled his forces and defeated the French army. On January 1, 1804, he proclaimed Haiti an independent country, the first black republic in the world.

Another uprising that has become a symbol of tragic resistance against a genocidal, if short-lived, empire was the armed struggle of the Jewish inhabitants of the Warsaw ghetto against the Nazis in April and May 1943. The uprising broke out when reports of the mass killings of

Jews who had been sent from Warsaw to Treblinka were received by those who remained in the ghetto. When the Nazis dispatched soldiers and police into the ghetto, 750 Jewish fighters opened fire on the Germans. In the one-sided struggle, the resisters held out for more than a month. In the end, when the Germans crushed the resistance, thousands of the survivors were shot, and the rest were sent to the death camps.

For the rest of this chapter, we will focus in greater detail on two historic struggles against imperial rule: one in Ireland and the other in India.

The Irish Quest for Freedom

One of the longest and most bitter struggles for independence was that waged by the people of Ireland against the British Empire. Before large numbers of emigrants set out from Britain to create a new world on the other side of the Atlantic, emigrants from Britain backed by the power of English armies colonized the island on the other side of the Irish Sea. The English conquest of Ireland began with Henry VIII's claim that he was the king of Ireland in 1541. The next century would see the small English presence around Dublin expand until the English exercised complete control of the island.

Irish resistance to British rule waxed and waned over a period of centuries. In 1800, the Act of Union made Ireland a part of the United Kingdom, which meant that from then on the Irish would elect members to the Parliament at Westminster. The Act of Union established the political setting within which the Irish struggle against the empire played itself out. The struggle involved a parliamentary element, as well as a bloody uprising that was put down with characteristic imperial viciousness.

In the early nineteenth century, Irish representation in the British House of Commons was dominated by the Anglo-Irish gentry under the extremely narrow franchise that applied throughout the United Kingdom. The franchise was gradually widened so that by the late nineteenth century it included the whole adult male population. The Irish National Party came to dominate Ireland's parliamentary caucus at Westminster and evolved a program and a strategy that brought Irish issues to the fore of British politics. The program was called Home Rule, a demand for status for Ireland roughly equivalent to that of the self-governing dominions in the empire such as Canada. And the strategy, which only became effective in the 1880s, was to seize an opportunity when either the Liberals or Conservatives, the two major parties, needed the support of the Irish nationalists to form a majority government. The nationalists hoped to compel one of the two major parties to adopt their program.

Long before the Irish nationalists became a potent political force in British politics, the lamentable condition of Ireland was there for all to see, at least for those who cared to look. In reality, if not in theory, Ireland was a British colony, ruled by Anglo-Irish landowners and populated by people who lived, for the most part, in abject poverty. The tragic condition of the population reached horrific proportions in the years following 1849, when a potato famine resulted in mass starvation in Ireland, a starvation so devastating that whole villages simply died and vanished. The famine struck Ireland at a time when the ideology of free trade and the free market were close to being dogma in the British establishment. Even though Britain could have intervened to save hundreds of thousands of people from starvation, very little was done on behalf of the Irish—not least because the ideology of the time did not suit such intervention. A million people died from starvation in the mid-nineteenth century and at least another million emigrated, principally to the United States and Canada. As a consequence, the population of Ireland was reduced by half.

What made the Irish situation especially complex in the nineteenth and twentieth centuries was the strategic value of the island to the British and the presence in Ireland of a Protestant minority that was determined to keep the island in the British Empire. The prospect of Ireland being seized by a hostile foreign power was regarded by the British with the greatest foreboding. Prior to Nelson's victory over the combined French and Spanish fleets at Trafalgar in 1805, the British constantly feared that Napoleon would dispatch a fleet to conquer Ireland. From Ireland, the French would be in a position to shut down the British sea routes to the rest of the world, the source of Britain's commercial and material strength. As long as the British navy ruled the seas, the British were never prepared to let Ireland fall into hostile hands.

The Anglo-Irish presence in Ireland dated back to the seventeenth century, when a sizable population of mainly Scottish Protestants settled in northern Ireland. Whenever it appeared that self-determination was likely to be achieved by Ireland, the Protestant minority made it abundantly clear that it would resort to force to avoid becoming a minority in a Catholic country.

It was William Ewart Gladstone, the giant of nineteenth-century British liberalism, who opened the door to the possible achievement of Irish Home Rule during his term as prime minister from 1880 to 1885. Gladstone took up the cause of Home Rule for a variety of reasons. He hoped that resolving the thorny question would open the way for his government to move on to other issues, and he feared that the Conservatives would gain seats in the upcoming election and that he would do well to have the Irish nationalists in his corner. He likely saw in Home Rule a generous gesture to a people that would revive the reforming spirit of the British Liberal Party at a time when rising social class antagonisms were threatening to bring a new left-wing, working-class agenda into British politics.[1]

Gladstone's initiative plunged his party into a crisis from which it would not fully recover for twenty years. Within the Liberal Party were forces led by Joseph Chamberlain, the radical, pro-imperialist demagogue who saw the devolution of even modest powers of self-government to Ireland as a grave threat to the very survival of the British Empire. As a consequence of divisions within the Liberal Party, among other things, Home Rule remained unrealized when the First World War broke out in 1914.

After this parliamentary struggle, events in Ireland took a violent turn that would change the course of history. On Easter Sunday 1916, a band of about one thousand Irish patriots led by the poet Patrick Pearse launched an armed revolt in Dublin. Among their number was the socialist labor leader James Connolly, famous for his militant efforts on behalf of working people in Ireland and on the British mainland. The republicans seized the Dublin post office and other sites in the center of the capital. Following in the footsteps of patriot leaders in other countries who had declared independence from empire for their peoples, Pearse proclaimed the birth of an Irish republic: "Irishmen and Irishwomen: in the name of God and of the dead generations from which she receives her old tradition of nationhood, Ireland, through us, summons her children to her flag, and strikes for her freedom. . . . We hereby proclaim the Irish Republic as a

Sovereign Independent State, and we pledge our lives and the lives of our comrades-at-arms to the cause of its freedom, its welfare, and of its exaltation among the nations."[2]

Though the uprising came as a shock to the British, who were fighting a world war against Germany, they responded by rushing troops across the Irish Sea from England. For three days the fighting continued. The British shelled rebel positions with artillery fire that had the effect of demolishing a portion of central Dublin. Forced to withdraw from the post office, Pearse decided he had no option but surrender. When the firing stopped, 64 Irish rebels and 130 British soldiers were dead. With the exception of a few limited actions elsewhere in the country, the popular rising of the Irish people on which the rebels had counted did not materialize.

Defeated, the rebels felt the full wrath of the British. Between May 3 and 10, following swift courts-martial, fifteen of the rebels were shot, executed in groups of two or three. Wounded during the uprising, James Connolly was court-martialed in his bed and was borne, tied to a chair, to his place of execution. Pearse and his brother Willie were also shot. At his court-martial, Pearse defiantly predicted that the cause of Irish independence would endure: "We seem to have lost. We have not lost. . . . You cannot conquer Ireland, you cannot extinguish the Irish passion for freedom. If our deed has not been sufficient to win freedom, then our children will win it with a better deed."[3]

More potent in death than during their rebellion, the martyrs of the Easter uprising became symbols of the viciousness of British rule. While the majority of Irish Catholics had not rallied to Pearse's call to arms, they were sickened by the vengeful response of the British. Although relatively few had died in the armed struggle in Dublin in comparison with other campaigns for national independence, the British position in Ireland never recovered.

As a consequence of the First World War and the Easter Rebellion of 1916, the ground on which the Irish struggle was based shifted fundamentally. Before 1914, Home Rule was the goal of most Irish nationalists. After the rebellion, Home Rule was a concept whose time had passed. Republicanism, a sharp break with the British Empire, was the ground on which the nationalists would henceforth position themselves. The transition did not occur suddenly, but the Irish National Party, the traditional vehicle of Home Rule, began to lose ground to Sinn Fein (Ourselves Alone), the party of the hard-liners who wanted outright separation from the empire. What made the situation of the National Party leadership especially difficult was that it was committed to trying to work out a deal with the Irish unionists (those who wanted to stay with the United Kingdom) that would allow all of Ireland to proceed to Home Rule. It was hoped that Ireland could thus avoid the looming partition between the Catholic south and Protestant Ulster. In the end, negotiations between the nationalists and the unionists came to naught, and it appeared that the likely outcome would be the partition of Ireland. This doomed the more moderate program of Home Rule in favor of the advocates of a sharper break.[4]

Following the failed attempt to negotiate a deal between nationalists and unionists that could have salvaged Home Rule, Sinn Fein surged ahead as the predominant voice of Irish freedom. With the British overwhelmingly focused on defeating the Germans on the French front, the British administration of Ireland, headquartered at Dublin Castle, began to lose its ability to govern the country. The seismic shift in Irish sentiment was revealed in the results of the British general election of December 1918. In Ireland, Sinn Fein won seventy-six seats (forty-seven of those elected were in jail), and the Unionists took twenty-six seats, while only six Home Rule advocates were elected.[5] A month after the election, the Sinn Fein MPs assembled in Dublin and proclaimed the establishment of the Republic of Ireland, with Éamon de Valera as its president. Acting through the Dáil Éireann (the Irish parliament, newly created by Sinn Fein), the government set about the task of creating an administration of its own, to challenge the authority of the British administration. The Dáil passed a resolution outlawing the Royal Irish Constabulary (the British-run police force) and called on the British to withdraw their troops from Ireland at once.

With two rival regimes in the country, the government of British prime minister David Lloyd George regarded the Irish situation as similar to that in the United States at the time of the secession of the southern states in 1861. During the "time of troubles" that continued for two years, the militants of the Irish Republican Army (IRA), dressed in civilian clothing, waged a guerilla war against the Royal Irish Constabulary and the British army, carrying out murderous assaults on them and then blending back into the Irish population at large. On a number of occasions, they carried out well-coordinated attacks on police stations and other British installations. In retaliation, the British struck back, not only at the IRA men, when they could get their hands on them, but on the local population, whose members they believed sheltered the guerilla fighters.

As the ugly war raged, the British government came up with a formula for achieving peace with the passage of a bill in Parliament in the spring of 1920. The Irish Home Rule bill was to partition Ireland into two states: the twenty-six counties in the south and the six counties in the north. There would be parliaments in Dublin and Belfast, but foreign and defense policies would remain firmly in the hands of the British.

Sinn Fein rejected the British plan and the war continued with de Valera touring the United States, where he was feted as a hero by Irish Americans. In the United States, he raised funds to sustain the Irish cause, and behind the scenes, he acquired funds to purchase armaments for the IRA fighters. On their side, the British recruited a brutish army, mostly composed of ex-servicemen, in places such as London, Glasgow, and Birmingham. These infamous members of the Black and Tans, as they were dubbed, replaced the regular police in parts of the country. They were notorious for their brutal attacks on civilian noncombatants and were seen by the Irish people as an army of occupation.

Tit-for-tat massacres reached a deadly climax on November 21, 1920, when IRA men gunned down twelve British military officers, claiming that they were intelligence agents. The same afternoon, members of the Royal Irish Constabulary Auxiliary opened fire on spectators at a Dublin football match, insisting they were returning the fire of IRA gunmen. Twelve were shot dead or crushed to death by the fleeing spectators.

In October 1921, the British government opened peace talks with Sinn Fein, and the two sides reached an agreement in early December. Under the terms of the Anglo-Irish Treaty, the twenty-six counties of the south became a dominion in the British Empire, the Irish Free State. The treaty also stipulated that the six counties of the north, in Protestant Ulster, were to be carved out of Ireland and were to remain in the United Kingdom. In addition, Ulster was to have its own local parliament.

Through the treaty, most of Catholic Ireland won self-government. But the treaty divided the nationalists into two bitterly opposed camps. The pragmatists, who were led by de Valera, reasoned that they had won as much as they could get from the British and that they would have to accept a deal that kept them in the British Empire, for a time at least. They also concluded that they did not have the strength to block the partition of Ireland, which would have pitted them against the British army and the militant fighters of the Ulster loyalists. In the Irish Dáil, de Valera's side carried the day in favor of the treaty by a margin of only seven votes. The hard-liners refused to live with the result. For them, the partition of Ireland was seen as the betrayal of a sacred cause. A new armed conflict erupted between the pragmatists and these hard-liners. De Valera and the pragmatists prevailed, but not before the fighting crossed the border into Ulster, which led in turn to violent reprisals against the Catholic minority in Ulster.

In 1949, Ireland seceded from the Commonwealth. Citizens of the Irish Republic retained the right to migrate freely to the UK. The tragic Irish struggles did not end with the establishment of an independent Irish state, however. In the north, armed conflict erupted in the 1970s. On one side were the Catholic nationalists, who fought to end what they saw as the unequal treatment of the Catholic minority in Ulster and to finish the job of creating a united and independent Ireland that would be governed from Dublin. On the other side were the Ulster Protestant loyalists, who were determined to keep the north in the United Kingdom and to sustain Protestant supremacy in their corner of Ireland. While the armed conflict has come to an end in the north, with the Catholic and Protestant militias disarming, the struggle to shape the future of Ulster is far from finished.

The Irish had won their freedom, but the legacy of empire was not so easily relegated to the past. As in other parts of the world, the consequences of British rule had included the establishment of a settler faction, the Protestants in Ulster, who would fight bitterly in opposition to the efforts of nationalists to achieve independence for their homeland. Today the context in which the Irish struggle continues is dramatically different from the situation in the 1920s. The British Empire is no more, and both the Irish Republic and the United Kingdom are members of a new federation, the European Union (EU). Ireland has thrived economically in the EU, and there is hope that ways can be found for Ireland's multiple identities to be preserved in a democratic setting that at last can transcend the desperate battles of the past.

India: The Struggle Against the Raj

The struggle of the people of India for independence from the British Empire eerily echoed the campaigns of the Irish for their freedom. While Ireland was Britain's first colony, India was the jewel of its empire. Following the British suppression of the great Indian rebellion of 1857, the struggle for Indian freedom took a different course. In the end, it was the building of one of history's most remarkable mass movements that led the people of India to their goal. As was the case with the British response to the Easter Rebellion in Ireland in 1916, a British massacre in India was seminal in hardening a people's determination to achieve national independence. The massacre occurred at Amritsar, the holy city of the Sikhs in the Punjab on April 3, 1919. Under orders from Brigadier-General R.E.H. Dyer, Indian army troops fired on a crowd of about twenty thousand demonstrators who were peacefully protesting for wider political rights. The demonstrators were effectively trapped within a walled area whose gates had been locked on British orders. The firing continued for twenty minutes until at last Dyer called a halt to it. Nearly four hundred Indians had been killed and more than a thousand wounded.[6]

Throughout India and in many parts of the British Empire, the public reacted with horror to the massacre and the public floggings and other punishments imposed by the British in its aftermath. An imperial Commission of Inquiry, while reprimanding Dyer for not warning the demonstrators at Amritsar to disperse and for not providing medical aid to the wounded, ended by taking no legal action against the commander. Dyer, although forced to take early retirement on half pay, retained his army pension.

To some British observers, however, Dyer was a hero, standing up for law and order at Amritsar. The novelist Maud Diver spoke for many of her fellow countrymen, both at home and in India, when she wrote: "Organized revolt is amenable only to the ultimate argument of force. Nothing, now, would serve but strong action and the compelling power of martial law. . . . At Amritsar strong action had already been taken. . . . The sobering effect of it spread in widening circles, bringing relief to thousands of both races."[7]

By the time of the atrocity at Amritsar, Mahatma Gandhi had already become one of the chief leaders of the Indian nationalist movement. The peaceful demonstration at Amritsar had been part of a nationwide movement led by Gandhi to oppose the Rowlatt Acts. Indian nationalists regarded the Acts as a betrayal because they continued the practice of heavy-handed British centralized control of India, in disregard of the declaration of the British Secretary of State for India, Edwin Montagu, that the British government favored "the progressive realization of responsible government in India as an integral part of the British Empire."[8]

Gandhi's response to the massacre was to state that further cooperation with this "satanic regime" was impossible.[9] Gandhi had been educated in England and called to the bar in London. He had learned his political skills in South Africa, where he spent two decades leading the struggle of the Indian population in that country against discrimination. By the time he returned to India in 1915, he had evolved a highly original strategy for the liberation of the subcontinent that differed from the approach taken by other English-educated Indian leaders.

It was the norm for nationalist leaders to wear Western dress and to present the case for responsible government in highly articulate English, their goal being to mobilize a small, educated Indian elite and to win the day by lobbying the British government and its representatives in India. The idea was to achieve victory by demonstrating that India had produced rational, effective political leaders into whose hands more and more authority could be entrusted.

Gandhi's approach was to mobilize a mass movement of a kind the world had never seen, a movement that would confront the well-armed British with peaceful but determined, nonviolent resistance. His chosen method of struggle was *satyagraha*, which he translated as meaning "soul force" or "love force." This described a state of being that could be attained by a man or a woman that would enable the person to develop the inner strength, faith, and determination to resist an unjust regime through nonviolent means.[10]

An adherent of this discipline would have to be capable of persevering in the face of physical repression, imprisonment, and the threat of death. It was a tactic ideally suited to challenging the British Empire at its most sensitive and potentially vulnerable point, its haughty claim to legitimacy. British imperial rule was justified to the British people and to those they governed as being just, principled, and grounded in a superior culture. The peoples of India, according to this view, were better off as a consequence of British rule, even if not all of them perceived this at all times. Gandhi's approach pierced this shield of self-righteousness.

His calculation was that the British—who had successfully played on the sectarian, caste, and regional divisions within India and who could easily meet force with superior force—could not cope with nonviolent protest. Gandhi recognized that Britain's rule of India's vast population with such a small force of Britons could only continue through the willing collaboration of Indians in every field of life, from the military to the government bureaucracy to the operation of the economy. Take that cooperation away and the seemingly impervious system of the British Raj would come tumbling down.

By 1906, Gandhi had abandoned Western dress, renouncing materialism and most physical pleasures in favor of a life of simplicity in all things. Soon the British found themselves face to face with a charismatic leader who had unleashed a spiritual and political force of a kind they found very difficult to counter. In 1935, Winston Churchill expressed the position of Tory imperial stalwarts who were determined to hang onto India at any cost and who saw Gandhi as an unscrupulous character, describing him as "a seditious Middle Temple lawyer, now posing as a fakir of a type well-known in the East, striding half-naked up the steps of the Viceregal Palace . . . there to negotiate and to parley on equal terms with the Representative of the King-Emperor."[11]

Gandhi differed from other Indian nationalist leaders in that he rejected the notion that Western education, science, and technology were superior to the ways of his own people. If India were to advance, he argued, it needed to establish cottage industries at the local level, in a way designed to undermine the India-wide and empire-wide economic operations that were at the heart of the British system. His tactics were not unlike those of the American patriots prior to the War of Independence who had organized campaigns against British imports and in favor of home-developed craft industries to meet the needs of the colonists.

In March 1930, Gandhi launched his most famous campaign against British rule, the protest against the hated salt tax. (The British administration forced Indians to import salt, on which they were required to pay a tax.) Gandhi's Dandi Salt March ended with thousands of Indians walking to the sea and breaking the law simply by picking up the salt that was there for the taking.

Indian nationalism amounted to much more than Gandhi's campaigns, crucial as they were. The Congress movement and later the Congress Party were the great political creations of the Indian movement for self-government. Jawaharlal Nehru, like Gandhi, educated in England, emerged as the paramount leader of this movement, which had its roots in the half-million villages of India.[12]

In the face of Indian nationalism, the strategy of the British government was one of slow retreat. Reforms to the system of British rule were made during the decades between the two world wars. Indians were brought in greater numbers into the top echelons of the administration, although the most sensitive jobs, those concerned with justice, police, and finance, remained in the hands of appointees from Britain. In 1935, the British government attempted some reforms with the Government of India Act, which introduced major elements of responsible government into Indian provinces but kept the central administration largely under the control of the British. The Congress Party was the major winner in the provincial elections that followed.

The reform of the mid-1930s ended by satisfying no one: not the nationalists, who were determined to achieve full self-government, and not the imperialist diehards, who believed that the British Empire was now on the verge of disintegration.

In the end, none of the parties involved in the struggle were to get everything they wanted. The Second World War intervened before India achieved independence, a war in which the subcontinent once again contributed mightily to the imperial war effort, this time in a war in which India itself was threatened with Japanese invasion. On August 15, 1947, not one but two new dominions, India and Pakistan, were established.

In a radio broadcast to the people of his country, Jawaharlal Nehru, India's first prime minister, declared that "a moment comes, which comes but rarely in history, when we step out from the old to the new, when an age ends, and when the soul of a nation long suppressed finds utterance."[13]

As in the case of Ireland, however, a wound had been slashed across liberation in the form of sectarianism and partition. During the early days of the political struggle for Indian self-government, most Muslims had supported the Congress Party, with only a minority backing the Muslim League. As time passed, however, many Muslims grew to believe that the goal of the Congress Party was to establish a Hindu Raj to replace the British Raj. From 1942 to 1947, sectarian violence tore the social fabric of the subcontinent apart.

As it became clear that Britain was indeed going to transfer full governmental authority to the people of India, the crucial question on the agenda was whether there would be one state or two. In the elections of 1945 the Congress Party hoped to win enough Muslim support to block the move toward the creation of a separate Muslim state, while the Muslim League wanted to create a separate entity called Pakistan. In the elections to India's central assembly, in which a portion of the seats were set aside for Muslim voters, the Muslim League polled a striking 86.6 percent of the vote. In the races for control of provincial governments, the Congress Party gained control in eight of the eleven provinces, with the Muslim League able to govern in only two, and the Congress Party coming to power in a coalition government in the Punjab. Even in the provinces with Muslim populations, the Muslim League polled less than half the votes.[14]

Despite the mixed results in the voting, there was a clear standoff between the Congress Party and the Muslim League, which continued to push for a separate Pakistan. While Britain's Labour government, under the leadership of Clement Attlee, continued to dither about how to complete the final transfer of power to the people of the subcontinent, violence in India played a huge role in setting the agenda. With partition in the offing, millions of Muslims and Hindus moved: Muslims to the territory that would become Pakistan and Hindus into areas that would stay a part of India. During the vast upheaval, between 250,000 and 600,000 refugees died, the victims of sectarian violence.[15]

What pushed the British government toward a final settlement was a series of mutinies among military personnel in India in 1946. The first, and most surprising, of the outbursts was a mutiny among British servicemen in the Royal Air Force, who were unhappy about the slow pace of repatriation to England and postwar demobilization. Later, personnel in the Indian air force and navy carried out their own mutinies in Bombay, Calcutta, Madras, and Karachi. The British government sent a mission to India to work out the details of the transfer of power. While the members of the mission considered schemes to avoid the partition of the subcontinent into two states, the strong stand taken by the Muslim League decided the issue.

There were to be two states: a vast Indian state, with a majority Hindu population and a considerable Muslim minority, and a smaller Pakistan, overwhelmingly Muslim. Pakistan was cut into two, with West and East Pakistan separated from each other by 1,600 kilometers of Indian territory. (In the early 1970s, East Pakistan achieved independence and became Bangladesh.)

In January 1948, Gandhi was shot dead, the victim of a plot by Hindu extremists who were bitterly opposed to his rejection of violence and his campaign to overcome sectarian hatred.

As was the case for Ireland, the legacy of the past still creates grave problems for the subcontinent. India and Pakistan confront each other warily, especially in Kashmir, a territory claimed by both sides. In Kashmir, Indian and Pakistani forces face each other along a de facto frontier that has often been a flashpoint for fighting. Adding to the problem in our time is the fact that both India and Pakistan have become nuclear powers. While tensions have eased somewhat between the two states, the risk of a nuclear showdown between these two heirs to the British Raj makes this one of the world's greatest danger spots.

IN OUR OWN ERA, resistance to imperial rule is a formidable challenge to the American Empire's notion of itself as a force for good. The invasions of Afghanistan and Iraq in 2001 and 2003, respectively, were undertaken by the United States and its allies—Afghanistan became a NATO mission, while Iraq was a mission of the so-called coalition of the willing—on the premise that short, sharp fights would be followed by successful regime changes in both countries. The U.S. military had been redesigned precisely to make use of its overwhelming firepower and logistical superiority to overcome any foe with a deployment of relatively small forces. The invasions, in both cases, worked well enough, with the armies of the

Taliban and Saddam Hussein rapidly defeated. What the Americans did not foresee was the extent to which Afghans and Iraqis, of various sects and persuasions, would act in concert to oust the invaders. The Bush administration made the case that the insurgencies that broke out in both countries in the aftermath of the invasions were largely the work of outsiders and Islamic fundamentalists working under the broad direction of Al Qaeda. What the administration did not want to acknowledge was that the cement that held the insurgencies together was Afghan and Iraqi nationalism, the desire of very important elements in both countries not to have their futures determined by outside invaders. It was empire itself that was the problem and the source of the resistance.

In addition to resistance to the American-led occupation of Iraq, a worldwide movement has grown up in opposition to war and to foreign occupations. The American invasion of Iraq in March 2003 was preceded a month earlier by the most massive global anti-war demonstration in history. Approximately ten million people in many countries, with enormous focal points in Rome and London, took to the streets to protest the preparations to invade Iraq. While the invasion was not deterred, the outpouring of determined opposition to this imperial adventure became a fact of global politics to which leaders had to pay attention. In the twenty-first century, outfitted with the latest communications technology, anti-imperialism is more organized, informed, and international in its scope than ever before. The unpopularity of the war went far beyond the millions who demonstrated. Only in the United States and Israel was the war truly popular in its early days. By the time of the third anniversary of the invasion, U.S. public opinion had turned sharply pessimistic about the outcome of the war, with a majority of Americans believing that Iraq was sinking into civil war. Only 44 percent of Americans polled believed that George W. Bush was doing a good job on the issues of terrorism and the war. In earlier days, massive majorities had stood by him on these questions. And only 36 percent of those polled said they thought the president was doing a good overall job. In an editorial, the *New York Times* warned that the "one lesson of U.S. war in Iraq is this: even a superpower cannot do certain things without overstretching itself."[16] It is quite possible that the writers of the editorial had in mind not only the overstretch of manpower, materiel, and money, but also the overstretch of going it alone in the face of hostile global opinion.

Observers who lived in earlier empires, notably the Spanish Empire, declared ruefully that as a consequence of their domination of other peoples, they were strongly disliked by people in other societies. Resentment is the inexorable outcome of societal structures that are based on inequality, on the rule by one people over others. For the Americans, the growth of anti-Americanism comes often as both a shock and a puzzle. How could so many parts of the world turn against a country that had been for so long the hope and refuge of humankind? Millions had come to America's shores to escape poverty and misrule and to make better lives for themselves. If white and Asian immigrants did better than black and Hispanic immigrants, the United States was nonetheless the road to opportunity for immense numbers.

At the end of the First World War, Europeans welcomed U.S. president Woodrow Wilson to the continent, hailing him as a man from another and better world who had come to save them from their terrible past. While disillusionment about the Treaty of Versailles soon set in, America did not lose its reputation among Europeans as a blessed land of freedom. Again, during the Second World War, Americans were perceived as liberators by Europeans and Asians. In the last days of the war, German soldiers strove to surrender to the Americans rather than the Russians. And German refugees exerted themselves to end up on the American side of the line in divided Germany.

With this enormous historical background of goodwill, reinforced by American mass media, cultural industries, and political leaders who constantly tell Americans that they live in the greatest country in the world, it is scarcely believable that so many people now have a negative view of the United States. And yet, public opinion polls report that in almost every country in the world, the United States is now seen more negatively than in the past. The reputation of the United States as a good country, and as a place where ordinary people could make a good life, has persisted for a long time. That immense goodwill has been rapidly depleted. It will not be quickly replenished.

The Legitimacy of Empire
in the Twenty-First Century

The end of empire has been anticipated in the past, sometimes apprehensively and sometimes gladly. The fall of the Roman Empire prompted foreboding and predictions that civilization itself was finished. After 1945, the demise of the great European empires was welcomed as opening a new age of equality. Both times, those who forecast the end of empire were so caught up in the dramas of their day that they lost sight of the longer sweep of history.

The collapse of the great European empires was the consequence of a vast shift in the system of global power after 1945. The British, French, and other European empires had been the great examples of late nineteenth-century capitalist empires. The Cold War brought two new empires to the fore, those of the Soviet Union and the United States. With the sudden and largely unanticipated collapse of the Soviet Empire in Eastern Europe and of the Soviet Union itself after 1989, the United States was left as the world's only superpower. It has emerged as a new kind of imperial power, one whose scope is more genuinely global than that of any earlier empire.

The end of the Cold War, by removing the ideological and geopolitical struggles between Soviet and American power, revealed the American global system much more clearly for what it was. The United States could no longer depict itself as the leader of the world's capitalist democracies. America was running an empire, and it was soon equipped with ideologues who conceived a rationale to justify its legitimacy.

From the start of its career as the world's only global imperial power, the United States has faced a legitimacy problem that has grown more serious over time. When the Americans failed to dismantle their military bases around the world and cash in the so-called peace dividend that derived from the end of the Cold War, it became clear that the United States had no intention of ceasing to be an imperial power. The change in America's status from first-among-equals in the struggle for freedom to imperial power prompted a basic shift in the attitudes of people around the world to the United States.

This process was not the same in all places, of course. In Eastern Europe, America was never more popular than in the halcyon days of the new democracies that followed the collapse of the Soviet puppet states. In this "New Europe," American power was a force for the liberation of countries whose peoples detested the Soviet Union. In Latin America, where people had lived under the shadow of American domination and frequent military interventions dating back to the early days of the American Republic, the idea that the United States was an imperial power was nothing new. Latin Americans had always known about American imperialism and had resisted it in various ways for well over a century. In Western Europe, "Old Europe," there was a similar wariness about American power in the decades following the end of the Second World War. The assumption that American business techniques were best had long bred resentment, as had the idea that Western Europe should leave it up to Washington to decide how to relate to the Soviet bloc. The French had regularly chafed against these signs of American imperial arrogance, and by the 1970s, the more compliant West Germans had concluded that relations with the Soviet bloc, and East Germany in particular, were too important to relegate to Washington. In the late 1960s and early 1970s, the Vietnam War had featured America on the television screens of the world as a militarist power that massacred villagers and used its advanced weaponry to subdue a country that wanted its independence from Western rule. Vietnam made America vastly unpopular in many parts of the world and helped fuel the youth radicalism of the period.

By the time the Soviet Union expired in late 1991, however, the United States had recovered from the internal wounds of the Vietnam War and from the anti-American sentiments the war had generated in other parts of the world. In the early days of post–Cold War triumphalism, a great many people celebrated the victory of liberal capitalism over its totalitarian foes of the twentieth century, Nazism and Communism. With Francis Fukuyama's manifesto *The End of History and the Last Man*, American power and the social system on which it rested were portrayed as natural and sure to dominate the world for the indefinite future. During the years of Bill Clinton's presidency,

American technological prowess and the establishment of the so-called new economy appeared to ensure American economic supremacy and to relegate the once-potent economic competitors in Japan and Western Europe to the sidelines. In addition, the new economy was not merely enriching a whole new cohort of capitalists in the high-tech sector; it seemed to have transcended the bad old days of the economic cycle. Boom and bust were deemed old hat along with industrial cities like Detroit or Cleveland. And underlining all this was the rise of the American military to a level of global domination greater than that of any military in human history. Apparently, America did not much need military allies any longer, not least because other militaries, such as those of Western Europe, were just too backward to be able to work seamlessly with the Americans. The easy military victories of the first Gulf War in 1991 and in Kosovo in 1998, in a war in which the United States had prevailed through the use of air power alone and had not suffered a single casualty in combat, seemed to confirm U.S. invincibility.

The speed with which the durability and legitimacy of the American Empire have been cast into doubt since those days in the late 1990s has been remarkable indeed. The dot-com crash that devastated the new economy in the early months of 2000 was the harbinger of the troubles to come, a sign while Clinton was still in power and before the terror attacks of September 11, 2001, that all was not well for the American imperium. Although the dot-com crash took the sheen off Clinton's last year in office, many Americans are bound to look back on his years in the White House as an era when many were enriched and a great opportunity to achieve social reform was squandered. The easy years were at an end before George W. Bush was sworn in as president on January 20, 2001.

It is often claimed that the terror attacks of September 11 changed the world. What is more accurate is that three major decisions taken by the Bush administration plunged the American Empire into crisis. The first decision, which pre-dated September 11, was an enormous tax cut that mainly benefited the affluent and the super-rich. The second and third decisions, growing out of the terror attacks, were the invasions of Afghanistan and Iraq, both of which caused a huge increase in American military spending. The policies of the Bush administration embroiled the United States in an interlocking, dual crisis that was geopolitical and economic in scope. The geopolitical crisis turned on whether the United States could continue to maintain its supremacy in the neighborhood of the Persian Gulf. The invasion of Iraq was a highly risky attempt to tighten the American grip on the petroleum-rich lands around the Gulf. If successful, the Bush administration would be rewarded with solid strategic gains, and, along the way, with the enrichment of key corporate backers of the Bush White House.

In a sanitized Iraq, remade in the socioeconomic image of the United States, Americans would establish permanent military bases and push rival contenders for Iraqi oil such as France and Russia aside in favor of Anglo-American oil interests. From Iraq, the Americans could keep a wary eye on Saudi Arabia, the country with the greatest oil reserves in the region and a country in which jihadist Islamic ideology had gained a strong enough position to pose a constant threat to the Saudi regime. Not unimportant in the scheme of things were the profits reaped by corporations such as Halliburton, with which Bush loyalists, most notably Vice-President Dick Cheney, had intimate ties.

The defeat of Saddam Hussein's armed forces came quickly, with Baghdad falling into American hands following a lightning drive of the U.S. military northwards from Kuwait. George W. Bush danced his jig of victory on the deck of a U.S. aircraft carrier. Then the real fighting began. Month after month, the insurgency against the occupation gained strength in Iraq. As the Kurdish, Sunni, and Shiite political leaders, who were prepared to work with the Americans and their allies, frequently quarreled with each other, those who had chosen the road of armed resistance broadened their alliance and grew ever more effective.

The Bush administration, under the direction of Defense Secretary Donald Rumsfeld, completed the reconstruction of the U.S. military. The new American military was a volunteer force, equipped with dazzling technology, both in its armaments and logistics. It boasted that it could fight and win two major wars simultaneously in different parts of the world. What the morass in Iraq revealed, however, was that the volunteer force was too thin on the ground to prevail in a lengthy occupation; a large number of reserve units had to be called up. The stresses of mobilizing reservists who had never expected to serve in a shooting war and of keeping units in Iraq for long periods contributed to flagging morale within the army and sagging support for the war at home. In the early months of 2006, retired American generals and military critics were not only calling for Rumsfeld's resignation, they were demanding a rethink of American military doctrine. What had appeared to be the most solid of the pillars on which the American Empire stood—its military—had shown itself to be much weaker than anyone had thought.

Because empires rely on the impression that they are invulnerable, continued or successful armed resistance is enormously damaging to the empire far beyond the region immediately affected. One consequence of the Iraq shambles for the United States has been to embolden potential foes of the United States in the Middle East and elsewhere in the world. The Islamic Republic of Iran, for instance, much troubled with its own domestic concerns, learned the lesson from Iraq that the United States would have a much more difficult time invading Iran than anyone had previously calculated. The result was that the Tehran regime felt it could take substantial risks in pushing ahead its program of uranium enrichment. For the Bush administration, facing declining support at home and growing doubts about its ability to cope abroad, Iran's challenge meant that Washington would have to consider another risky military adventure—the bombing of Iran's nuclear facilities. Empires cannot allow themselves to look weak, and when they do they sometimes take risks that can make them look even weaker.

Absent the Iraq debacle, the Bush administration could have afforded to deal with the Iranian nuclear challenge by mobilizing the other major powers and by bringing various kinds of economic and political pressures to bear on Tehran. After Iraq, the issue became a naked test of American power. And the whole world, not least the American people, was watching.

The Iraq miscalculation prompted many governments in different regions of the world to take actions that could be regarded as "soft" rejections of American power. In Latin America, the consequence was to reinforce the tendency of the region's left-of-center governments to back away from supporting the American-initiated Free Trade Area of the Americas. In Western Europe, the tendency among political elites everywhere except in the UK (and to some extent France since the election of Nicolas Sarkozy as president of the republic in the spring of

2007) was to see American global policy as reckless and to seek ways to counterbalance the initiatives of the Bush administration. In Asia, the momentum of many countries drawing closer to China, for commercial reasons, was accelerated.

America's heightened military spending in the Middle East was directly related to the emergence of an economic crisis. A number of key economic indicators of American economic performance warned that a basic realignment in global economic relations could be in the offing. The American current account, perennially in deficit, was plumbing new lows. As the most basic indicator of the American commercial relationship with the rest of the world, the U.S. current account revealed that in terms of both trade in goods and capital flows, the United States was in a sharply negative position. In 2006, Americans were importing far more goods than they were exporting, to the tune of about $800 billion a year, with China replacing Japan as the country with the largest trade surplus with the United States. On the other side of the current account ledger, the United States is facing growing indebtedness to the rest of the world. Far from being the net creditor country it had been before 1986, the United States was now, by a long margin, the world's leading debtor nation, in debt to the tune of more than $2 trillion.

Its plunge into debt was a sign of its weakening position as the overseer of the global economic system. The other major area of malaise in the U.S. economic performance was the federal government deficit. In 2006, the deficit was running at about $250 billion a year, with American military spending at roughly double that level. Economic forecasts and the plans of the Bush administration made it clear that the United States was likely to run a sizable deficit over the medium-term future.

With the price of crude oil touching one hundred dollars a barrel in January 2008 and threatening to go higher, partly as a consequence of the American showdown with Iran, the U.S. dollar was in decline against other major currencies. Not only was the high price of petroleum threatening to push the world into recession, but the U.S. dollar's position as the global reserve currency was becoming ever more precarious. The Euro has been considered as a potential alternative reserve currency, and even though the economic performance of the leading Euro countries has been sluggish, the countries of the Euro zone have a rock-solid current account performance. For countries highly dependent on selling raw materials, particularly crude oil and natural gas, the temptation to denominate their sales in Euros rather than in depreciating dollars has been growing ever stronger. If the U.S. dollar were to lose its position as global reserve currency, either partially or generally, it would hit the American economy with price shocks in the broad area of primary products, most importantly petroleum. In addition, the freedom of the United States to run a continuous current account deficit would be sharply curtailed. This is because major central banks and corporations would be bound to shift their holdings to a considerable extent from dollars to Euros, a development that would accelerate the downward pressure on the American dollar and force a sharp hike in U.S. interest rates to prevent a flight of foreign capital from U.S. securities.

While other major countries would have a strong interest in managing such a transition from dollar to Euro as responsibly as possible, the risk of a severe crisis could not be ruled out. Not since the end of the First World War has the world seen a transition of the kind that could be in the offing. Moreover, the world economy is enormously more global in its functioning than it was eight or nine decades ago, with capital and currency transfers from market to market dwarfing those made in the days when the pound was floundering and the dollar was taking its place.

Both the geopolitical and economic aspects of the crisis of the American Empire are forcing major choices onto the American political agenda, and some of those choices are likely to be highly unpalatable. On the geopolitical side, the United States is faced with the need to decide its future policy in the Middle East. The strategy of the Bush administration—relying on Israel as America's most important ally in the region and pursuing the objective of regime change in Afghanistan and Iraq—has proved disastrous. Liberals and a growing number of conservatives are demanding a reassessment of American foreign policy, resulting in serious divisions on the American political right. While the discussion of the power of the Israeli lobby in American politics has so far been limited to a few academics and a few journals and newspapers, the fact that it has been occurring at all is a sign of change.

In March 2006, the *London Review of Books* published a lengthy article titled "The Israel Lobby" by John Mearsheimer and Stephen Walt, the former a professor of political science at the University of Chicago and the latter a professor of international affairs at the Kennedy School of Government at Harvard. The article, a shortened version of a study undertaken by the two academics, was published in England because a suitable venue could not be found for its publication in the United States. Mearsheimer and Walt made the case that the powerful Israeli lobby in the United States had succeeded over decades in steering American foreign policy in the Middle East toward an unswerving allegiance to Israel, to the detriment of the interests of the United States. The article concluded that the Israeli lobby's influence made it impossible for the United States to play a decisive role in resolving the Israeli–Palestinian conflict. The continuing conflict gave extremists a powerful recruiting tool and increased the danger of terrorism in both the United States and Europe. The influence of the lobby, the authors claimed, increased the influence of those in the United States who were pressing for military attacks on Iran and Syria to achieve regime change in those countries. American efforts to prevent other countries such as Iran from developing nuclear weapons, the authors argued, made the United States appear hypocritical given Washington's failure to oppose the existence of Israel's nuclear arsenal.

The article, which at first was almost completely ignored in the mainstream American media, drew widespread condemnation from critics, who suggested that the authors had reinforced age-old conspiracy theories about the power of the Jews in manipulating the media and in steering politics on behalf of their own agenda. What was surprising was not the criticism meted out to the two academics, but the fact that their work saw the light of day and was widely read. A taboo had been broken.

Along with reconsideration of the American relationship with Israel, the debacle in Iraq has already prompted calls for a different U.S. policy stance toward the Islamic world. The consequence of the Bush administration's policies had been to provoke an almost universal enmity among Muslims toward the United States, bringing to the brink of fruition the notion of a war of civilizations. "Realists" (the term is used to describe a self-designated group of thinkers and does not imply that they are more rational than others) such as Francis Fukuyama have called for the United States to back away from this precipice and to adopt a policy that renounces calls for regime change in Islamic countries, de-emphasizes the "war on terror" as the centerpiece of American foreign policy, and is more fine-tuned in seeking working relationships with Islamic countries. Realists were bound to demand a ramping down of the American crusade to spread democracy throughout the world, seen by them as a too-aggressive attempt to enhance American power that was making more enemies than friends for the United States.

Nearly four years after the invasion of the country by the "coalition of the willing," Iraq was sinking into civil war. The execution of Saddam Hussein on December 30, 2006, cast into clear relief the divisions within the country. In Shiite and Kurdish districts of Iraq, celebrants took to the streets, firing guns in the air and cheering the death of the former tyrant. In the Sunni heartland, where Saddam was buried, hundreds came out to mourn him, vowing revenge for the hanging of their leader. The American occupiers have been ineffectual, as sectarian violence drives Iraq toward balkanization.

Also in peril as a consequence of Iraq's descent into chaos is the global strategy that has been pursued by the neo-conservative school of American foreign policy. Not satisfied with the status quo, the neo-conservatives have set out to increase the global supremacy of the United States. During the halcyon days of the Bush administration in the aftermath of September 11, 2001, the use of military power was seen as the crucial way to transform societies whose regimes were hostile to Washington. War could be used as the means for creating democratic, liberal societies in countries such as Afghanistan and Iraq. Along with the drive to export an American-style version of liberty to other countries, the Bush administration proclaimed its determination to ensure that the United States remain the world's dominant military power, able to face down challenges from friendly and hostile regimes alike.

By the end of 2006, the Bush administration's policies were in tatters as witnessed by the failing wars in Iraq and Afghanistan, its relationships with many countries around the world, and the rising crisis caused by America's inability to finance its military operations and keep its fiscal house in order. In Iraq, the administration's political and military strategies were exposed as threadbare. Far from being received as liberators in the country, the American occupiers provoked not only a massive and growing resistance to their presence but a deep internecine conflict among the elements that made up Iraqi society. Sunnis and Shiites were at each other's throats and the city of Baghdad was reduced to a cauldron of warring neighborhoods, with local militias defending their own turf and the central authority unable to establish law and order. Thousands of people who had the means to do so were fleeing the city every week. The American planners of the invasion had utterly failed to predict the kind of calamity that would descend on the society as a consequence of their overthrow of Saddam Hussein's regime.

Contributing to the chaos in Iraq was the American military doctrine, espoused by the U.S. Department of Defense under Secretary Donald Rumsfeld, Vice-President Dick Cheney, and other neo-conservative stalwarts. Ignoring the advice and warnings of Pentagon generals that Iraq could only be pacified with a much larger American and allied occupation force, Rumsfeld had insisted that a force of about 140,000 American troops could get the job done.

For the first few months, things appeared to go well for the Americans in Iraq. By the end of 2003 and certainly by the end of 2004, however, the writing was on the wall for the Rumsfeld strategy. The American occupying force was too small. The generals were right and Rumsfeld was wrong. And it was not a mistake that could easily be corrected. The U.S. army had been reshaped according to the Rumsfeld doctrine. Changing it would require a long period of reorganization and vastly increased military expenditures. In the meantime, Iraq had passed the point of no return. A much larger occupying force, which might have been effective against the insurgency and the descent into sectarian violence two or three years earlier, could no longer do the job by the end of 2006.

With the tenets of the Bush administration in disarray, the door was open to the alternative doctrines of the realist school. James Baker, the patrician Republican from the first Bush administration, was interested in the global power of the United States and making the world safe for American enterprise. In the Baker-Hamilton report, establishing democracy in Iraq was discarded as a major objective. What these elders wanted was pacification in the Persian Gulf. James Baker was prepared to deal with the governments of Iran and Syria, not because he liked them, but because they exercised power in the region. Keep your friends close and your enemies closer, could be his motto.

The realists aspired to making deals where necessary. Their goal was to maintain a global, and in the Middle East a regional, order in which American geopolitical and business interests were paramount. To achieve their objectives, the realists were not inclined to make sacrifices on behalf of Israel, as the neo-conservatives were prepared to do.

The publication of the Baker-Hamilton report was one episode in the power struggle between the neo-conservatives and the realists. The Bush administration, while on the defensive, continued to have warlike ambitions in the Middle East and Central Asia. The neo-conservatives in Washington and the Israeli government have been keeping a wary eye on Iran as a potential threat in the region, a threat that could be countered by an aerial assault on the country. The pretext for such an assault would be the refusal of the Iranian government to give up plans to develop a nuclear program, allegedly for the purpose of generating nuclear power. The Bush administration and nuclear-armed Israel (the best estimate is that Israel possesses about two hundred nuclear missiles) claimed that Iran was determined to produce nuclear weapons.

For the neo-conservatives, who have seen their power draining away, the prospect of an air war against Iran's nuclear facilities and its military-industrial complex was a tempting one. Thwarted in Iraq and Afghanistan in lengthy ground wars, which have become highly unpopular with the American people, the prospect of an air war in which U.S. power could be displayed to maximum effect was seen by some as a way to propel the Americans to victory in the larger regional struggle.

On January 7, 2007, the *Sunday Times* of London reported that Israeli pilots were training to carry out a pinpoint attack on three Iranian targets believed to house nuclear facilities and uranium enrichment sites. The *Sunday Times* said that Israeli planes had flown to Gibraltar to practice for the three-thousand-kilometer return flight to Iran, possibly by way of Turkey. The story included speculation from unnamed Israeli military sources that to destroy facilities housed many meters underground, the Israelis could use low-yield nuclear weapons.

Meanwhile, in Washington, leading Democratic Senator John D. Rockefeller IV of West Virginia, Senate Majority Leader Harry Reid of

Nevada, and Joseph Biden of Delaware warned Americans that the Bush administration was preparing public opinion for an attack on Iran at a time when the United States did not possess the military resources for such an attack and had neither the support of its allies nor the backing of Congress.

In the aftermath of the November 2006 Congressional elections and the report of the Iraq Study Group, the Bush administration decided on a short-term strategy of sending more troops to Iraq. In an address to the American people on January 10, 2007, Bush held out the hope that "victory will bring something new in the Arab world—a functioning democracy that polices its territory, upholds the rule of law, respects fundamental human liberties, and answers to its people." The real emphasis in the speech was not on remaking the Middle East, but on bloodying the noses of the insurgents and strengthening the Iraqi government so that the United States could hand over the security job to the Iraqis.

The new Bush strategy fell between two stools. To neo-conservatives, those who remained committed to achieving victory in Iraq, the additional troops were not enough. They wanted fifty thousand or more reinforcements to crush the insurgency. And they wanted a commitment that the troops would stay until victory was achieved. At the other end of the political spectrum were those who wanted a firm commitment that American troops would begin coming home soon. Americans had been migrating toward this position on the war for some time. Most Americans were no longer in a mood to be aroused by stirring words about liberating the Iraqis. They wanted out of this conflict as soon as possible. Not enough of a reinforcement to please the neo-cons and not a clear enough commitment to pull out of Iraq to please the majority of Americans— that was the awkward position in which the president now found himself.

What was happening was very similar to the American situation in Vietnam in the last two years before the North Vietnamese and the National Liberation Front seized Saigon in 1975. When Richard Nixon was elected president in 1968, his mandate was ambiguous—he pledged to get Americans out of a war they had come to detest, while still promising to win it. In office, Nixon tried to achieve victory by broadening the conflict into Cambodia and Laos. All this was for naught. The Nixon White House came to the view—with an important input from the great realist of the day, Henry Kissinger—that the United States had to make a deal with North Vietnam to allow it to withdraw from the war, and further that it had to make an opening to China to further divide the Communist superpowers, the Soviet Union and China, against each other. On the road to the deal with North Vietnam, which was achieved in 1973, Washington's emphasis was to bring about the "Vietnamization" of the war: U.S. units would progressively withdraw from their fighting role and South Vietnamese units, with training from the Americans, would take their place. Following elections in South Vietnam, the question was whether the regime there could stand without being powerfully supported by tens of thousands of U.S. soldiers.

In the end, of course, South Vietnam collapsed, and the American presence in the country came to an end. The American defeat in the war did not, however, lead to a collapse of the U.S. position in Asia as many had forecast. The dominoes, as the countries in the region had been called, did not follow Vietnam into the Communist camp. Instead, something quite unforeseen transpired. The Nixon administration made its historic opening to China with the president's visit to Beijing. Having insisted in the past that the Communist world was a single juggernaut that must be resisted, a Republican administration faced reality and took advantage of the chasm of mistrust that had grown up between Beijing and Moscow. The new strategy was to balance off the two Communist giants by drawing closer to each one in different ways.

The new approach bore fruit for the Americans. It played an important part in increasing the pressure on the Soviet Union and its empire that eventually caused its demise a decade and a half later. Moreover, these overtures with China played a key role in opening up the world's largest country to capitalism and the West. Over the longer term, the Americans were helping create their next imperial challenger, but that is another story.

George W. Bush, who never wanted the Iraq mission to be compared to Vietnam, was faithfully following in the footsteps of Richard Nixon, who escalated the war in Southeast Asia to prepare the conditions for U.S. withdrawal. Bush was doing the same thing in Iraq. Bush's decision to send more troops to Iraq should not be interpreted as determination on the part of Washington to fight through to final victory. Indeed, Bush hinted at that in his speech when he said that "victory will not look like the ones our fathers and grandfathers achieved. There will be no surrender ceremony on the deck of a battleship." In the pithy language of stock-market analysts, Bush's new strategy may turn out to be a "dead cat bounce." (This refers to a brief market rally that occurs after the market crashes, to be followed by a further decline.) What was clear by the beginning of 2007 was that the United States was no longer committed to winning the fight in Iraq. What was at issue now was the withdrawal strategy.

Bush's policy of sending reinforcements to Iraq was a rejection of the recommendations of the Iraq Study Group. It also flew in the face of the message American voters sent when they handed both houses of Congress to the Democrats in the elections in November 2006. The Bush White House, however, had lost much of its freedom to set U.S. policy. As the Americans prepare to leave, Iraq could disintegrate into its constituent parts. If that were to occur, the paramount American and Western objective in the country would be to maintain their hold on Iraqi petroleum. The Americans could end up pulling their forces out of Iraq and setting up a large and permanent presence in Kuwait from which they could oversee the petroleum reserves of the Persian Gulf.

The present period in the United States should be seen as an interregnum. The age of neo-conservative control of policymaking has ended. But it is not fully clear what will come next.

The early jockeying for position among presidential hopefuls for 2008 in both the Republican and Democratic camps took shape around the Iraq question. The debate had two focal points. The first concerned the positions taken by potential candidates in the vote in the U.S. Senate in October 2002 authorizing Bush to use force if necessary to strip Saddam Hussein of his weapons of mass destruction. The second was the position taken by would-be presidential candidates on the Bush plan to send reinforcements to Iraq in January 2007.

The U.S. Senate vote in October 2002 was later used by the Bush administration as authorization for its March 2003 invasion of Iraq. The vote played a pivotal role in shaping perceptions of heavyweight U.S. senators. John Kerry, for instance, voted for the resolution, declaring his support for the proposition that it could become necessary to use force to strip the Iraqi dictator of his weapons of mass destruction. After the invasion, when it was revealed that Iraq had possessed no weapons of mass destruction, Kerry denounced Bush for having misled the country. He repudiated his 2002 vote in the Senate. That change of position was used with effect by Republicans during the 2004 presidential campaign to portray the Democratic standard bearer as a flip-flop artist. Two other Democratic senators with presidential aspirations for 2008, who also voted for the 2002 resolution, were John Edwards and Hillary Clinton. Edwards has since repudiated his 2002 vote and is playing a leading role in denouncing Bush's strategy in Iraq. Clinton has been more cautious, noting that if Americans knew then what they later learned, there would have been no such vote. Presidential contender Barack Obama, the junior senator from Illinois, had the advantage of not having been in the Senate in 2002 for the fateful vote.

On the Republican side, John McCain, who wanted his party's 2008 nomination, had voted for the 2002 resolution and stood staunchly behind that vote, and fellow candidate Rudy Giuliani, the former mayor of New York, took a similarly pro-war stance.

McCain defined himself as the hawk's hawk. I remember hearing him speak at an outdoor rally in Rochester, New York, in March 2000 during the campaign for his party's nomination. A Vietnam veteran, McCain declared that what he had learned from that conflict was that the United States should never go to war again without the willingness to do everything necessary to prevail. He has stuck to that position ever since. While he backed Bush on the war, he believed the United States should have sent a much larger number of troops. McCain's problem was that the country as a whole was negative about the war, and that included some high-profile Republicans. Senator Chuck Hagel of Nebraska, also a Vietnam veteran, had long since become a critic of Bush's handling of the war. Senator Sam Brownback of Kansas, who was making a run for the Republican nomination, was trying to set himself up as an alternative to McCain among conservatives. He repudiated the Bush administration's decision to send additional troops to Iraq. While traveling in Iraq in January 2007, Brownback said that he did not believe that sending more troops was the answer. "Iraq requires a political rather than a military solution," he said. Following meetings with the Iraqi prime minister, the Kansas senator said he did not believe that the United States should increase its involvement in Iraq until Sunnis and Shiites stop "shooting at each other." While Brownback had supported the war in the past, he later moved away from administration positions. He called for the division of Iraq into autonomous Kurdish, Sunni, and Shiite regions within a loosely configured federation. He declared that he generally supported the approach of the Iraq Study Group.

Rethinking the American Middle Eastern position is bound to be accompanied by efforts to make the American Empire sustainable economically. This raises the thorny and interrelated questions of the size of the U.S. defense budget and the problem of the American government's burgeoning deficits and debt. The Romans faced similar issues when they decided to build Hadrian's Wall and to abandon most of the Germanic lands, as did the British when they had to finance their great wars against France during the eighteenth century. For the American Empire to survive, it will have to achieve a level of funding that is sustainable. Either the costs of empire will have to be pared back or greater funding for the imperial project will have to be sustained.

Cutting the U.S. defense budget cannot easily be done as long as the Americans occupy Afghanistan and Iraq. Over the longer term, cutting defense spending is an option that segments of the American political leadership are likely to consider. Whatever the United States does about the defense budget, the overall budget deficit is a broader problem that cannot go unresolved. Previous empires, the Romans and the French, foundered on an inability to finance their operations. While Bill Clinton managed during the 1990s, through the imposition of a tax increase, to pull Washington's finances into the black, it will be exceedingly difficult for the United States to summon the political will to repeat that exercise. Failure to deal with the government deficit can only mean more borrowing by the United States, much of it from foreigners. That borrowing will add to the problems of the American dollar and to the country's growing indebtedness.

Everywhere one looks, the United States faces a series of interrelated problems. While the American Empire is by no means in imminent peril of collapse, it could be forced to pull back from some of its more exposed positions in world trouble spots, in particular the Middle East. In the process, it is likely that the United States will have to consider moving over to a more multilateral strategy, bringing other major powers into its confidence, so that the burdens of empire can be shared with the Western Europeans, the Japanese, and others. Accepting the restraints that would accompany multilateralism would be no easy thing for the American leadership, certainly the neo-conservative leadership that has been at the helm under George W. Bush. For the neo-conservatives, sharing power with the Europeans and the Japanese has been anathema, a sure way to blunt the effectiveness of American power in sensitive regions of the world.

The challenges that now confront the American Empire are similar to the problems faced by previous empires—problems of imperial over-stretch and the challenge of fashioning legitimacy for its rule. What makes it especially difficult for the American political leadership to cope with these challenges is the extent to which the norms of American political culture confuse the issues and make it difficult to confront them directly. Only the occasional ideological outrider such as the maverick neo-conservative Charles Krauthammer has had the temerity to say that the United States should stop shying away from the word "empire," and then to add for good measure that "we could use a colonial office in the state department."[1] It is no easy thing to plan for the long-term viability of an empire in a political culture in which the very existence of the empire needs to be constantly denied, at least in public discourse.

Previous empires always recognized the need for the top elites in the society to understand their role in maintaining the empire. Sometimes their roles were cloaked in religion and in the idea of rulers as gods, as in the case of the Egyptian pharaohs. Rulers of empires that endured for long periods of time had a clear view of their role and what needed to be done to sustain it. The British ruling class had a surer understanding of the role it needed to play to sustain its empire than did the French ruling class during the eighteenth century. Never in the period of their dominance did the British lose their sense of cultural superiority, the key claim to their right to rule. While it was critiqued and questioned from time to time, the legitimacy of the empire was never denied.

The Athenian Empire, brilliant but short-lived as was its career, was always plagued by an unresolved question of legitimacy. The Athenians believed, as an integral part of their political culture, in the right of city-states to self-rule. Initially, when they constructed the Confederacy of Delos, the Athenians were able to cloak their dominance under the rubric of an alliance in which Athens was first among equals. With the abandonment of the confederacy and the creation of an Athenian Empire that was plain for all to see, the problem of legitimacy returned to haunt the leaders of Athens. The question was never resolved, among either Athenians or those they colonized.

The American Empire faces a legitimacy challenge both at home and abroad. The point has already been made that because the United States was born from an anti-imperialist revolution, Americans are highly resistant to the idea that their country has become an empire. Not only does the Declaration of Independence announce the right of Americans to enter the world as an independent state, it also heralds the right of all peoples to self-government. While the Declaration lists the wrongs inflicted on the Thirteen Colonies that led its authors to take the dramatic step of dissolving "all political connection" with Great Britain, its opening lines pronounce the rights of all peoples to "assume among the powers of the earth, the separate and equal station to which the Laws of Nature and Nature's God entitle them." While the authors declare "Prudence . . . will dictate that Governments long established should not be changed for light and transient causes," whenever any form of government becomes destructive of the unalienable rights of men to "Life, Liberty and the pursuit of Happiness," they have the right "to alter or abolish" such a government and to institute a new government. In addition, the proclamation that "all men are created equal" further emphasizes the inequality inherent in all forms of empire.

Along with the U.S. Constitution, the Declaration of Independence lies at the heart of the American civic religion of national values. To state that the United States has established an empire is to blaspheme against the Declaration. The Athenians, in their perverse way, under similar circumstances, imposed their own model democratic constitutions on the city-states that they brought within their empire. A nation that will not admit that it is an empire is not well suited to rule other peoples over the long term. This is especially true of the nation's elite, those who must insist on the martial discipline, the self-sacrifice, and the willingness to shoulder the human and financial burdens of empire during difficult times.

Like the Athenians, the Americans insist on pushing their system of government on peoples conquered by their military. And while the United States may aspire to secure special deals for its corporations on a country's soil and to establish permanent military bases for its armed forces, the system of government it champions incorporates the ideals of the American Declaration of Independence, namely that all men are created equal and have the right to self-government. While that contradiction promotes cynicism about the wide gap between American values and practice, it also has the effect of promoting the dissolution of the empire the United States is establishing. Constitutions written for other countries under the bayonets of American soldiers and under the tutelage of American officials perversely become training manuals that preach the right of dependent countries to self-determination. To acknowledge the existence of their empire is for Americans to turn their backs on one of their most cherished values. This is much more than a matter of semantics. Americans cannot get around this dilemma by simply proclaiming that the United States is a superpower and not an imperial power.

During the first century B.C., the Romans had to grapple with a parallel, but by no means identical, problem. By the time of the civil wars, the Romans had established their imperial sway over much of the Mediterranean. Unlike the Americans, the Romans had no deep-seated ideological aversion to empire. Nonetheless, the transition from republic to empire was exceptionally traumatic for the Romans. The idea of the virtuous citizen-soldier as the archetypical figure of the society was replaced by that of the emperor, the godlike embodiment of the new imperial ethos.

Could the Americans endure such a transformation of their identity to enable their elites to plan for the long-term management of an empire? The American civic religion, based on the Declaration of Independence and the Constitution, contains within it the germ of imperial ambition, cloaked though it is in the garb of the doctrine of national self-determination. From well before the American Revolution and its seminal accompanying documents, colonists who were becoming Americans developed the idea that theirs was a "special providence," that their society was a City on a Hill, a shining example to the rest of the world, and a refuge for those seeking liberty.

Not many decades after the founding of their republic, the Americans developed the Monroe Doctrine of 1823, which contained a strong imperialist proclamation. The United States announced to the world that it would not tolerate any new holdings being established by imperial powers in the western hemisphere. In keeping with the spirit of the Declaration of Independence, the Americans were setting themselves up as the guardians of the right of the other nations of the hemisphere to self-determination. At the same time, though, America was proclaiming itself to be a great power and relegating its neighbors to the status of lesser states within their sphere of influence.

During the eras of American imperial assertiveness, from the short-lived age of Wilsonianism at the end of the First World War, and through the Cold War, America legitimated its expansionism under the rubric of defending freedom against autocracy and totalitarianism. In the post–Cold War period, legitimation was achieved through the claim that America was the "indispensable nation" in the global system and more latterly through George W. Bush's doctrine that it is America's vocation to spread freedom to all people of the world. The Bush doctrine has proved to be a highly costly justification for empire, both abroad and at home. Foreigners, elites, and citizens alike have reacted strongly against the claim that the United States has the right to pursue regime change in countries such as Iran, North Korea, and even Venezuela.

The freedom doctrine, while it is capable of mobilizing Americans for short periods, has proved to be a poor basis for rallying the American people for extended periods of time. When things do not go well in a place like Iraq, Americans quickly conclude that Iraqis, with their interminable sectarian disputes, do not value democracy. Popular enthusiasm for lengthy occupations of other countries in the face of armed resistance has always been difficult to sustain in the United States. Although the Americans persevered in fighting a long and bloody guerilla war to victory in the Philippines a century ago, opposition to that war generated the first major anti-imperialist movement in American history.

More recent American missions in Vietnam and Iraq have provoked widespread opposition much more rapidly. In Vietnam, the American will to achieve victory was not great enough to overcome the fierce determination of the North Vietnamese and the National Liberation Front in

South Vietnam. The Iraq occupation has been crumbling as a consequence of the insurgency and the flagging support for the war at home.

The freedom doctrine does not offer American elites and the American people enough of an incentive to discipline themselves to win bloody, costly, and lengthy struggles. The major alternative justification for winning lengthy wars of occupation is to argue that victory is in the vital national interests of Americans, both to safeguard their own national security and to maintain access to critical resources such as oil. Naturally, the self-interest case has been vigorously made during America's wars. The argument that Communist expansionism had to be resisted worked well enough during the general standoff against the Soviet Union in the era of the Cold War. While the case was repeatedly made by the Johnson and Nixon administrations during the Vietnam War, it failed to rally Americans to pay the price necessary to achieve victory.

Since the demise of the Soviet Union, it has proved more difficult to find durable reasons for Americans to carry the day in their military missions. The terror attacks of September 11, 2001, served to unite Americans in support of the invasion of Afghanistan and during the initial phases of the assault on Iraq. However, by 2006, the Bush administration's insistence that the war on terror was a great struggle on a par with the world wars and the Cold War was a palpable failure. Repeated alarms about potential new terrorist attacks on their homeland had less and less effect on the people of the United States. Moreover, the cynicism that followed the revelation that weapons of mass destruction in Iraq did not exist undermined support for the mission. Worse still, the revelations about the Abu Ghraib prison atrocities and the realization that the United States was constructing its own gulag in places such as Guantanamo tore apart the idea that the U.S. mission in Iraq was genuinely about the pursuit of freedom. Both the Bush administration's low ratings in the polls and the flagging support for the war were signs of the declining legitimacy of the Iraq mission.

The ambivalence of the American people and the American elite about the imperial project has made it difficult for their rulers to see missions such as those in Vietnam and Iraq through to victory. Successful empires in the past were able to call on greater solidarity from both the general population and members of the elite to make sacrifices to achieve imperial goals. For example, in the eighteenth and nineteenth centuries, the

British could rely on a constant supply of recruits for both the army and the navy, sometimes bolstered by the efforts of press gangs whose members forcibly seized men and carried them off to serve on the ships of the Royal Navy. Without that ready source of men, the British imperial system could never have been created or sustained. In the major battles of the imperial wars right down to Waterloo in 1815, this supply of men was the indispensable backbone of British power. In the United States today, while a form of "economic draft" exists, which pressures the poor from disadvantaged regions to join the armed forces, the willingness to stay on indefinitely no matter how high the casualties can no longer be depended upon. While Americans were prepared to accept mass casualties during the two world wars, today even small body bag counts provoke a political reaction. This dramatically limits the ability of the United States to endure long struggles of occupation against strongly rooted insurgencies.

If the American people do not have the stomach for lengthy imperial wars, neither do important elements of the American elite. As things went badly for the American operation in Iraq in 2006, retired generals were quick to call for the resignation of U.S. Defense Secretary Donald Rumsfeld, and important political critics came forward to call for a revision of U.S. strategy abroad. In the Vietnam War, it was the growth of serious divisions within the American corporate and political elite, as well as among Americans at large, that finally forced the Nixon administration to wind down the war.

In the face of stubborn resistance, elite opinion in the United States tends to splinter in a number of directions. Stoic dedication to a lengthy and discouraging cause is not something to which the American elites are inured. In part, this can be explained by the fact that the United States has been an immensely privileged country, occupying an enormous territory, blessed with weak neighbors, and separated from dangerous foes by two oceans. It is not difficult to see why members of the American elite can grow weary of struggles in unpromising places. The stakes can appear not to be high enough for the leading elements of American society to summon up the resolve to achieve victory. Resolve for the elites does not, at present, mean volunteering to serve in the armed forces. The volunteer force of the United States, made up as it is largely of people from the poor and working class, is very much insulated from the upper classes and

THE PERILS OF EMPIRE

elites, who do not, in most cases, have to fear that their own sons and daughters will die in battle. Resolve for the elites, therefore, has more to do with financing a war than actually fighting it.

The American upper classes resent paying taxes. Mobilizing them to pay for a war on the frontiers of the empire is a political exercise fraught with risk. In the American political system, leaders who make the case for financial sacrifice on the part of the rich and the affluent can expect to be challenged by potential leaders who are willing to offer this crucial constituency a better deal. In the Republican Party, the party of neo-conservatism that has promoted recent imperial wars, the mere suggestion of tax increases is anathema. This contradiction creates serious problems for the financing of American wars. It points up the difficulty that arises in a society in which the elite cannot be appealed to directly in the name of imperial loyalty. The republican virtues of the American Revolution and the strong commitment in the upper classes toward an untrammeled market-oriented society retain their potency. Altering this individualist culture, which measures rewards in personal terms and which regards "business as the business of America," in favor of more martial values is no easy thing to achieve.

What are the prospects that a more consistently imperial and martial culture will arise in the United States? As things currently stand, the chances are slim. What could change this situation would be either a confrontation with a great power, say with China, or a terrorist attack on a much larger scale than the one that occurred on September 11, 2001.

Barring an immense catastrophe, it is difficult to see how the American elite can be culturally transformed to become a disciplined and consistent imperial ruling order. At present, the prevailing pressures in American society militate against such a change. Indeed, the pressures are mostly in the opposite direction. In the near future, the excesses of American economic policy are bound to force a painful period of adaptation and restructuring. The accumulated debt to foreigners, the current account deficit, and Washington's budget deficit will all have to be faced, either through a protracted period of adjustment, the famed "soft landing," or through a hard landing that necessitates rapid adaptation. Such a hard landing could occur as the result of a major recession caused by a spike in oil prices to the range of one hundred dollars a barrel, the bursting of the property price bubble (long overdue in both the United States and the United Kingdom), or a U.S. military show-down with Iran. These adjustments, when they come, are virtually guar-anteed to force radical changes in the economic relationship of both the United States and the UK (which has pursued a similar economic strat-egy) with the rest of the world. The sky-high trade surpluses of China, and to a lesser extent of Japan, will have to be corrected and scaled back. These developments will generate two further effects worth noting: the end of China's wide-open market in the United States, which will neces-sitate serious adjustments to Chinese economic policy, and pressure on the United States (and the UK) to ramp up the goods-producing sectors of their economies.

What is coming is no less than the dethroning of the United States as the central economy around which the global system revolves. The First World War had similar consequences for the British, who felt the pain of adjustment for decades afterward. At the end of the great cycle of changes to come, neither of the major English-speaking countries will be posi-tioned at the apex of the global economy. This is not to predict that the United States will have an unimportant economic role to play or will cease to be productive. On the other hand, Americans will no longer enjoy the extra benefits that have gone with presiding over the world's central economy. As debtors, they will be pushed down the ladder of the world division of labor in favor of the world's more financially sound creditor economies, likely the Japanese, Europeans, and Chinese, among others.

These transformative events are sure to have an impact on the willing-ness of Americans and their elites to sustain their empire. Faced with a declining role in the global economy and the material consequences of their indebtedness, political leaders are sure to propose a number of strategies to deal with these calamities. The responses will be informed by the traditions of American political culture. Undoubtedly, one wing of American opinion is bound to be sharply hostile to a world that has done such terrible things to America. They will preach isolation from an evil world while lashing out and seeking to dominate it. Isolation and domination—these reactions are endemic among those Americans who are particularly attached to the notion that the United States is a unique society, endowed by God to play a special role in the world.

Other streams of thought will have an influence as well. Those Americans, including major elements of the business community and the elites, who have considered themselves multilateralists will want America to back away from the path of being the world's solitary imperial titan. They will not want to dispense with the fruits of empire, but will seek to have the United States imbed itself in a far-reaching regime of international organizations, rules, and treaties. For them, the advantage of this route is that it will allow the United States to adapt to changed economic and geostrategic conditions. If higher taxes become necessary in the United States, and this is almost certain to be the case, this tendency will push for America to reduce its defense spending. Proponents of this line of thinking will want the United States to rely for its security on a system of relationships around the world in which many other countries bear the burden of security. In return for this, they will want the United States to sign on to the international agreements that the Bush administration has turned its back on—the Nuclear Test Ban Treaty, the Anti-Land Mines Treaty, the International Criminal Court, and the Kyoto Accord and future environmental agreements. In short, they will want the United States to end its splendid isolation and come in from the cold. The outcome will depend on developments in the rest of the world, not least in the Americas, where the rising Hispanic influence in the United States is bound to be a factor in the creation of a new American political culture.

The struggle over which of these tendencies will prevail will have immense implications for the rest of the world. If a militarist regime that seeks to rely on American military power to dominate much of the world is established, the United States will become a dark force in the twenty-first century, more authoritarian at home and deeply resented abroad. If a more multilateralist tendency prevails, the world can look forward not to the immediate end of the American Empire but to a long-term shift away from empire toward an international regime in which a myriad of voices, tendencies, peoples, and ideas have their place in shaping the world.

ACKNOWLEDGMENTS

I am much indebted to my literary agent, Jackie Kaiser, who was instrumental in helping shape this project.

Diane Turbide has been a highly supportive editor, offering cogent advice and encouragement at every stage. Jim Leahy did a fine job copy editing the manuscript. I am grateful to Tracy Bordian at Penguin, who oversaw the production of this book.

Thanks to my son Jonathan for the research he did for this book.

My spouse, Sandy, to whom this book is dedicated, is always the one who shares these projects, lives with them, and offers invaluable input.

NOTES

Chapter 1

1. Michael Ignatieff, *Empire Lite: Nation-building in Bosnia, Kosovo and Afghanistan* (Penguin Canada, Toronto, 2003), 1.
2. Niall Ferguson, *Empire: The Rise and Demise of the British World Order and the Lessons for Global Power* (Basic Books, New York, 2002), 367–70.
3. Ibid.
4. Zbigniew Brzezinski, *The Grand Chessboard: American Primacy and Its Geostrategic Imperatives* (Basic Books, New York, 1997), 10.
5. Ibid., 24.
6. Ibid., 25.
7. Ibid., 38.
8. Ibid., 198.
9. Project for the New American Century, *Rebuilding America's Defenses: Strategy, Forces and Resources for a New Century*, A Report of the Project for the New American Century, September 2000 (Project for the New American Century, Washington, DC, 2000), i.
10. Ibid., i.
11. Ibid., ii.
12. Ibid., 1.
13. Ibid., 8.
14. Ibid., v.
15. Ibid., 12.
16. Ibid., 3.
17. Ibid., 19.
18. Ibid., 16.
19. Ibid., 51.
20. Ibid., 52.
21. Ibid., 54.
22. Ignatieff, *Empire Lite*, 2.
23. Michael Ignatieff, "The Burden," *The New York Times Magazine*, January 5, 2003.
24. Ibid.
25. Francis Fukuyama, *America at the Crossroads: Democracy, Power, and the Neoconservative Legacy* (Yale University Press, London and New Haven, 2006), ix–x.
26. Ibid., 84.
27. Ibid., 101.
28. Ibid., 189.
29. Ibid., 189–90.
30. Zbigniew Brzezinski, *The Choice: Global Domination or Global Leadership* (Basic Books, New York, 2004), 203.

Chapter 2

1. Cited in John Strachey, *The End of Empire* (Victor Gollancz, London, 1959), 324–25.
2. Kathryn A. Bard, "The Emergence of the Egyptian State," in Ian

Shaw, ed., *The Oxford History of Ancient Egypt* (Oxford University Press, Oxford, 2002), 81.

3. Michael Mandelbaum, *The Case for Goliath: How America Acts as the World's Government in the Twenty-First Century* (Public Affairs, New York, 2005), 225–26.

Chapter 3

1. John Keegan, *A History of Warfare* (Vintage Books, New York, 1994), 130.
2. Stephan Seidlmayer, "The First Intermediate Period, 2160–2055 B.C.," in Ian Shaw, ed., *The Oxford History of Ancient Egypt* (Oxford University Press, Oxford, 2002), 120–21.
3. Ibid., 122.
4. Ibid., 128–29.
5. Ian Shaw, "Egypt and the Outside World," in Ian Shaw, ed., *The Oxford History of Ancient Egypt* (Oxford University Press, Oxford, 2002), 315–17.
6. Ibid., 325.
7. Ibid., 324–25.
8. Ibid., 320–22.
9. Ibid., 329.
10. Alan B. Lloyd, "The Late Period, 664–332 B.C.," in Ian Shaw, ed., *The Oxford History of Ancient Egypt* (Oxford University Press, Oxford, 2002), 384.
11. Ibid., 384, 385.
12. Ibid., 390.
13. Ibid., 396, 397.

Chapter 4

1. J.B. Bury, *A History of Greece* (The Modern Library, New York, 1913), 322.
2. Ibid., 323.
3. Ibid., 324.
4. Ibid., 324.
5. Ibid., 324–25.
6. Ibid., 326.
7. Ibid., 329–30.
8. Ibid., 333–34.

Chapter 5

1. Jacques Gernet, *A History of Chinese Civilization* (Cambridge University Press, Cambridge, 1982), 62, 102–3.
2. Ibid., 107–9.
3. Ibid., 109–10.
4. M. Cary, *A History of Rome: Down to the Reign of Constantine* (Macmillan, London, 1957), 669–70.
5. J.M. Roberts, *The New Penguin History of the World* (Penguin Books, London, 2004), 457.
6. Gernet, *History of Chinese Civilization*, 710, 731.

Chapter 6

1. John Keegan, *A History of Warfare* (Vintage Books, New York, 1994), 265.
2. Ibid., 265.
3. William Harris, *War and Imperialism in Republican Rome* (Oxford, 1979), 48, as cited in Keegan, *History of Warfare*, 266.
4. Walter Russell Mead, *Special Providence: American Foreign*

Policy and How It Changed the World (Routledge, New York and London, 2002), 218–21.
5. Keegan, *History of Warfare*, 264.
6. Ibid., 268.
7. M. Cary, *A History of Rome: Down to the Reign of Constantine* (Macmillan, London, 1957), 505–6.
8. Ellen Meiksins Wood, *Empire of Capital* (Verso, London, 2003), 31.
9. Cary, *History of Rome*, 550–52.
10. Ibid., 617–18.
11. Ibid., 657–58.
12. John Strachey, *The End of Empire* (Victor Gollancz, London, 1959), 330.
13. Ibid., 330.
14. Edward Gibbon, *The History of the Decline and Fall of the Roman Empire*, cited in Bertrand Russell, *History of Western Philosophy* (Unwin Paperbacks, London, 1979), 268.
15. Ibid., 268–69.
16. Wood, *Empire of Capital*, 36.

Chapter 7
1. Hugh Thomas, *Rivers of Gold: The Rise of the Spanish Empire, from Columbus to Magellan* (Random House, New York, 2005), 3–6.
2. Ibid., 69–73.
3. Ibid., 78–83.
4. Paul Kennedy, *The Rise and Fall of the Great Powers: Economic Change and Military Conflict from 1500 to 2000* (Fontana Press, London, 1989), 31.

5. Henry Kamen, *Empire: How Spain Became a World Power 1492–1763* (Harper Collins, New York, 2003), 96.
6. Ibid., 99.
7. Ibid., 100–1.
8. Ibid., 101–2.
9. Ibid., 102–3.
10. Ibid., 493.
11. Ibid., 107–8.
12. Ibid.
13. Ibid., 109.
14. Ibid., 285.
15. Ibid., 49–50.
16. Ibid., 203, 205.
17. Ibid., 208, 220.
18. Ibid., 285–86.
19. Ibid., 286.
20. Ibid., 504.
21. Ibid., 294–95.
22. Ibid., 295–96.
23. Ibid., 443.
24. Ibid., 445.
25. Ibid., 509.
26. Ibid., 509–10.
27. Ibid., 507.
28. Ibid.
29. Thomas, *Rivers of Gold*, 536.

Chapter 8
1. Denis Judd, *Empire: The British Imperial Experience from 1765 to the Present* (Phoenix Press, London, 2001), 46–47.
2. Ibid., 77.
3. Ibid., 77–78.
4. Ibid., 78.
5. Niall Ferguson, *Empire: The Rise and Demise of the British World*

Order and the Lessons for Global Power (Basic Books, New York, 2002), 4.

6. Daniel J. Boorstin, *The Americans: The Colonial Experience* (Vintage Books, New York, 1958), 7.

7. P.J. Cain and A.G. Hopkins, *British Imperialism 1688–2000*, 2nd ed. (Longman, Edinburgh, 2002), 77.

8. Ibid., 79.

9. Ibid., 90.

10. Ibid., 66.

11. Ibid., 648.

12. Ibid., 651.

Chapter 10

1. Niall Ferguson, *Colossus: The Rise and Fall of the American Empire* (Allen Lane, Penguin, London, 2004), 301.

2. Michael Klare, *Blood and Oil* (Penguin Books, London, 2005), 12–13.

3. Ibid., 16–17.

4. Ibid., 19.

5. Ibid., 36–37.

Chapter 11

1. Tom Engelhardt, "Winners and Losers: Moving Out of the Superpower Orbit," commondreams.org, May 2005.

Chapter 12

1. Robert Kagan and William Kristol, eds, *Present Dangers: Crisis and Opportunity in American Foreign and Defense Policy* (Encounter Books, San Francisco, 2000), 59.

Chapter 13

1. Denis Judd, *Empire: The British Imperial Experience from 1765 to the Present* (Phoenix, London, 2001), 45–46.

2. Ibid., 242.

3. Ibid., 243.

4. Alvin Jackson, *Home Rule: An Irish History 1800–2000* (Phoenix, London, 2004), 204–13.

5. Lawrence James, *The Rise and Fall of the British Empire* (Abacus, London, 1998), 376.

6. Judd, *Empire*, 258.

7. Ibid., 259.

8. Ibid., 250.

9. Ibid., 259.

10. James, *Rise and Fall of the British Empire*, 416.

11. Judd, *Empire*, 271.

12. John Strachey, *The End of Empire* (Victor Gollancz, London, 1959), 132.

13. Judd, *Empire*, 323.

14. Ibid., 334, 335.

15. Ibid., 324.

16. *The New York Times*, March 18, 2006.

Chapter 14

1. *The Guardian*, May 10, 2006.

Abu Ghraib prison, 227
Abyssinia, 117
Acapulco, 106
Acheson, Dean, 11
Act of Union (1800), 192
Actium, battle of (31 B.C.), 55
Aegean Sea, 54, 55, 61
Aegina (Greece), 66
Afghanistan, 54, 75: Soviet invasion of (1979), 156, 165; U.S. invasion of (2001), 3, 25, 30, 148, 155–56, 165, 166, 204, 215, 227
Africa, 41, 51, 121, 126; slave trade, 102, 109, 112, 113 (See also North Africa; South Africa)
agriculture, 45, 48, 53, 55, 77, 89, 122, 123, 181
Al Qaeda, 3, 16, 151, 165, 205
Albright, Madeleine, 16
Alexander the Great, 54–55, 68
Alexandria, 55
Allende, Salvador, 169
Almansa, battle of (1707), 110
Amenemhet I (ruler, 12th dynasty), 50
America at the Crossroads (Fukuyama), 27
American Civil War, 160
American Empire: challenges to, 146; comparisons, 18–20, 68, 69, 158–59; and imperialist overstretch, 146; and last empire concept, 20; structure of, 158; term, 5; (See also United States)
American exceptionalism, 29, 30, 31
American Republic, 208
American Revolution, 103, 119, 139, 141, 146, 189, 190, 191, 225, 229
American triumphalism, 15, 16, 208
American War of Independence, 201
Amoy (China), 77
Amritsar massacre (1919), 199–200
Anatolia, 51
Angell, Norman, 129, 131
Anglo-Irish Treaty (1921), 197–98
Ankhtifi (administrator, Egypt), 49–50
Anschluss, 143
anti-Americanism, 29, 30, 171, 172, 186, 206, 208, 214, 215
Anti-Ballistic Missile (ABM) Treaty, 24, 33
Anti–Corn Law League, 129
anti-globalization movement, 17
anti-imperialism, 205, 224, 226

Anti–Land Mines Treaty, 33, 231
anti-war movement, 205
Arab-Israeli War (1973), 163
Arabia, 88
Aragon (Spain), 93, 94, 104, 107
Aramaic language, 54
Aramco, 163
Argentina, 12, 169
Arizona, Hispanic population, 175
Armenia, 88
Army of Bengal, 116
art/architecture, 50–51, 53, 81, 101
Assyria, 12, 88
Athenian Empire, 6, 8: decline of, 64–68; democracy, 69; demographics, 61; division with Sparta, 64–66; economy, 60–61, 62; foreign policy, 66–67; govt., 63, 66, 69; justice system, 64, 66; legacy of, 59; and legitimacy, 64, 68, 223–24; member state categories, 60, 62; military, 59–62; slavery in, 59, 61, 65–66; subject states, 62–64, 68; and taxation, 59, 61, 63 (See also Confederacy of Delos)
Athens, 59, 60, 64: war with Sparta. See Punic Wars
Atahualpa (Incan leader), 99–101
atomic bomb, 161
Attlee, Clement, 203
Augustus, Emperor (of Rome), 55, 83, 86, 87, 88
Australia, 121, 191
Austria, 30, 104, 109–10, 143
Austria-Hungary, 131, 134 (See also Dual Alliance)
Austro-Hungarian Empire, 81
"axis of evil," 30, 115
Ayatollah Khomeini, 164
Azores, 94
Aztec Empire, 12, 96, 97–99

Babylonian Empire, 45
Baker-Hamilton report, 216, 217
Baker, James, 1, 152, 216–17
ballistic missiles, 23, 24–25
Bangladesh, 204
Bank of England, 125, 128, 153, 185
Barcelona, 94, 110
Bard, Kathryn, 43

Bath (Roman Britain), 42
Bechtel (engineering firm), 159
Belgium, 39, 133, 143, 190
Bengal, 115
Bidden, Joseph, 218
bin Laden, Osama, 3, 151, 165
Bismarck, Otto von, 27, 30, 31, 120
Black and Tans, 197
Black Hole of Calcutta, 115
Bloom, Allan, 27
Boeing Company, 83
Boer War (1899), 118, 126, 130, 156
Boetia, 67
Bolívar, Simón, 171
Bolshevism, 142
borderless world, 13–14, 16–17
Boxer Rebellion (1899), 78
Brandenburg Gate (Berlin), 81
Brazil, 160, 169, 171
Bretton Woods (1944), 33, 39, 140, 149, 184
Bright, John, 129
Brilliant Pebbles project, 24–25
Britain: classism in, 124; colonies, 115, 117,
    118–19, 121, 139, 141; cultural superiority
    of, 115, 200–1, 223; dissolution of
    empire, 140; economy, 117, 120, 121,
    122, 124–25, 128–29, 153–54, 158–59,
    160, 185; –France relations, 110, 119, 120,
    121, 124, 131, 139–40; and gentlemanly
    capitalism, 121–23, 124; –Germany
    relations, 128, 136, 140. 143; govt., 124–25;
    imperial overstretch, 137–42; in India,
    116–18, 139, 158, 199–204; Irish resistance
    to. See Ireland, struggle for independence;
    –Japan relations, 131; and legitimacy, 42;
    military, 119–20, 130–32, 138, 139–40,
    227–28; nationalism, 124, 126–27; Roman,
    87–88; –Russia relations, 131, 180; taxation,
    120, 121, 139, 140; –U.S. comparisons, 128
British East India Company, 77
British Imperialism (Cain/Hopkins), 122–23
British Liberal Party, 194
British North America Empire, 119
British Raj. See Britain, in India; India,
    struggle for independence
Brownback, Sam, 221–22
Brzezinski, Zbigniew, 18–19, 20, 31–32, 169
Bulgaria, 88
Bush (George Sr.) administration, 152, 216
Bush (George W.) administration, 3–4, 16,
    21, 28, 30–31, 151–52, 166, 169, 170, 205,
    209–12, 213, 215–18, 221–22, 227, 231

Bush, George (Sr.), 166
Bush, George W., 1–2, 3, 21, 23, 25, 27, 115,
    128, 146, 148, 150–51, 156, 157, 158, 165,
    166–67, 172–74, 182, 186, 205, 209, 210,
    219–20, 223, 226

Caesar Augustus, Emperor (of Rome), 81, 87
Cain, P.J., 122–23
Cajamarca (Peru), 99, 100, 101
California, Hispanic population, 175
Cambodia, 218
Campanella, Tommaso, 103
Canada, 53, 162, 191
Canadian Pacific Railway, 125
Canary Islands, 94, 95
Cannae (Italy), 82, 92
Canton (China), 77
Cape of Good Hope, 117
capitalism, 6, 12, 39, 112, 113, 154
    (See also gentlemanly capitalism;
    liberal capitalism; mercantilism)
Cappadocia, 88
Caracas (Venezuela), 171
caravels, 95
Carr Center for Human Rights Policy, 26
Carter, Jimmy, 18, 164
Carthage, 82, 92, 179–80 (See also Punic Wars)
Carystus (Greece), 61
Case for Goliath, The (Mandelbaum), 43
Castile (Spain), 93, 94, 103–4, 107, 108
Castilian language, 108
Castilian monarchy, 103–4
Castro, Fidel, 170, 171, 172
centurions, 86
Ch'ang-an (city), 73
Chalcis (Greece), 64
Chamberlain, Joseph, 194
Chan-Chiang region (Kwangtung), 78
chariots, 50, 56
Charles I, King (of England), 119
Charles of Hapsburg, emperor (Holy Roman
    Empire), 104, 109
Chavez, Hugo, 157, 169–72, 174
Ch'in dynasty, 72
Ch'ing dynasty, 76
Ch'ing-tao (Shantung), 77
Cheng, Prince (of Ch'in)("First Emperor"), 72
Chiang Kai-shek, 78
Chile, 99, 169
China: bureaucracy, 75; dynasties, 72, 76;
    economy, 15, 75–76, 160, 177, 179,
    180–81, 184, 212, 230; –Europe

comparisons, 73–74, 77; –Japan relations, 78, 182–83, 187; military, 73, 75, 76; nationalism, 178; and oil, 163, 170, 177, 181; political culture, 71, 73–74; taxation, 71, 73, 74; –U.S. relations, 4, 15, 23–24, 40, 148, 155, 156, 157, 177–87, 230
Chin Empire, 75, 76
Chinese Civil War (1949), 178
Chios, 62
Choice, The (Brzezinski), 31
Cheney, Dick, 3, 21, 210, 216
Cholulan people, 97–98
Christianity, 41–42, 91, 94, 97, 113
Churchill, Winston, 140, 162, 201
Cithaeron (Greece), 59
city-states, 7, 8, 46, 59, 61, 64, 223, 224
classical economics, 124
Claudius, Emperor (of Rome), 87
Clemenceau, Georges, 147
Cleopatra, Queen (of Egypt), 7, 55
climate change, 167
Clinton administration, 16, 21, 22, 24, 148
Clinton, Bill, 208–9, 222
Clinton, Hillary, 221
Closing of the American Mind, The (Bloom), 27
coalition of the willing, 204, 215
Cobden, Richard, 129
Cold War, 12, 13, 19, 152, 153, 154, 156, 179, 180, 207, 226
Columbus, Christopher, 93–94
Colombia, 99
Commentary Magazine, 28
Commodus, Emperor (of Rome), 89
Communism, 13, 15, 129, 146, 153, 208, 219, 227
Communist Party (China), 178
Communist Party (Soviet), 144–45
comparative advantage, theory of, 124
Comprehensive Test Ban Treaty (CTBT), 22
concentration camps, 130, 192
Confederacy of Delos, 59–60, 63, 68, 64, 184, 223–24 (*See also* Athenian Empire)
Confucianism, 75
Congress of Berlin (1885), 27
Congress Party (India), 202, 203
Connolly, James, 194, 195
conquistadores, 95, 96–97, 112–13, 139
Conservative Party (Britain), 125
Corinth, 66, 67
Corn Laws, 125, 129
corporations, 83, 210, 225
Cortés (governing assembly), 111

Cortés, Hernando, 97–99
Council of Areopagus, 66
Council of Five Hundred, 66
Cromwell, Oliver, 119
Cuba, 97, 98, 99
cuneiform, 45, 47
Curzon, Lord, 117
Cusco (Peru), 99
cyberspace, U.S. domination of, 22, 24
Cyrenaica (Ancient Greece), 55
Czechoslovakia, 145, 190

da Silva, Lula, 171
Dáil Éireann (Irish parliament), 196, 198
Dandi Salt March, 201–2
Darwin, Charles, 40
de Isaba, Marcos, 110
de Valera, Éamon, 196, 197, 198
Declaration of Independence, 146–47, 191, 224, 225, 226
Defense Policy Guidance (DPG), 21
defensive weapons system, 23
Delos, 63. *See also* Confederacy of Delos
democracy, 8, 32, 24, 59, 66, 68, 69, 83, 215, 218, 224
demonstration effect, 157
Denmark, 143
Desert Storm (1991), 165
Dessalines, Jean-Jacques, 191
Dhahran (Saudi Arabia), 163
Diamond Jubilee (Queen Victoria), 126–27
diamond trade, 118
direct democracy, 69
Disraeli, Benjamin, 125
Diver, Maud, 199
Domition, Emperor (of Rome), 89
dot-com crash, 209
Drake, Sir Francis, 139
dreadnoughts, 130, 140
Dual Alliance (1879), 127
Dyer, R.E.H., 199

eagle, symbol, 81
East Germany, 145, 208
East India Company, 117, 139
Easter Rebellion (1916), 194–95, 199
Edwards, John, 221
Egyptian Empire: agriculture, 48, 53, 55; demographics, 53; dynasties/kingdoms, 36–47, 49, 50, 51; economy, 52; invasions/conquest of, 47, 53–55, 118; kings of, 47, 48, 50; legacy of, 45–48, 56–57;

Egyptian Empire: agriculture (*continued*)
longevity of, 6, 7, 46, 52, 55–57; military,
50–51, 52–53, 56; and monuments,
pyramids, 46, 47, 48; social hierarchy, 43,
47–48; structure of state, 48–50; and
taxation, 52
Eighteenth Dynasty, 50
Eisenhower, Dwight D., 83
elites. *See* empire, and elites
Empire and Communications (Innis), 56
empire: concept of, 2–5; defined, 11, 12; and
divine purpose, 103, 113, 147, 156;
and elites, 223, 224, 225, 228–29; and
geopolitical position, 17; and legitimacy,
42–43, 189, 207–31; link with slavery,
37, 38 (*See also* slave labour); longevity
of, 7–8, 189; and military conquest,
11–12, 56; rationale for, 40–42, 115–16,
117, 145, 226; resistance against. *See*
revolts, rebellions, resistance; types of,
6–7, 38–39; and warfare, 86–87
Empire of the Tsars, 13
encomienda system, 96–97, 102
End of History and the Last Man, The
(Fukuyama), 27, 129–30, 208
Engels, Friedrich, 37, 38
English Civil War, 119
English language, 185
Enlightenment, 141
Entente Cordiale (1905), 131
ephors (magistrates), 65
Epidaurus, 66
Erythrae, 63
Estates General (1789), 141
Euro, 212–13
Europe: –China comparisons, 73–74, 77;
defense identity, 24; and oil supply, 163
European Union (EU), 24, 160, 198–99
evolution, theory of, 40, 132
exchange rate system, 149
Exxon Corporation, 161

failed states concept, 26–27
fascism, 129, 153
Ferdinand, King (of Spain), 93, 94, 104
Ferguson, Niall, 17–19, 155–56
feudalism, 73–74, 77, 112, 141
First British Empire, 139
First Han dynasty, 72
First World War, 8, 39, 78, 129, 130, 133–34,
140, 153, 206, 213, 226, 230
Foochow (China), 77
formal imperialism, 118, 126

former Yugoslavia, 16
Fox, Vicente, 172, 174
France, 6, 12, 15, 19: –Britain relations, 110,
119, 131, 139–40; –China relations, 78;
economy, 120, 121, 124, 141; –Germany
relations, 30, 127, 143; and imperial
overstretch, 140–42; military, 142; –Russia
relations, 127, 131; taxation, 141; –U.S.
relations, 208
francs-tireurs, 190
free trade, 122, 125–26, 128–29, 184
Free Trade Area of the Americas (FTAA), 17,
170, 171, 211
French language, 141
French Revolution, 15, 120, 141–42
Friedman, Milton, 154–55
Frum, David, 3
Fukuyama, Francis, 27–31, 129–30, 208,
214–15

galleons, 95, 106, 139
Gandhi, Mahatma, 200–2, 204
Gates, Robert, 152
GATT (General Agreement on Tariffs and
Trade), 33, 184
gentlemanly capitalism, 121–23, 124
geographical isolation: Egypt, 52, 53, 55; US,
53, 69
George, David Lloyd, 196
Germany: –Britain relations, 128, 130, 143;
–China relations, 77–78; –France relations,
127, 132, 133–34, 143; and imperial over-
stretch, 142–43; military, 130, 132–33; and
racism, 40–41; –Russia relations, 132, 133,
143; –U.S. relations, 208
Gibbon, Edward, 89, 91
Gibraltar, 110
Giuliani, Rudy, 221
Gladstone, Sir William Ewart, 194
glasnost, 145
global empire, 39–40
global environmental crisis, 155, 160, 167
global missile defence, 24
globalization, 16, 176, 128–30, 171
Glorious Revolution (1688), 119, 122–23
gold trade, 107, 108, 109, 113, 118, 138, 139
Gorbachev, Mikhail, 145, 146
Gore, Al, 167
Government of India Act (1935), 202
Granada (Spain), 93
Grand Chessboard, The (Brzezinski), 18, 169
Grande Armée, 142
Great Depression, 142, 153

"great game" (British/Russian rivalry), 131, 180
Great Illusion, The (Angell), 129
Great Wall of China, 73, 88
green labor, 155
Greenspan, Alan, 172
Grenada (Caribbean), 119
Guantanamo, 227
Guatemala, 169
Gulf Wars, 16, 165–66, 209

Hadrian, 87
Hadrian's Wall, 87–88, 222
Hagel, Chuck, 221
Haiti, 91
Halliburton Energy Services, 83, 210
Hamilton, Lee, 1, 152
Han-Chinese empire, 6, 72, 73–77
Hannibal, 82
Hapsburg monarchy, 104, 109
hard power, 43
Harris, William, 84
Hawaiian Islands, 106
helots (Sparta), 65, 66, 189
Henry VIII, King (of England), 192
Hero of Alexandria, 88
hieroglyphics, 47–48
high-tech sector, 209
history, end of, 13–14, 15
Hitler, Adolf, 2, 40–41, 142–43, 161
Hobson, J.A., 126
Holy Roman Empire, 104
Hong Kong, 77
Hopkins, A.G., 122, 123
hoplites (soldiers, Athens), 66
Hsien-yang (China), 73
Hsiung-nu people, 73
Hungary, 144–45
Hurricane Katrina, 186
Hussein, Saddam, 164, 165, 166, 205, 210, 215, 216, 220
Hyksos people, 50

Ibn Saud, King (of Saudi Arabia), 162–63
Iberian Peninsula, 105, 109
Ignatieff, Michael, 26–27, 31, 155–56
illegal immigrants, 172–74, 175
imperial parliament, 111
imperial strategy, 32 (See also isolationism; multilateralism; unilateralism)
imperial symbols, 19
imperialism. See empire; formal imperialism; informal imperialism

Imperialism (Hobson), 126
Inca Empire, 12, 96, 99–101
Inconvenient Truth, An (Gore), 167
India, 29, 54, 75, 76, 155: British rule in, 116–18, 139; economy, 160, 182; –Japan relations, 202; military, 117, 204; and oil, 163; struggle for independence, 199–204
Indian Mutiny (1857), 116–17, 199
Indus states, 12
industrial revolution(s), 77, 88, 121, 124, 126
inequality, link to empire, 38, 224
informal imperialism, 118
Innis, Harold, 56
International Criminal Court, 33, 231
International Monetary Fund (IMF), 17, 33, 171, 184
Iran, 1, 30, 75, 226:–Iraq War (1980s), 164–65; oil reserves, 162, 164, 181; revolution in, 164; threat of air war against, 217–18, 230; –US relations, 4, 152, 183, 211, 214
Iraq, 30, 75: U.S. invasion of (2003), 3, 25, 27, 31, 43, 115, 148, 155–56, 159, 165, 166, 173, 183, 204, 205, 209, 210, 215, 220–21, 227; and oil reserves, 162, 220; war, 1–2, 28, 29, 150–51, 152, 156, 157–58, 159, 166–67, 186, 205–6, 210–11, 215–18, 219–20, 226–27, 228
Iraq Study Group, 1, 152, 220, 218, 222
Ireland, 116: British conquest of, 119; struggle for self-determination, 192–99
Irish Free State, 197
Irish Home Rule, 116, 192–93, 194, 195–96
Irish Home Rule Bill (1920), 197
Irish National Party, 192, 195–96
Irish potato famine (1849), 193
Irish Republican Army (IRA), 196–97
iron production, 56, 77
irrigation, 53, 71, 73
Isabella, Queen (of Spain), 93, 94
Islam/Islamic world, 155–56, 214–15
Islamic fundamentalists, 23, 164–66, 205, 210
isolationism, 14, 32, 34, 151, 230, 231
isolationism-unilaterialism, 151
Israel, 155, 157, 163, 205, 213, 217
"Israel Lobby, The" (Mearsheimer/Walt), 213–14
Isthmus of Panama, 99

Jacksonian nationalists, 30
Japan, 6, 39: –Britain relations, 131; –China relations, 78, 182–83, 187; economy, 15, 106, 149–50, 160, 177, 182, 209, 212, 230; military, 182–82; and oil, 163; –U.S. relations, 143

Jews, 94, 191–92, 214
Johns Hopkins University School of
  Advanced International Studies, 43
Johnson administration, 227
Jordan, 1
Junta Central (Spain), 111
Jutland, Battle of (1916), 130

Kagan, Robert, 3, 20, 187
Kan Ying, 76
Kashmir, 204
Keegan, John, 46, 84, 86
Kennedy School of Government (Harvard),
  26, 214
Kerry, John, 150–51, 220–21
Keynes, John Maynard, 33
Khrushchev, Nikita, 145
Kim Jong-II, 4
Kingdom of Punt (Africa), 51
Kissinger, Henry, 30, 169, 186, 219
Kitchener, Lord, 133
Kosovo, 209
Krauthammer, Charles, 223
Kristol, Irving, 28
Kristol, William, 3, 20, 28, 187
Kurds, 166, 210, 215, 222
Kuwait, 162, 165, 210, 220
Kwangtung (China), 78
Kyoto Accord, 33, 231

Laos, 218
Late Period (Egypt), 53
Later Han dynasty, 72
Latin America–US relations, 155, 157, 169–75,
  208, 211(See also specific countries)
legions, 81, 86, 111
Lesbos, 62, 63
liberal capitalism, 129, 208
liberal internationalists, 30
liberty, link to inequality, 38
little Englanders, 125, 129
Liu Pang, 73
London, financial sector, 120, 122, 123,
  134, 139
London Review of Books, 213–14
Long Walls (fortifications), 60, 67, 68
Louis XIV, King (of France), 109, 139, 140, 141
L'Ouverture, Toussaint, 191
Luzon (Philippines), 106

McCain, John, 221
Macedon, 54, 55, 62, 67

Macedonia, 68, 82
Mackinder, Harold, 19–20
Madeira, 94
Madrid, 94
Magellan, Ferdinand, 104–5
magnetic compass, 77
Manchu dynasty, 76
Manchuria, 75, 78
Mandelbaum, Michael, 43
Manila, 106–7
maniples (fighting unit), 86
Mao Zedong, 78
Mark Antony, 55
Marshall Plan, 177
Martin, Paul, 26
Marx, Karl, 20, 37
Marxism, 14, 15
Massachusetts (British colony), 119
Matsu, 179
Mauretania, 88
Mayan civilization, 12
Mead, Walter Russell, 84–85
Mearsheimer, John, 213–14
Memphis (Egypt), 52
Menes, King (of Egypt), 46
mercantile empires, 6, 12, 38–39, 94
mercantilism, 112, 124, 125, 129,
  139, 159
meritocracy, 74–75
Mesopotamia, 45, 48, 53, 55, 88
Messenia, 66
Messina (Sicily), 82
metics (resident aliens), 60–61
Metternich, Count, 30
Mexica Empire, 97–99
Mexican-American War (1846–48), 175
Mexican labor, 172
Mexican immigration, 172–73
Mexico, 53, 97–102, 106–7, 162, 169, 172,
  194–85
Middle Kingdom (Egypt), 47, 50, 51, 52
military-industrial complex, 83, 217
Mill, James, 123
Mill, John Stuart, 123
Ming dynasty, 76
missile defence, 23, 24–25
missionaries, 41–42, 123
monetarism, 154
Mongols, 76, 84
Monroe Doctrine (1823), 147, 226
Montagu, Edwin, 200
Montezuma, 97, 98

monuments (Egypt), 46, 47, 48, 50
Morgan, Henry, 95, 119, 139
Morocco, 94
Mossadegh government (Iran), 164
multilateralism, 14, 18, 32–33, 34, 222–23, 231
Munro, Russ, H., 187
Muslim League, 203–4

NAFTA (North American Free Trade Agreement), 170, 171, 172, 174
Nanking, bombing/massacres (1937), 182
Naples, 103, 104
Napoleon, 111, 142, 191, 193
Napoleonic era, 119, 141
Napoleonic Wars, 120, 124, 140
NASDAQ, 150
National Guard, 156
National Interest (periodical), 28
National Liberation Front, 226–27, 218
National Security Strategy (NSS), 28, 29
NATO (North Atlantic Treaty Organization), 24, 66, 204
Navigation Acts, 125
Naxos (Greece), 61
Nazi-Soviet Pact (1939), 143
Nazism, 2, 40, 142, 153, 185, 190, 191–92, 208
Nehru, Jawaharlal, 202
neo-colonialism, 39
neo-conservatism , 16, 21–32, 152, 154, 155, 186, 187, 215, 217, 218, 220, 223, 229
neo-liberalism, 171
Netherlands, 104, 109–10, 138, 143
New Carthage (Spain), 84
New Deal, 153
new economy, 209
New France, 141
New Kingdom (Egypt), 47, 50
New Mexico, Hispanic population, 175
New Spain, 105, 106
New York: financial centre, 134, 140; attacks on. See 9/11 terror attacks
New York Times, 81, 205
New York Times Magazine, 31
New Zealand, 121
Nigeria, 160, 162
Nile River, 46, 53
Nile Valley, 46, 52, 53, 55
9/11 terror attacks, 3, 16, 17, 23, 25, 26, 28, 30, 156, 165, 166, 172, 173, 209, 215, 227, 229
Ningpo (China), 77
Nixon administration, 218–19, 227, 228
Nixon, Richard, 149, 186, 218

nomenklatura (Soviet govt. class), 144
non-violent protest, 200–1
North Africa, 88, 93
North Korea, 4, 30, 157, 226
Norway, 143
Nubia (Africa), 50, 51
Nuclear Non-Proliferation Treaty, 182
Nuclear Test Ban Treaty, 231
nuclear weapons, 4, 22, 28, 33, 180, 182, 187, 204, 211, 214, 217, 231
Nyasaland (Africa), 117

Obama, Barak, 221
offensive weapons system, 23
oil embargo (1973), 164
oil industry, 155, 160–64 (*See also* specific countries)
Old Kingdom (Egypt), 47, 48–49
Olympics (2008), 183
One China policy, 178
Operation Barbarossa, 143
Opium Wars, 77
Outer Mongolia, 78
overstretch. *See* imperial overstretch

Pakistan, 75, 182, 202, 203 (*See also* India, struggle for independence; Partition)
Palais Bourbon (Paris), 81
Palestine, 50, 51
Panama, 99
Paris Commune, 190
Paris Peace Talks (1919), 78
Parthian Empire, 75, 76
Partition (India/Pakistan), 203–4
partisan resistance movements, 190
Patriotes (Lower Canada), 191
Pax Britannica, 140, 153
peace dividend, 149
Peace of Westphalia (1648), 28–29
Pearl Harbor (1941), 78, 143, 161
Pearse, Patrick, 194–95
Pearse, Willie, 195
peasant empires. *See* slave/peasant empires
peasant revolts, 190
Peking, 76, 77, 78
Peloponnesian War, 67–68
People's Republic of China, 78
perestroika, 145
Pericles, 66, 67
Perle, Richard, 3
Persian Empire, 54, 59, 60, 67, 68
phalanx formation (warfare), 85

pharaohs, 43, 47, 48, 50, 56, 223
Philip II, Emperor (Holy Roman Empire), 104
Philip V, King (of Macedonia), 82
Philip V, King (of Spain), 109, 110
Philippines, 105–7, 226
Photodynastic period (Egypt), 36
pictograms, 45
Pinochet, Augusto, 169
Piraeus (port), 60, 67
pirates, 38, 61, 139
Pizarro, Francisco, 99–101
pluralism, 19, 20
Podhoretz, Norman, 28
Poland, 143, 144, 145, 190
popular culture (U.S.), 19, 32, 42, 185, 206
Portugal, 38, 94, 95, 101, 105, 109
Potosi (Bolivia), 107
pre-emptive war, 28–31, 151
Present Dangers (Kagan/Kristol), 187
preventive wars, 28–29, 30
printing, 77
privateers, 139
Project for the New American Century, 16,
    20–26
Ptolemaic Empire, 55
proto-empires, 12, 37, 40
Public Interest, The (periodical), 28
Punic Wars, 82, 84, 92, 179–80
Puritans, 119
Putin, Valdimir, 145–46
Pyongyang (North Korea), 4
pyramids, 46, 47, 48, 57

Qatar, oil reserves, 162
Quemoy, 179

Reagan administration, 24–24
Reagan, Ronald, 3, 154, 164
realists, foreign policy, 30, 31, 214–17
rebellions. See revolts, rebellions, resistance
Rebuilding America's Defenses (2000), 21–25
Red Army, 145
red scare, 153
Reformers (Upper Canada), 191
Reid, Harry, 217–18
Reign of Terror (French Revolution), 190
Renaissance, 89
Republican Party, 229 (*See also* neo-
    conservatism)
revolts, rebellions, resistance, 189–231
Revolution in Military Affairs (RMA), 24
Rhodes, Cecil, 118, 126

Rice, Conoleezza, 170
Rockefeller, John D., 161, 217–18
rogue states, 23, 28, 40
Roman Empire, 7, 11–12, 14, 15, 55:
    decline/fall of, 89–92, 120, 207;
    developments/innovations, 88;
    economy/trade, 75–76, 88, 89, 90; govt.,
    83; and imperial overstretch, 137–38;
    legacy of, 81; legitimacy of, 42; longevity
    of, 81; military, 81–82, 83–87, 90, 91–92;
    slavery in, 38, 74, 81, 82, 86–87, 88–89;
    social & ruling structures, 90; scope of,
    87–88; taxation, 90, 91, 137–38;
    transition from republic, 83; –U.S. com-
    parisons, 81
Roman Republic, 82–83, 121
Romania, 88, 149
Roosevelt (FDR) administration, 161
Roosevelt, Franklin D., 143, 153, 162–63
Roosevelt, Theodore (Teddy), 11
Rosetta Stone, 47–48
Rowlatt Acts, 200
Royal Air Force, 203–4
Royal Irish Constabulary, 196–97
Royal Navy, 7–8, 128, 130, 140, 142, 147,
    153, 228
Rumsfeld, Donald, 3, 4, 152, 170, 210–11,
    216, 228
Russell, Bertrand, 89
Russia: –Britain relations, 131, 180; –China
    relations; –France relations, 127, 131, 142;
    –Germany relations, 127; and oil, 163
    (*See also* Soviet Empire)

salt tax, 201–2
Samos, 62, 63
Sante Fe (Spain), 93
Sarkozy, Nicolas, 211–12
satrap, 54
satyagraha (peaceful resistance), 200–1
Saudi Arabia, 157, 162–5, 210
Schlieffen Plan, 132–33
Scipio Africanus (general), 82, 84
scribes, 47
Second British Empire, 124
Second German Reich, 30
Second International period (Egypt), 47
Second World War, 7, 13, 39, 78, 85, 86, 92,
    129, 140, 142–43, 160, 161, 184, 190, 202,
    206, 208
Seeley, Sir John, 118
Seleucid Empire, 55

Seven Years' War, 141
Seville, 109
Shah of Iran, 164
Shanghai, 77
Shantung, 77, 89
Shaw, Ian, 52
Shiites, 165–66, 210, 215, 216, 222
"shock and awe" technique, 43
Sian, 73
Sicily, 67, 82, 104
silk trade, 75–76, 106, 109, 138
silver trade, 107, 108, 109, 113, 138, 139
Sinai, 51
Sinn Fein, 196, 197
Sixth Dynasty (Egypt), 49
slave labor/slavery, 6, 37, 38: Athenian Empire,
    59, 61, 65; Egypt, 50, 51; Rome, 81, 82,
    86–87; Spain, 94, 96, 102, 112, 113; U.S., 147
slave/peasant empires, 6, 12, 38, 71
slave revolts, 66, 189–90, 191
slave trade, 61, 77, 96, 102, 119
Smith, Adam, 124
social Darwinism, 131–32
socialism, 146
soft power, 30, 32, 42–43, 123
Somalia, 16
South Africa, 118, 200 (See also Boer War)
South America, Spain's incursions into,
    99–101 (See also Latin America)
South China, 73
sovereign states, 39–40, 146, 158
Soviet Union: collapse of, 2, 13, 15, 129, 143,
    144–46, 149, 207, 208; economy, 144;
    –Germany relations, 142, 143; govt., 144;
    and imperial overstretch, 144–46; military,
    92, 144–45 (See also Cold War; Russia)
space, weaponization of, 22–23, 24–25
Spain, 6, 39, 93, 108, 111: Asian outposts,
    105–7, Bourbon rule in, 109–10; –Britain
    relations, 118–19; –China relations, 106;
    conquests, New World, 96–103, 112–13;
    decline/end of empire, 109–10; diseases
    brought to New World, 102; dynastic
    alliances, 104, 113, 138; economy/trade,
    94, 107–8, 109, 138; and European
    holdings, 103–4; growth of, 94–95; and
    imperial overstretch, 138–39; legacy of,
    112; military, 96, 109–10, 113, 138; slavery
    in, 94, 102, 109, 112, 113; technological
    developments, 94–95
Spanish-American War (1898), 112
Spanish Armada, defeat of (1588), 7, 138

Spanish language, 175 (See also Castilian
    language)
Sparta, 59, 62, 64–68, 189
Spartacus, 189–90
specie (gold & silver) exports, 108–9
"splendid isolation," 34, 128–29, 231
Stalin, Joseph, 143, 162
Standard Oil Company of California
    (SOCAL), 161, 162
Star Wars program, 24
state sovereignty, 28–29
States of the Yellow River, 12
stock market crash (1929), 185
stone tablets, 56
Stracey, John, 89
Strauss, Leo, 27
subject states, 62–64, 68
suburbs, 161
Sudan, 50, 52, 117
Sudetenland, 144
Suez Canal, 117
sugar trade, 113, 138, 139, 191
Sumer, 12, 45
Sun Yat-sen, 76
Sung dynasty, 76, 77
Sunnis, 165–66, 210, 216, 222
survival of fittest, 40
Syracuse (Sicily), 67
Syria, 1, 50, 51, 55, 152, 157, 214, 216–17

Taipei, 178, 179
Taiwan, 78, 157, 178–79, 187
Taliban, 165, 205
T'ang dynasty, 76
Tehran embassy, hostage taking, 164
Tenochtitlan (Mexico), 97, 98, 99
terrorism, 3, 16, 17, 23, 28, 29, 31, 151, 155, 183,
    205, 227, 229 (See also 9/11 terror attacks)
Texas, Hispanic population, 175
Texas Air National Guard, 1
textile production, 77, 108
Thasos (island, Aegean Sea), 62
Thatcher, Margaret, 4, 154
Thebes, 49, 50, 52
Third Intermediate Period (Egypt), 53
Third Reich, 40–41, 142
Thirteen Colonies, 103, 139, 141, 190, 191, 224
Thirty Years' War, 29
Thomas, Hugh, 113
Thrace, 62
Tibet, 71, 183
Timurids, 84

Tlaxcalans, 97, 98
Trafalgar, Battle of (1805), 8, 193
Treaty of Nanking (1842), 77
Treaty of Paris (1783), 191
Treaty of Utrecht (1713), 110
Treaty of Versailles (1919), 206
Treblinka concentration camp, 192
tribute (inu). See Egyptian Empire, taxation
Triple Alliance, 131
Triple Entente, 131
triremes (warships), 54, 61
Tyler, Wat, 190

UN Security Council, 179, 183
unilateralism, 14–15, 18, 22, 29, 32–34,
    128, 151
United Arab Emirates (UAE), oil, 162
United Fruit Company, 26, 169
United Nations, 178–79, 183
United States: –Britain relations, 230; –China
    relations, 4, 15, 23–24, 40, 148, 155, 156,
    157, 177–87, 219, 230; cultural industries,
    19, 32, 42, 185–86, 206, 223; –East Asia
    relations, 20, 23–24; economy, 4, 15, 33,
    92, 148–50, 153, 159–64, 177, 180–81,
    184–85, 209, 212–13, 222, 229–30; elite.
    See empire, and elites; –Europe relations,
    24; freedom doctrine, 226–27; –Germany
    relations, 143, 149; Hispanic influence in,
    172–75, 231; and immigration issue,
    174–75; and imperial overstretch, 137,
    146–48, 152–53, 156, 205–6, 223; –India
    relations, 182; –Iran relations, 4; –Islamic
    relations, 155–56, 164–65, 214–15; –Israel
    relations, 155, 163; –Japan relations, 143,
    148, 149–50, 161, 182, 209; –Latin
    America relations, 155, 157, 169–75, 208,
    211; legitimacy of, 42, 207–31, 223,
    224–26; military, 4, 19, 20–25, 84–85, 91,
    92, 144, 148, 150–51, 161, 163, 178,
    204–5, 209–11, 215–16, 222, 228, 231;
    nationalism/nativism, 173, 206, 230;
    –North Korea relations, 4; oil, 155,
    160–64, 181, 212, 213, 230; role of, 3, 13,
    14–15, 43; –Saudi relations, 162–63, 166;
    slavery in, 147; –Soviet relations, 219 (See
    also Cold War); taxation, 121, 148, 149,
    209, 222, 229, 231 (See also neo-conser-
    vatism; multilateralism; unilateralism)
U.S. Armed Forces, 22
U.S. Constitution, 224
U.S. Department of Defense, 21, 25, 216

U.S. Department of Energy, 162
U.S. dollar, 4, 15, 33, 149, 184, 212–13, 222
U.S. Federal Reserve, 172, 184–85
U.S. Space Command, 25
U.S. Space Forces, 22–23, 25
U.S. State Department, 163
USS Abraham Lincoln, 1, 210
utopianism, 14, 15, 16, 27

Venetian Empire, 38, 102
Venezuela, 162, 169–70, 171, 172, 226
Versailles, 141, 181
Vesey, Denmark, 190–91
Victoria, Queen (of England), 126–27
Vietnam, 1, 73
Vietnam War, 13, 88, 149, 154, 157, 208,
    218–19, 221, 226–27, 228
Vietnamization, 219
Virginia (British colony), 119
von Schlieffen, Count Alfred, 132, 133

Wal-Mart, 180–81
Walt, Stephen, 213–14
War of the Austrian Succession, 141
War of the Spanish Succession, 141
war on terror, 23, 215, 227
Warring States, age of, 72, 73
Warsaw ghetto uprising, 191–92
Warsaw Pact, 144
Waterloo, battle of (1815), 15, 120, 124, 140,
    142, 228
Wealth of Nations (Smith), 124
weapons of mass destruction (WMD), 28,
    220–21
Wei-Hai region (China), 77–78
Weimar Republic, 142
West Indies, 119, 139
Willughby, Francis, 108
Wilson, Woodrow, 206
Wilsonianism, 30–31, 226
Wolfowitz, Paul, 3, 20, 25, 27, 166
Wood, Ellen Meiksins, 87, 91
World Bank, 33, 171
World Trade Organization, 17, 183

Yalta Conference (1945), 162
Yeltsin, Boris, 145
Yucatán, 97
Yugoslavia, 190

Zacatecas (Mexico), 107
Zama (North Africa), 82